1992
BEST NEWSPAPER WRITING

WINNERS: THE AMERICAN SOCIETY OF
NEWSPAPER EDITORS COMPETITION

EDITED BY KAREN F. BROWN

ISBN 0-935742-21-2
ISSN 0195-895X
LC 80-646604

Printed in the United States of America

Copies of *Best Newspaper Writing 1992* may be ordered
directly from The Poynter Institute. Earlier editions are also
available in limited quantities. Please contact the Institute
for further ordering information.

For Don Fry,

director of writing programs,
The Poynter Institute.

A writer's captain and coach,
mentor and friend.

About this series

JUNE 1992

The Poynter Institute for Media Studies proudly publishes the 14th volume of its series *Best Newspaper Writing*, valued since 1979 by students, teachers, and professionals as an indispensable text on clear, effective, and graceful newswriting.

As in past years, *Best Newspaper Writing* is a joint venture of the Institute and the American Society of Newspaper Editors. In 1978, ASNE made the improvement of newspaper writing one of its primary goals. The Society inaugurated a contest to select the best writing from newspapers in the United States and Canada, and to reward the winning writers with $2,500 prizes. The Institute volunteered to spread the gospel of good writing by publishing the winning entries along with notes, commentaries, and interviews. That first volume, *Best Newspaper Writing 1979,* sold out long ago and has become a collector's item.

The first six editions of *Best Newspaper Writing* were edited by Dr. Roy Peter Clark, who was then director of the Institute's writing programs and is now dean of the faculty. Clark was one of the first newspaper writing coaches and has been a national leader in the movement to make newspapers more readable, more interesting, and more accurate. Dr. Don Fry, an associate of the Institute and current director of Poynter writing programs, co-edited the 1985 volume with Clark. Fry then took over the series from 1986 to 1989, adding the annual bibliographies. In 1990, Fry was joined as co-editor by Poynter colleague Dr. Karen F. Brown, who has edited the series since 1991.

Brown holds degrees from Michigan State, Tennessee State, and the University of Tennessee, and has taught at Poynter since 1986. Previously, she was on the mass communications faculties of Tennessee State University and the University of South

Florida, and was a reporter for the *Nashville Banner, Macon Telegraph and News,* and the *St. Petersburg Times.*

The 1992 award categories are non-deadline writing, deadline writing, short newswriting, editorial writing, and commentary. A committee of 11 editors, chaired by Ellen Goodman, associate editor of *The Boston Globe,* judged this year's entries:

Joann Byrd, *The Herald,* Everett, Wash.

Judith Clabes, *The Kentucky Post,* Covington

Linda Cunningham, *Rockford* (Ill.) *Register Star*

Jack Fuller, *Chicago Tribune*

Jane Healy, *The Orlando* (Fla.) *Sentinel*

Don Marsh, *The Charleston* (W.Va.) *Gazette*

Ted Natt, *The Daily News,* Longview, Wash.

Eugene Patterson, St. Petersburg, Fla.

Robert Pittman, St. Petersburg, Fla.

C. Michael Pride, *Concord* (N.H.) *Monitor*

The Institute congratulates the winners and finalists of the ASNE Distinguished Writing Awards, and thanks the judges for their fine work and dedication to good writing.

* * *

Founded in 1975 by the late Nelson Poynter, chairman of the *St. Petersburg Times* and its Washington affiliate, *Congressional Quarterly,* the Institute was bequeathed Poynter's controlling stock in the Times Publishing Company in 1978. It invests its dividends in educational activities in four areas of print and broadcast journalism: writing, graphics, management, and ethics. The faculty teaches beginning and mid-career professionals as well as news executives, publishes teaching tools such as this book, and conducts educational and research projects, all of which seek the same goal: to raise levels of excellence in newspapers and the communications media generally.

Robert J. Haiman, President
The Poynter Institute

Acknowledgments

Anchorage Daily News and Doug O'Harra
The Boston Globe and Colin Nickerson
Concord Monitor and John Fensterwald
The Des Moines Register and Tom Alex
Los Angeles Times and Robert Jones
Minneapolis *Star Tribune* and Paul McEnroe
Newsday and Adrian Peracchio
Philadelphia Daily News and Marianne Costantinou
The Philadephia Inquirer, Russell Eshleman Jr., and
  Carol Morello
Providence Journal-Bulletin and G. Wayne Miller
Richmond Times-Dispatch and Thomas Harvey Holt
The Sacramento Bee and Peter Dexter
The Washington Post, Henry Allen, and Paul
  Hendrickson

We wish to thank the following people for their generous
assistance in producing this volume: Bobbi Alsina, Don Fry,
Luz Nelida Miranda, and Joyce Olson of The Poynter Institute
staff; editorial assistant Lisa Compton, production assistant
Foster Barnes, and proofreader Nancy Oliver; and of course,
the authors and their editors.

*Cover illustration by photographer Michel Tcherevkoff
through The Image Bank Florida*

Book design by Billie M. Keirstead

Contents

Introduction

In 1946, George Orwell penned an essay on why he became a writer. Somewhere after his anecdotal lead, "nut graph," and background block, he described his idiosyncrasies. From them, he derived "four great motives for writing," aside from the need to make a living.

The motives closely parallel reasons The Poynter Institute continues to publish the series *Best Newspaper Writing*.

■ **Aesthetic enthusiasm**. Orwell said writers write because of "a desire to share an experience which one feels is valuable and ought not to be missed." We produce this book as a means of celebrating good writing. Much of the writing in daily newspapers continues to be mediocre. Readers and journalists often overlook good writing in the steady rush to the next assignment or deadline. This book showcases writing that goes beyond informing: writing that engages, entertains, and endures.

■ **Historical.** Writers "desire to see things as they are," to find truths and "store them up for the use of posterity," Orwell wrote. The truths we seek are on the nature of good writing. We record the stories of journalists, and their conversations on how they got the stories. We're interested in preserving techniques for generating innovative story ideas, for gaining depth in reporting, for converting cumbersome notes into concise, flowing copy. This series stores the accumulated wisdom of excellent writers.

■ **Political.** Orwell defined his third motive for writing as the "desire to push the world in a certain direction." We look at this series as a way of reforming journalism. We hope it provides food for thought to writers who hunger for new forms of writing and editing. We've heard that this series has helped jump-start stalled veterans and focused the aim of student journalists. We hope the comments will guide editors who have their eyes on the prize of good writing, but don't know the path.

■ **Sheer egoism**. Orwell said writers have "a desire to seem clever, to be talked about, to be remembered after death." Forthrightness required Orwell to include the category "egoism." He was, after all, writing more than 1,800 words on the topic "Why I Write." Frankly, this category has little application to the purposes of *Best Newspaper Writing*. We do enjoy talking with important journalists and seeing our name on the book's cover. But our motive is love of the industry. It's also the desire to just have fun.

Karen F. Brown

BEST
NEWSPAPER
WRITING
1992

G. Wayne Miller
Non-Deadline Writing

Writing had a hold on George Wayne Miller years before he considered a career in journalism. The works
of Edgar Allen Poe first enticed Miller to a love of the
language. But Poe was soon surpassed by H.P. Lovecraft as Miller's favorite author. "Lovecraft was a resident of Providence," Miller said. "He wrote in the
early part of this century. And he was like Poe in the
sense that he set a very dark mood. He was good with
detail."

Inspired by writers like these, Miller wrote poetry
and short stories during high school and while attending Harvard College. Then he graduated to writing
novels and free-lance articles as he began reporting
for newspapers. For years, he wrote for newspapers
during the day and practiced other forms of writing at
home. This year his interests came together. His
award-winning series is about a Boston surgeon who
is also the subject of a book Miller has written for
Random House.

Providence Journal-Bulletin

Working wonders: Day 1

NOVEMBER 17, 1991

On the morning her world was turned on end, Jean Brinegar lay in a hospital bed, overwhelmed with pride. Katie was the daughter she'd always wanted —a blue-eyed infant who had her mother's fair skin and her father's red hair. She weighed 7 pounds 5-1/2 ounces. At birth, she'd scored 9 of a possible 10 on her Apgar, a test that broadly assesses a new-born's health.

Exhausted by eight hours of labor, Jean closed her eyes. Her thoughts drifted to her home in Vermont's Green Mountains, to her gardens, to the bonnets and smocks she already had for her daughter, to her only other child, a son.

In the nursery, Katie was quiet on that Aug. 17, 1989.

Her father, Terry Brinegar, was downstairs in the cafeteria. He needed coffee and a good meal. He'd been up all night, too, helping Jean through her contractions, cutting Katie's umbilical cord, holding his little girl, counting her fingers and toes and taking small delight that she had 10 of each.

Jean dozed.

In the nursery, a crowd was assembling around Katie. A doctor opened a sterile package and began threading a tube through her nose. Katie flailed, but she was no match. The doctor got the tube down into her stomach. Next they'd have to get a line into a vein.

Jean stirred.

Her obstetrician had come into her room. In a suspiciously flat voice, she told Jean that there had been a more thorough examination of Katie. She had a disturbing discovery to report.

Your child has no anal opening.

They're putting in an IV now.

Where nature should have given Katie three openings down below, there was only one: what looked like, but could not be positively identified as, a urethra, which drains urine from the bladder. It was anyone's guess what things were like inside Katie. This much could be confirmed: Without an adequate outlet for her intestines, she needed surgery—soon—or she would die.

When Terry returned a few minutes later, Jean had lost it.

Oh my God, our poor baby, she said.

Terry embraced Jean—and then he did something quite typical for him.

He took action. A construction worker and ex-Marine who's had to fight for most of the good things he's gotten out of life, Terry, 34, went looking for the doctors to hear their plan. He would let them do nothing without his okay.

Everything's going to be all right, he said to Jean. *Whatever it takes, we're going to make it. Our baby and us.*

The doctors told Terry that their hospital, a small community facility of no particular distinction, couldn't possibly handle Katie, who was unlike any baby they'd ever seen. Even as they spoke, an ambulance with a newborn-care team was en route from the Medical Center Hospital of Vermont in Burlington, largest and most sophisticated of Vermont's 14 hospitals. It was a sound plan, Terry agreed, the best that could be expected. And still it felt like being dropped into deep woods without compass or map.

"Prognosis is somewhat guarded until the extent of the malformations can be better defined," a doctor wrote on her transfer papers. As the ambulance was receiving Katrin B. Brinegar, no one was betting she would live.

Terry helped settle Jean, still crying and sore, onto the back seat of their car. They headed after their daughter.

For the Brinegars, these were the beginning steps of a long, uncertain journey that would take them to medicine's remotest outpost—to a hospital and a surgeon many believe are the best in the world at what they do.

NO CASE TOO DAUNTING

Dr. W. Hardy Hendren III is the chief of surgery at Children's Hospital, Boston. Among his other titles is Robert E. Gross Professor of Surgery, Harvard Medical School. It commemorates Hendren's mentor, the father of pediatric surgery.

Guided by the philosophy that "it's better to fix things than just remove them," Hendren thrives on cases that are an ordinary physician's nightmare.

Prune Belly.

Mermaid Baby Syndrome.

Cloaca.

Megaureter.

Pseudohermaphroditism.

Rhabdomyosarcoma.

Hendren has stationed himself on the leading edge of science and surgery, where nature's worst mistakes taunt medicine's best minds. Starting with bad tissue, or misplaced or missing tissue, or tissue mutilated by someone else, Hendren sifts through grotesque physical confusion, then sets about rebuilding people. Nothing is too weird for Hendren. Nothing is too hopeless. No one is refused. If surgery were law, Hendren's operating room would be the court of last appeal.

Born with a bad esophagus?

Hendren can make a new one out of a piece of colon, a versatile tissue he can also fashion into a vagina or a makeshift bladder.

Bladder too small to maintain continence?

Hendren can enlarge it with a wedge of stomach.

Urethra malformed?

Hendren can roll tissue into a tube and build a perfectly good substitute.

Perhaps a third of Hendren's time is spent reversing bad outcomes by doctors who probably should never have tackled such complicated cases but did so anyway, perhaps because their egos hid the truth, which was that they were in over their heads.

Hendren is an average-sized man.

His hair is graying and thinning. Except for the nails, always clipped and clean, his fingers provide no clue to the thousands of children he's made normal. They do not tell of the several sets of Siamese twins he's successfully separated, or how he operated on his best friend, also a surgeon, to save his life from cancer, or about the family dog Hendren put under the knife—twice—at the Massachusetts General Hospital. They do not tell the story of his left hand, which he cut clowning around when he was a boy and which a surgeon sewed up badly, leaving Hendren forever without full use of his left thumb.

Hendren's hands do not say anything of the man who trained them to perform: Dr. Robert E. Gross, an eccentric genius who, at a pivotal point in his prize pupil's professional development, drove Hendren away.

Nor do they tell of Sandy, Hendren's firstborn and only daughter, a child afflicted with diabetes, which no surgeon can cure. Sandy was 7 when her father diagnosed her disease. Thirty years later, as she lay in irreversible coma, her family surrounding her, he disconnected her from the machines and let her die.

You remember his eyes.

Steely blue, framed by wire-rim glasses, they can sparkle with pleasure at a story well told—or burn through your skull if, God forbid, you've bumbled at his operating table. After such an embarrassment, you will remember your rebuke. Ordinarily, Hendren speaks with impeccable grammar and an authority virtually no one ever challenges, and his manners are those of a well-bred Southerner. When he's angry—and nothing angers him more than stupidity—Hendren's words cut.

"A case like this doesn't allow you to put in a single mistaken stitch—not a one," he said during a reconstructive operation that went 14 uninterrupted hours, about average for his most difficult cases. "One bad stitch in here and you have a leak. One leak and you can have a dead patient."

FIRST STEP: COLOSTOMY

Katie Brinegar's arrival in Burlington was heralded. This was one for the textbooks.

As she lay in intensive care, no specialist, it seemed, could leave her alone. No intern or resident could resist a look. Cardiologists investigated her heart. Urologists and radiologists attempted to define her anatomy. Geneticists interviewed her parents. An ultrasonographer examined her spine. A neurosurgeon's opinion was sought. Ultimately, her overall management fell to Dr. Allen F. Browne, a pediatric surgeon.

Browne was the only children's surgeon in Vermont that August of 1989.

There was nothing unusual about that.

Fewer than 500 members of the prestigious American College of Surgeons—barely 1 percent of total membership—specialize in operating on children. In all of North America, only 20 new pediatric surgeons graduate from advanced fellowship programs each year; like prize athletes, the best are recruited coast to coast through letters and calls and promises of professional and financial rewards. Most migrate toward urban centers and teaching hospitals, among them, the Medical Center Hospital of Vermont, affiliated with the University of Vermont College of Medicine.

As he took Katie to the O.R. on the second day of her life, Browne had two goals.

The first was to ensure her survival.

Although there was evidence that her intestines somehow were linked to her single opening— when he probed around inside her, gas bubbled up from somewhere—there was nothing to sustain normal bowel function. Left untouched, Katie's intestines would back up. She would slowly poison herself and she would die in a matter of days.

Browne solved that by fashioning an opening in her left lower abdomen and exiting the bowel through it, a routine operation known as a colostomy. Katie would need a bag, but she would survive.

Browne's second objective was to begin sorting out her anatomy, a job that would take more than a year.

Browne already knew, from a preoperative ultrasound, that Katie had only one kidney: the right. After examining her with an endoscope, an optical instrument that provides remarkable views of the interiors of about any organ you can stick something into, he knew that she did not have a normal urethra.

With Katie opened up on his table, Browne learned more. He learned that her bladder appeared OK, at least on the outside. He found a uterus—but only one ovary, one Fallopian tube. There is nothing in the record to suggest he saw a vagina, only an abnormal chamber known as a cloaca. Emptying into it were three systems that, in the normal female, have separate outlets.

"A very rare malformation in which all of the organ systems—the urinary tract, the genital tract, and the gastrointestinal tract—converge in the pelvis," Dr. W. Hardy Hendren III, the world's cloaca expert, has written.

"This is normal in the bird, but a disaster when it occurs in the human!"

A 1-IN-50,000 BABY

As bad as Katie's problems were, they could have been worse, much worse.

Children with cloacal anomalies typically have one or more of a host of associated defects, all of which can be traced to the very beginning of pregnancy, when embryological tissue is dividing and growing and miraculously fashioning itself into recognizable structures.

Some cloaca babies are born with an esophagus that dead-ends before reaching the stomach. Some have an esophagus with an abnormal connection to the trachea. Some have extra fingers, or webbed fingers, or stunted fingers. Some are missing limbs. Some are missing ribs or ears.

In perhaps the worst cases, some cloaca babies begin life with their mixed-up guts spilling out of a hole in their abdomens, a calamitous condition called cloacal exstrophy. Aesthetically and every other way, cloacal exstrophy is a nightmare.

As Browne operated on their daughter, a 1-in-50,000 baby, Terry and Jean had different outlooks.

Maybe if I only have her for a short period of

time it's better than not having had her at all, Jean thought.

"She's going to be fine," Terry kept telling his wife. "She's going to be wonderful."

SKILL, STAMINA, MEMORY

Early in life, Hendren learned these lessons:

That one must take risks; that few problems are without solutions; that one must never give up; that even the most fleeting lapse in confidence can sink the surgeon—and patient—as quickly as it can down the naval aviator, which Hendren was at 20 years of age.

Aided by a memory that can instantly recall names of patients and the most minute details of operations 35 years ago, Hendren was a schoolboy when he began to study human anatomy. Everything about the body fascinated Hendren; no organ or tissue lacked appeal.

Beginning in medical school, he learned heart surgery, thoracic surgery, vascular surgery, urological surgery, plastic surgery, general surgery on adults and on babies. He learned that fixing children is an investment in humanity lasting 60 or 70 or 80 or more years.

He could not learn stamina, not to the limits where he takes it.

Hour after hour, from morning into night and sometimes straight through to dawn, Hendren stands at his O.R. table. On and on and on he goes, telling the occasional joke, teaching residents, lambasting liberals, working in wordless harmony with the personal scrub nurse who's been with him for 30 years as he meticulously takes apart—and then meticulously reconstructs—children whose Frankensteinian insides would have killed them not many years ago.

During one case, the rebuilding of a child whose defective urinary system had progressively deteriorated in several operations at another hospital, Hendren worked 23 hours with but three breaks: once to eat a bowl of fruit; another time for a grilled ham-and-cheese sandwich; and a third time, at 3 a.m., for microwave popcorn (buttered), a can of cran-apple juice, and two glasses of milk. Hendren finished at 7 a.m. After napping an hour, he showered and shaved, did two hours of surgery on another child, then spent most of the day preparing his defense of a malpractice suit—a suit so weak it was dropped before reaching trial, but not before so angering Hendren that he still cannot speak of it without his blood boiling.

Hendren is 65.

Seventeen years ago, he lost most of his colon to an operation that cured him of cancer.

THE CAUSE IS UNKNOWN

Eight days after she was born, the Brinegars brought Katie home.

Home was better than hospital, but the manmade hole in their baby's side and the plastic bag that fit over it were disgusting.

"You've got this pink blob sticking out of your daughter's belly that stool comes out of," Jean thought. "It was like some sort of growth."

Terry and Jean had barely mastered colostomy care when the infection struck—a creeping yeast invasion that turned Katie's belly into an oozing, red mess. Unversed in such affairs, a visiting nurse suggested alcohol swabs. The Brinegars had never really heard a baby scream until they tried those.

A doctor eventually prescribed the proper, less painful treatment, but he could not ease the inevitable self-questioning.

What could have caused such a deformity?
Was it something in the water?
Something in the air?

The Brinegars live in the Vermont woods, in as pretty and pristine a spot as northern New England has to offer. There are no landfills nearby, no toxic-waste dumps, no factories belching chemicals, no high-tension lines, no known contaminants in their well. A stream running across their property supports a robust population of native brook trout.

Jean, 40, was raised a Catholic. She knew about guilt.

I must have done something wrong.

But what? She hadn't had a drink during her pregnancy, hadn't done drugs, had cut her cigarette habit to next to nothing, had rested and watched what she ate and been afforded the best of 20th-century prenatal care.

Terry examined his past, wondering if any clues were hidden there. Years before, in another life entirely, he'd used drugs.

The doctors assured the Brinegars that the cause—or causes—of cloaca are unknown, that the best guesses are a virus, or some environmental agent as yet unidentified, or some genetic mutation that cannot be predicted or prevented. All they could say for sure was that during the very early development of the embryo, something had gone radically awry inside Jean.

"If you examine early pregnancy in almost anyone, you can always find something" that seems suspicious but cannot be proven as the cause, says Dr. Bruce R. Korf, head of the Children's Hospital Birth Defects Center.

Maybe it was the mosquito repellent.

A professional gardener who sells flowers and herbs, Jean was no stranger to that.

Maybe it was the acetaminophen.

Before knowing she was pregnant, Jean had taken an over-the-counter drug to relieve what she'd mistakenly believed were menstrual cramps.

How could nature do this to us?

FAMILY COMES FIRST

Today, at the peak of a 40-year career, Hendren has a curriculum vitae that runs to 23 single-spaced typewritten pages.

Some entries seem inconsequential.

For example, his honorary membership in the Brazilian Society of Surgery. Or that in 1972 he received second prize from the Biological Photographers Association. Or that he once delivered the William P. Burpeau Memorial Lecture in Newark, N.J.

But other entries reveal more of the man.

At the top of the first page, directly beneath the place and date of his birth, is the name of his wife: Eleanor McKenna of Wilmington, Del., whom he married one winter day in 1947 after a courtship of barely four months. Below that are the names and particulars of their five children. Three of their sons are surgeons. The fourth is a lawyer. And their daughter Sandy, who is buried beneath tall pines in a graveyard at an Episcopal church.

Below, still on page one, is his military record and the fact that at age 20 he was qualified to land warplanes on an aircraft carrier. Heading a long list of awards and honors is his Eagle Scout status, attained in 1941 in Kansas City, Mo., where Hendren, who has two sisters, grew up.

He has lectured and operated in virtually every major city in the U.S., as well as in Shanghai, Beijing, Hong Kong, Warsaw, Moscow, Medellin, Rio de Janeiro, Dublin, Liverpool, Lyon, Tokyo, Rotterdam, Salzburg, Bern, and many other foreign cities. In midcareer, he took a two-month sabbatical to operate in Malawi, an impoverished African nation where medicine was barely into this century. This week, he is operating in Damascus, Syria, part of a humanitarian mission that includes some of America's most esteemed physicians. He is paying his own way and working for free.

Hendren estimates he has performed more than 20,000 surgeries. He could, if he so chose, come up with the exact count. In the library of his oceanfront home in Duxbury, on Boston's South Shore, he has bound volumes of typewritten reports of his every operation. They take up two shelves of a bookcase. Nearly every week, another 20 or 30 pages are added.

Except for the Nobel Prize, which his friend and Children's colleague Dr. Joseph E. Murray received last year, Hendren has enjoyed most of the accolades that can be bestowed on a surgeon.

WHAT KIND OF LIFE?
Surgery had saved Katie's life, but what kind of life would it be?

Sexual relations and children would be impossible. Katie would have a bag on her side, and it didn't take a colostomy expert to foresee how nasty it could get in the classroom or on the playground, how easily a single accident could traumatize a little girl for life.

In Burlington, Dr. Browne had told Jean and Terry that it should be possible to reconstruct Katie. The results could not be predicted precisely—her anatomy was still very much a mystery—but at a minimum, a skilled surgeon could get rid of the colostomy bag. A highly skilled surgeon might be able to do more.

Jean's sister, Beth Thompson, is a librarian with the New York Public Library. Armed with the word "cloaca" and a graphic impression of her niece's deformity, she went hunting through journals, abstracts, textbooks, and reference works. There, among the chronicles of surgery's rarest cases, one name kept appearing more than any other.

The Brinegars went to Browne, who was about to relocate to Maine.

What do you know about this Hardy Hendren at Boston Children's?

You couldn't ask for any better, Browne told the Brinegars. *He's the one who wrote the book on all this.*

THE DOCTOR IS IN

Around Thanksgiving 1989—when the Brinegars' new life had settled into a steady rhythm, when finally they could dare to imagine graduations and proms and christenings—Terry Brinegar placed a call to 300 Longwood Ave., Boston.

He waited for the phone to be answered.

What if Hendren's practice was closed? The local doctor can get too busy to take on new patients, never mind an international authority at one of the world's foremost medical institutions. As amazing as he might be, Hendren certainly hadn't found the Fountain of Youth. What if he was planning to retire? What if he'd started turning over his toughest cases to the younger doctors he was training? What if he was picky about insurance? What if?

A secretary came on the line. Dr. Hendren isn't here, she informed Terry. Dr. Hendren is in the operating room.

Dr. Browne sent a letter about our daughter, Terry said. We were hoping for an appointment.

Oh, yes, the secretary said. Let me look at The Book.

Here it was November and The Book, a Bible-sized daily minder, already had entries to the end of next year. Operations were circled in red; hospital meetings and office visits and birthdays, including the birthday of Hendren's daughter, dead five years, were written in blue.

A busy book, but an utterly democratic one. Among Hendren's thousands of patients are the son of a prominent congressman, a Saudi Arabian prince, the adopted daughter of a lesbian, grandchildren of several people on the Forbes 400 list of the richest people in America. Others haven't a penny; for them, Hendren waives his fees, which for a tough case run into the thousands. More than 25 percent of Hendren's work is done for free.

"The important thing," he says, "is we fix the kids."

How about February? his secretary said to Terry Brinegar.

BOUND FOR BOSTON

On a cold, cloudy morning in February 1990, the Brinegars drank one last cup of coffee, set the wood stove for the day, and rushed Katie to their car. The sun was still behind the Green Mountains as they headed down to Boston.

They were thinking about Hendren.

Since learning his name, they'd heard a thing or two about the man. They'd heard his nickname, Hardly Human, and its origin had been the subject of some debate. Did it refer to his stamina in the O.R.? The fact that he took on cases no one else dared try? Or was it a reference to his bedside manner, which, the Brinegars had been told, was not his strongest suit? Hendren could be demanding, cold, curt, impatient when questioned, intensely intolerant of ignorance. Or so they'd heard.

They drove south and then east to Boston, eventually onto Longwood Avenue and the heart of America's medical mecca: a 20-block neighborhood that includes the Harvard Medical School, the Harvard School of Public Health, the Dana-Farber Cancer Institute, Brigham and Women's Hospital, Massachusetts College of Pharmacy, Joslin Diabetes Center, Beth Israel Hospital, Countway Library of Medicine, Deaconess Hospital, and Children's.

The Brinegars parked, then hurried across Longwood and up the hospital's main drive, dwarfed by the architecture around it. Children's is several buildings: broad and tall, granite and brick, old and new, each testimony to an institution that has flourished because the brains attracted here have been the best. Past taxicabs the Brinegars went, past handicapped vans, past security guards and shivering cigarette smokers, whose habit is banned inside the door. In the lobby, a bright and spacious place, they saw giant stuffed animals and a glass elevator and pay phones that are nearly always in use.

On their way by, they dropped pennies into the wishing pool.

Observations and questions

1) Miller's story opens with a powerful contrast: "On the morning her world was turned on end, Jean Brinegar lay in a hospital bed, overwhelmed with pride." Notice the contrasting elements at the end of the first clause and at the end of the sentence. Also notice how contrast continues on the first page of the story.

2) Foreshadowing appears throughout the story. One example is the last paragraph on page 3: "For the Brinegars, these were the beginning steps of a long, uncertain journey that would take them to medicine's remotest outpost—to a hospital and a surgeon many believe are the best in the world at what they do." Find other examples. How does this technique serve the reader? How does it serve the writer?

3) One method of presenting a lot of information in a readable form is to create lists. On page 8, Miller lists lessons that Hendren learned early in life. The paragraph is a digest for the reader of what Miller has learned from extensive research. What other purposes are served by the list?

4) In his article "We Mustn't Let Words Fail Us," Gary Blonston writes: "There are ways to compel my people to read. There are some things words can do that pictures can't." One way to engage readers is to play with language. On page 13, Miller uses the phrase "The Book, a Bible-sized daily minder." What are some of the comparisons alluded to by using the metaphor of a datebook as a Bible?

5) Another way of playing with the language is the use of grouping and repetition on page 14. Consider the phrases "broad and tall, granite and brick, old and new." What is gained by giving the description in sets rather than in one series? What is the value of the repetition of "past" in the next sentence? When do such devices work?

Working wonders: Day 2

NOVEMBER 18, 1991

The P-47s were coming again. Hardy Hendren could hear their propellers, could feel the thunder of their engines, faint but getting louder, getting closer, until the windows were rattling and he could concentrate on his studies no more.

Out of their dorm and into autumn sunshine they poured—Hendren and his classmates, teen-agers all, not a girl among the lot, spreading out onto the lawns and playing fields of the private boarding school in Shenandoah Virginia, a most picturesque part of that genteel state.

They exploded into view: fighter planes from a nearby training field, so low you could all but touch their wings.

The cockpits were open. You could see the pilots—boys who fancied themselves men, with their goggles and helmets and their hands on the stick. You could see the pilots' grins, wide as a tarmac. You could just about smell the exhaust and oil and gasoline. A shiver ran down your spine and soon you couldn't help yourself—you were shouting and waving, and the fighter pilots were waving back.

War was everywhere that fall of '42. It consumed the newspapers, the Saturday-afternoon newsreels, the radio broadcasts. Inevitably, it had found Woodberry Forest School, opened half a century earlier to give Southerners of standing the foundation they would need for a successful life.

"To give moral and religious guidance," Woodberry's founder had set as one of his goals, "to help young pupils in forming correct habits of study, and to direct such physical exercises as are needful for healthy development."

Hendren's father, W. Hardy Hendren Jr., had made good use of Woodberry values since he himself had attended. Born in Virginia to a line of Hendrens that included a weaver, a militiaman in George Washington's army, a Confederate major, and a Baptist preacher and slave owner, Hendren's father was a businessman and commercial film-maker. While a young boy, Hendren's father had been taken by fortune to New Orleans, where he'd later married and had three children, including his only son.

That son was 7 when the Hendrens moved to Kansas City, Mo.

The young Hendren was a bit of a tease, a bit of a flirt, a boy fascinated by motor scooters and Erector sets and living creatures you found under logs. Sometime around the day that he caught and dissected a tadpole with his pocketknife, he decided he wanted to be a doctor—and not just any kind of doctor, but the kind who's good with his hands.

Surgeons always have work, the boy figured. *Surgeons make people better.*

Hendren attended a public grammar school and graduated to a public high school in Kansas City. A good but not yet brilliant student, he took Latin his freshman year—and flunked. His parents blamed his teacher, who did not count Hendren among her favorite pupils.

It was a miserable year. Such promise, sadly unfulfilled. Despite the Depression, which had tightened the family purse strings, Mr. Hendren decreed that come fall, it was Woodberry for his boy.

But first, the boy would have to attend summer school.

A LONG WAIT

On their first visit to Children's Hospital, the Brinegars left the lobby wishing pool and found their way down halls and up an elevator to the Department of Surgery. The waiting area, large and loaded with toys, was jammed. Infants slept in mothers' arms. Toddlers scurried. Teen-agers read magazines or watched the TV.

Business as usual.

Last year, 12,767 surgical procedures were performed at Children's. Surgical patients accounted for many of the 1.6 million laboratory tests and the 94,806 x-rays and related radiological procedures. In all, almost 16,000 patients were seen at Children's last year; 345 were from Rhode Island, and 184 were from foreign countries.

An hour passed, and the Brinegars waited.

Two hours, and still no sign of Hendren.

Katie crawled. Katie smiled her endearing smile. Katie tugged at her colostomy bag. Katie, 6 months old, wanted her dolly. Katie wanted someone else's dolly. Katie fussed. Katie took a bottle, and her parents took turns holding her and reading to her, and once again they were reminded why Jason, Jean's son from an earlier marriage, had given his half-sister the nickname that had stuck: Katie Beast, usually shortened to Katie B. If you looked for it, you could see fire—Terry's fire—in Katie B.'s eyes.

"Mr. and Mrs. Brinegar?"

Dorothy Enos, Hendren's nurse, was calling their turn. An unfailingly polite woman, Enos sets strangers at ease. The sole exception might be new surgical residents, who learn through the grapevine that the one person at Children's who will stand up to the chief is the nurse he's employed for 30 years.

Enos brought the Brinegars into a small examining room.

"Dr. Hendren will be right with you," she said. "Please have a seat."

IT STARTED WITH A DANCE

Jean was waiting tables to supplement her gardener's income that spring evening in 1988 when she and her girlfriend, Marian, decided to go out on the town.

The hangout was called Dad's; a local band, the Spiders, was on stage. Jean and Marian got up close but didn't take the floor. The rest of their crowd had yet to arrive.

"Are you here to dance—or just stand in my way?"

Jean turned. A man with red hair and a pierced ear was eyeing her.

"Dance," Jean said.

And so they did—number after number.

Between dances, they talked. Terry was divorced, childless, muscular, witty, a construction worker whose wanderings had taken him just about everywhere, most recently to a bridge project near the house Jean had inherited from her grandmother. Terry was interested in Jean's gardens. He was interested in her son, Jason, a grammar-schooler, and the fact that she was separated from her husband and was never going back. He thought she was funny and attractive and almost—almost—as good a dancer as he.

Outside, in the cool spring night, they kissed.

That fall, Jean's marriage over, Terry moved in.

At first, Jean charged him rent.

HEADING FOR HANOVER

A year before the P-47s, on a cloudy and cool day a generation would never forget, Hendren and his dorm mates had gathered around a radio in their proctor's room. President Roosevelt was addressing the nation.

"Yesterday—Dec. 7, 1941, a date which will live in infamy—the United States of America was suddenly and deliberately attacked by naval and air forces of the Empire of Japan," the president said.

"No matter how long it may take to overcome this premeditated invasion, the American people in their righteous might will win through to absolute victory. We will not only defend ourselves to the uttermost but will make it very certain that this form of treachery shall never again endanger us.

"We shall gain the inevitable triumph, so help us God."

Hendren was 15, a sophomore who'd struggled his first year at prep school with his old nemesis, Latin, but was now near the head of his class. Listening to FDR, he knew that if the war went long, he would serve—would postpone his medical dreams and go off to defend his country. For a youngster raised in the heartland, a boy whose ancestor had marched alongside George Washington, it was all very simple.

When warplanes buzzed Woodberry that next autumn, the autumn of '42, Hendren wrote letters. One was to Dartmouth College, which he'd decided he wanted to attend. Two others went to the Army and Navy. He particularly wanted information on military aviation.

In June 1943, Hendren graduated cum laude from Woodberry. He was barely home when he went down and introduced himself to the Navy.

An excellent candidate, the recruiter told him —except for your weight. At 117 pounds, Hendren was 3 pounds too light. He gorged on bananas and water until he was nearly sick, then went back and stepped on the scale again. He was still shy a pound. But the recruiter, liking everything else he'd seen, particularly the kid's success on the Woodberry wrestling team, gave it to him.

Hendren headed off to Hanover, N.H. On the long train ride north, he and a buddy from Kansas City toasted their futures with a bottle of Irish whiskey. They got bombed.

"When the Class of '47 steps out at the Inn Corner after a five-mile ride—or walk—from the Vermont metropolis of White River Junction, the first impression will be that of a slightly smaller Newport or Parris Island," *The Dartmouth,* a school newspaper, declared. "For at the same time that the three hundred odd additions to the civilian college make their Hanover debut, men now enrolled in the various Naval and Marine reserves will return to the college on active military duty."

Hendren began his freshman year.

In October, the Navy called. Hendren was 17.

A HAND FROM UNCLE SAM

Hendren had never flown before, although his father had, during the First World War. Like his dad, Hendren had the knack. He advanced quickly. He seemed certain to see action, probably in the Pacific.

And then America started to win.

Pressure to produce new pilots slackened. Future fliers were steered into a holding pattern. By the time two atomic bombs were dropped in August

1945 and Japan was left with no choice but surrender, Hendren was still in pilot training. He was told
he could leave the Navy, but he stayed on—less for
patriotism now than to achieve his goal of winning
his wings.

On Oct. 4, 1946, after final training, he made repeated landings and takeoffs on the *Saipan,* a carrier
cruising the Gulf of Mexico. He was awarded Wings
of Gold, signifying his status as a naval aviator.

Hendren would be in the reserves for another
eight years, but his full-time flying was over. Riding a 1933 Harley all the way from Pensacola, Fla.,
Hendren went home to Kansas City to get on with
his life.

On a visit to Woodberry Forest soon after his return, Hendren met a stewardess for Trans World
Airways. He wanted Eleanor McKenna's hand almost from the moment he met her. Although his father worried that marriage would interfere with
doctor training, Hendren married Eleanor early in
1947.

The newlyweds went off to Dartmouth, where
Hendren resumed his premedical education. He
was 21; his bride, 20. It wasn't long before his father was crediting Eleanor with being a key to his
son's success in the long road to becoming a surgeon.

It was a point of pride for the son, made independent by war, not to rely on this father for support.
But Uncle Sam was OK. Hendren qualified for the
GI Bill and that helped. He worked in Dartmouth's
medical library, built and sold fine furniture, was a
reunion-weekend dormitory clerk. He and Eleanor
sold their blood. They cooked on a hot plate and
heated with kerosene, which cost 5 cents a gallon.
They washed their clothes in a sink.

In late 1947, Sandy, their first child, was born.
Hendren was there, just as he would be there the
day she died.

Sandy was daddy's darling, a blond-haired girl
who had Hardy's blue eyes and Eleanor's easy-
going personality and the sense of humor both parents share. Like her dad, Sandy would be drawn to

medicine. Like her mom, she should show a talent for music. She was a natural at the piano. Her voice, strong and pure and sweet, would, in time, grace semiprofessional stages around New England.

Sandy was 7 when Hendren diagnosed her diabetes, which would be alleviated but not cured by diet and insulin. Not even surgery would be able to save Sandy.

In 1950, the year Douglas Hardy, their first son, was born, Hendren left Dartmouth. He had a bachelor's degree and two years of medical school. He was bound for Harvard Medical School and Boston, where his reputation would begin to grow and grow, eventually threatening to rival that of Dr. Robert E. Gross, Hendren's mentor.

'I SEE WE HAVE A PROBLEM'

Just when Jean and Terry were sure Katie B. was going to lose it altogether, the door to the examining room opened and a bespectacled man in a white lab coat appeared. He offered his hand and apologized for being late.

"I'm Doctor Hendren," he said. "I see we have a problem here."

He was younger looking than the Brinegars had imagined, more smiling, but his tone—reassuring, authoritative but not stern—was what they'd expected.

"All right," Hendren said. "Let's have a look."

The Brinegars put Katie on the examining table and unsnapped her outfit. Hendren looked. He probed. He took photographs with the Nikon camera he's had for 25 years. He scribbled some notes. He questioned the Brinegars. He consulted records sent from Vermont, taking particular note of Katie's solitary kidney. In his head, he began to rough out a new anatomy for her. He knew already that she would need at least two operations, and probably more.

"What we're going to do first," he announced with the conviction of a physician whose patients almost never seek second opinions, "is see how her ureter is working, how the kidney is working. Because you can live with a colostomy, but you can't live without a kidney."

Hendren wanted Katie back soon to run a series of tests and bring her into the O.R. for a hard look at her insides. Once he had a better handle on her anatomy, he'd schedule her reconstruction.

Hendren had started to dress Katie. He was having trouble with the snaps.

"You're going to have to do this," he said to Jean. "I'm not very good with my hands."

The Brinegars were speechless.

Hardy Hendren winked.

ADOPTION IS AN OPTION

Jean grew up on Long Island and spent several years in Buffalo before landing in Vermont, where her grandmother lived. At 37, Jean was letting go of her dream of having a little girl. She'd started giving all the baby things away—Jason's baby clothes, his toys, even his crib.

Son of a machinist, fourth of six children, Terry was born in Illinois. He spent his boyhood in Chicago, Iowa, and Kansas. After high school, Terry enlisted in the Marines. He was stationed down South when he got into a fight that briefly landed him in the U.S. Disciplinary Barracks at Fort Leavenworth, Kan.

Out of the Marines, on the outs with his father, Terry hit the road. In Colorado, he learned construction. He stayed in ski country some four years before the restlessness returned and he had to move, this time to Oklahoma, where his family had relocated, and where he and his father finally reconciled. Terry married a woman named Terry, had no children, was divorced, was left bitter, moved to Texas. He made it to superintendent. Good work at good wages brought him to New England, where he met Jean.

As their relationship intensified, the topic of kids came up.

Terry told Jean he didn't think he'd be able to father a child: Years before, a doctor had said that infection had damaged, apparently irreversibly, the anatomy that delivers sperm. Jean could accept that. But would he consider adopting? Terry said he would.

'I CAN'T WAIT TO HOLD YOU'

As Christmas 1988 approached, Terry and Jean had embarked on a new life together. They'd done their pickling, cut their wood, taken the snow shovels out of storage. The freezer was full of salmon Terry had caught. With any luck, there'd soon be fresh venison in there, too.

I feel like I'm pregnant.

You can't be, Terry said. *The doctor said I can't have kids.*

Jean bought a home pregnancy kit. The next morning, Terry woke her before dawn. Jean took the test.

The result was positive.

We're going to have a baby!

Because of her age, Jean wanted amniocentesis. The doctor had some trouble drawing the sample, but the results showed nothing abnormal. Although amnio detects only a limited number of defects, they include two that parents dread: spina bifida and Down's syndrome.

Everything's negative, the voice on the phone said. *We find nothing wrong with your baby.*

The Brinegars were thrilled.

Would you like to know the sex? they were asked.

Jean did.

Terry didn't.

Jean prevailed. It was the girl she'd always wanted.

As late spring gave way to early summer, a busy season for people who make a living off the land, Jean could feel her unborn child move. At a baby shower, her gifts included dresses. She held one in front of her belly. "She's going to look great in this one!" she said to her friends.

Alone, she'd whisper to Katie: *I can't wait for you to come out. I can't wait to see you. I can't wait to hold you.*

She's going off the deep end now! Terry would joke.

At around 11 p.m. on Aug. 16, 1989, Jean's water broke.

SMOKERS BEWARE

Although his office appointments invariably back up, once you're in with Hendren, he's yours for as long as you want. He answers all of your questions. He hears your complaints. He hands you his card, which includes his home phone number, and urges you to call anytime, for any reason.

If you're carrying a pack of Marlboros in your shirt pocket, as Terry Brinegar was, watch out.

Even though Hendren was due on a plane in a couple of hours—he was bound for Dublin, where he would lecture, operate, and be made an honorary member of the Royal College of Surgeons—he has time for one of his sermons.

He begins by citing statistics. He explains how smoking jeopardizes not only hearts but also bladders, how there is a demonstrable link between cigarettes and other cancers, a matter he believes should be of profound concern to parents of a young baby. He says he's never met a smoker diagnosed with lung cancer who didn't immediately quit, "as if that could redeem them—get them down off the cross—which of course it can't."

He says that he himself had a smoking habit—until the day in 1974 that his colon cancer was diagnosed. He does not raise his shirt to show the Brinegars his scar from the surgery that cured him, at the expense of a substantial piece of his insides, although he sometimes does to drive the point home.

Cancer has been a bogeyman in Hendren's life. Lung cancer claimed the lives of his father and father-in-law and the father of his nurse, all smokers. One of his physician friends at Children's recently died of cancer. His best friend, also a surgeon, might have died of kidney cancer if Hendren hadn't cut it out of him in a nine-hour operation that had a high potential for failure. Some of Hendren's most horrific cases have been infants and children with tumors.

One was a 19-month-old boy whose bladder and prostate Hendren had to remove as the only way of saving his life. The operation was a success. After a follow-up exam, Hendren discovered that the toddler's mother smoked.

"Celebrate the good news that your son is cured of cancer," he said as a packed O.R. waiting room watched in undisguised amazement. "Quit."

"I'd like to…"

"Open that bag," Hendren said. "Go on."

The mother opened her handbag. There was a pack of cigarettes.

"Take them in your hand."

The mother did.

"Now crush them."

The mother couldn't.

"Go on."

Still she couldn't.

Hendren gently took the pack from her, mangled it, then tossed it into a trash barrel.

"Do you have another pack?"

"No."

"Where's that lighter?"

She didn't have one. She had matches, which she handed to Hendren. He tossed them away.

"There," Hendren said. "You've quit."

"It's almost a feeling of relief," the mother said.

Hendren hugged the woman and kissed her on the cheek. "I like kissing women who don't smoke," he said as he disappeared for his next case.

MAKING IT IN BOSTON

There were plenty of smokers in the Harvard Medical School Class of 1952. There were cigarette smokers, pipe smokers, smokers of cigars. The class yearbook, the *Aesculapiad,* had their photographs, along with one of a young doctor coyly fingering a cigarette. The caption: "Throat Specialist."

The Class of '52 had a sense of humor—a wickedly irreverent one. "Feeney's Funeral Parlor. When Your Diagnosis Fails," reads a full-page yearbook ad cooked up by Jim Feeney, Hendren's lab partner at Dartmouth College. "Little kiddies from the entire civilized world, and even a few from as far west as Albany, flock to this fabled institution," is how Children's is described.

They were a confident bunch—mostly male, mostly white, charging into a world where the physician was still supreme. Consumerism, malpractice, affirmative action, contemporary nursing with its unions and management responsibilities—all that belonged to an alien world, one that lay on the other end of the Eisenhower Era.

Hendren excelled at Harvard Medical. He was secretary-treasurer of his class. His talent for surgery was apparent on his first trip to the dog lab. In a campaign that enraged deans who thought the old ways worked just fine, Hendren spearheaded a national effort to improve the system that "matches" medical school graduates with training programs of their choice.

"Future plans," the *Aesculapiad* said of Hendren. "Surgery in Kansas City."

Hendren was an intern at Massachusetts General Hospital for a year, then a resident there in general adult surgery. In 1955 and 1956, he furthered his training at Children's, whose chief surgeon, Dr. Robert E. Gross, was already a legend. Encouraged by his mentor, Hendren earned a reputation as one to watch—maybe even, someday, one who'd rival Gross himself. Hendren returned to The General in 1957, becoming chief surgical resident in 1958.

That year, Hendren was offered the job of head pediatric surgeon at the children's hospital in his hometown.

"I think you can make it here in Boston," Gross said, and invited him back to Children's as one of his top assistants. Hendren accepted.

A FIRST LOOK

On March 8, 1990, Katie B. visited Hendren's table for the first time.

As anesthesiologists set about removing consciousness and the ability to feel pain, Hendren watched through a window from an adjacent room, where he was parked before a stainless-steel trough. Controlling the spigot with his foot, he scrubbed his forearms and hands with a plastic-bristled brush saturated with anti-bacterial soap. In the O.R., dirt can kill.

Katie Brinegar was on her back, her legs in stirrups. Sterile towels and drapes covered all of her body except for her bottom, which Hendren had painted with Betadine, a brown solution that annihilates germs.

Today was not Katie B.'s reconstruction, but the procedure was not a simple one, either.

Katie had a cloaca.

Hendren went into the room, dried his hands, and put on a gown and gloves.

"Chair, please," he said.

Enos rolled up a black stool. Hendren sat. A resident handed him an endoscope, an optical instrument used to visualize the interiors of organs.

As gently as if he'd been examining Ming china, Hendren inserted the scope into Katie.

"Camera, please."

Hendren attached a miniature camera to the eyepiece. Dorothy adjusted the light and got ready to record.

"Can everyone see that?"

The inside of Katie's bladder appeared on the video monitor, larger than life. It didn't look normal at all.

Observations and questions

1) The second day of the story begins in 1942. In the blocks that follow, Miller shifts readers to the present chronological progress of the story, back to 1988, then to 1941 through 1950, back to the present, then to 1988-89, then 1952, and back to the present. How is Miller able to make such shifts without confusing readers?

2) In the article "Five Frames to Support Your Articles," Jane Harrigan discusses the use of the hourglass structure; spatial, scenic, and parallel narratives; and the variable distance story. Miller begins this story by reconstructing a scene. What are some of the elements of good scene reconstruction employed in this section?

3) Writing an authoritative narrative requires extensive research. Consider the section "Heading for Hanover" that begins on page 19. What sources seem to have been used to produce this section?

4) The story begins with the focus on P-47 fighter planes. Notice how airplanes are a unifying device in the piece. Where do they appear and what do they indicate in the narrative?

5) After introducing readers to the principal characters in "Day 1," Miller gives their backgrounds in "Day 2." Why is this extensive background needed?

Working wonders: Day 3

What Hardy Hendren found inside Katie Brinegar on March 8, 1990, was anatomic anarchy. As residents and nurses watched on the video monitor, Hendren, eye to scope, discovered just how profoundly Katie was deformed.

There was the urogenital sinus, a passageway that mimicked, but could not replace, the urethra nature hadn't given her. There was a vagina, attached to the sinus. There was a cervix. Sometimes, cloaca patients have two cervixes, two vaginas, two uteri —two sets of reproductive organs with little chance of either ever working—but Hendren didn't find any evidence of duplication, not today.

Near the vagina was a freak of nature: a fistula, or passage, joining rectum to bladder neck. Next to the fistula were two other openings, which Hendren suspected also were connected to the rectum.

Another problem was Katie's single ureter.

Normally, ureters, which come in pairs and drain urine from the kidneys, enter the bladder through holes that are readily recognizable. Katie's ureter entered through a weird crater—hidden so well that Hendren, even with his experience and his scope, never did actually see it today. He pinned down its approximate location by loading dye into Katie's veins and waiting for her kidney to excrete it. When the kidney did, about four minutes later, blue streamed out of a corner of her bladder. The ureter had to be down in there.

This wouldn't do. Because of the ureter's oddball attachment to the bladder, Hendren knew that urine was backwashing into Katie's lone kidney. Uncorrected, it would become infected. Infection would do damage, often severe and irreversible.

Katie would have one option then: a transplant, which not everyone survives.

"This is a very unusual anatomy, although I have

seen it several previous times," he wrote in her record. "It will be a tough cloaca to repair because of this abnormal position of the various structures."

There was some good news.

With Katie under, Hendren electrically stimulated the area on her bottom where her anus should have been, and found good, strong muscle—muscle that contracted normally. It was a promising omen. Sew her rectum into the exact middle of that muscle, and Katie would have an excellent shot at continence.

By the time Katie was being wheeled to recovery, Hendren had his strategy. Barring any surprises —which happen so often with cloacas they're not properly surprises—he envisioned a three-stage reconstruction, starting with an operation to relocate that oddball ureter.

With six hours on the O.R. table already, Katie, age 7 months, faced a possible 24 hours or more of additional surgery—and untold weeks of recuperation, with no guarantee of success.

Stage 1 was scheduled for April 30, 1990.

A MEDAL FOR HENDREN

The auditorium at Tufts University School of Medicine is packed today: A famous professor from Harvard, that medical school across town, is receiving a medal.

Doctors, like journalists, are fond of bestowing accolades on one another. In medicine, the Orvar Swenson Medal is significant. It honors a genuine giant in pediatric surgery, a man who, like Hendren, devised ways of erasing the worst deformities. Like Hendren, Swenson studied under Dr. Robert E. Gross, father of the field. And like Hendren, he was driven from Children's when his reputation began to rival Gross's.

"I came because of Hardy Hendren," says the man who is to introduce him, Dr. Martin W. Abrams, a pediatric surgeon from New York who has referred some of his toughest cases to Hendren. "There is no man I respect more in the field of pediatric surgery than my friend."

"Many years ago," Abrams tells his audience, which includes Dr. Frank DeLuca, one of the pediatric surgeons at Rhode Island Hospital, "Hardy and I were attending a meeting out in California. I had suffered from polio when I was a kid, and my back went out on me as we were walking down the hall in the main part of the hotel, and Hardy said to me: 'Stop.'

"So I stopped. When Hardy tells me to stop, I stop."

The audience laughs. Most know Hendren or have heard plenty about him. They know what Abrams means.

"He said, 'Stand there.' And he got behind me and he put his arms under mine and he said, 'Now, you lie back.'

"Now this was in front of a whole bunch of people in a hotel. And I said, 'What are you going to do?' He said, 'I'm going to lift you up on me.' I said, 'You're kidding me.'

"And he said, 'No, I'm not. You're going to hear your back crack and then you're going to feel better.'

"So in the middle of this room, he lifted me up, he bent back like this, and I heard *crack, crack, crack, crack, crack*. And I felt better. I walked away from there saying: 'This man knows something that I don't know.'"

GREAT PROGRESS SINCE 1955

Hardy Hendren takes the podium. He's not getting the Orvar Swenson Medal without delivering an original lecture.

First, Hendren pays tribute to Swenson, 81, who has driven down from retirement in Maine. Swenson pioneered correction of Hirschsprung's disease, a nightmarish bowel defect that hitherto had been untreatable. As a student at Harvard Medical School in 1951, Hendren had heard plenty about Dr. Swenson.

"It was always with admiration, respect, and with great warmth as well, which other surgeons don't always feel for colleagues," Hendren says.

Academic doctors almost never lecture without a trayful of slides; their reluctance to do so is something of an inside joke. Hendren asks for his first: a photograph of the autopsied organs of a cloaca baby who died in 1955, when reconstruction was fantasy.

"I would like to talk on the subject of cloaca, which, as you know, is a congenital persistence of an early embryologic stage where everything empties into a single chamber. Cloaca is, in Greek, the word for sewer."

He points to the screen.

"This is the second cloaca that I had occasion to see, many years ago, in 1955. We'd had one that came into Children's when I was a new resident there. We didn't know what to do for it and the baby died. The family refused a postmortem, saying, 'Well, if no one knows what to do for the baby, if nobody's ever seen one just like this before, you probably never will again.'"

The slide tray advances.

'I WENT TO A DANCE!'

Hendren has seen 109 cloacas, by far the most in the world. The patients come from 25 states and 12 foreign nations.

He describes to his Swenson audience how he tackled this variation, and that unusual one, and this other very complicated one here. Unlike the standard surgical presentation, confined to technique, Hendren also shows portraits of patients after they've been cured. All are smiling. Most are children.

One is a young woman in a red dress.

She, Hendren says, "is a girl who came from a very fine institution and her surgery had been done many, many years ago, before we sort of understood much about this. At age 20, she wore diapers. She was totally incontinent of urine and she was totally incontinent of stool."

Hendren took her to his O.R. "She came back for her first postoperative visit and she walked in and she said: 'Guess what? Last Friday night, I went to a dance! And it's the first time I ever felt I could go to a dance! And I was wearing real panties just like everybody else. I didn't have on diapers.'

"And that was a profound thing to her socially, to get that fixed. She has subsequently become married and is leading a normal life in New York City."

Hendren closes with a call to arms.

"The things that I'd like to stress are that these are all tough cases, they're all different one from another—but nearly all of them have a pretty good way to get solved if you're willing to roll up your sleeves and do it."

Hendren gets a standing ovation. Guests surround him, eager to shake his hand. "Awesome," says one surgeon, no slouch himself.

"When he's gone," Abrams observes, "there are going to be a lot of kids getting screwed up again."

KATIE B. WOULD HAVE DIED

A century ago, Katie B. probably would have died. If, miraculously, she had survived, her life wouldn't have been worth living.

That's what her doctor might have said.

"The imperfection is one of a peculiarly delicate character and one that, should life be spared and prolonged, would only entail misery upon the unfortunate victim of it," a surgical text published in 1860 declared.

"The manner in which such a malformation would operate upon the mind, should the patient thus afflicted arrive at the age of reflection, can well be imagined when we take into account the disgusting and the repulsive nature of the deformity itself."

The 19th century saw few advances in treatment of cloaca. Progress in the early 1900s was similarly slow, in part because of the complexity of the deformity, in part because its great rarity and high mortality made extensive experimentation impossible—and for this one, there are no good animal models. Well into the second half of this century, leading hospitals and surgeons still didn't know what to do.

So they did nothing—or mucked around, to no one's benefit.

At Hendren's medical ceremony, Swenson spoke of the '40s and '50s. He remembered "having patients come to Children's with the most bizarre anomalies of the genital and urinary systems. I hated to see them come along because regardless of what we did, we made them worse, it seemed."

By the 1960s, advances in surgical technique hinted of hope. But only a handful of doctors—among them Hardy Hendren, the first chief of pediatric surgery at the Massachusetts General Hospital, a man who had seen his first cloaca as a Children's resident—made pursuit of a cure their personal crusade.

UP AT 5:30, WORKING BY 7

There have been days in Hendren's career that he has not worked 15 or more hours, but there have not been many. A few were in 1974, when he was recovering from his colon-cancer operation. Even then, he saw patients from his bed at Massachusetts General Hospital. It has ever been thus. One can envision the young Hendren casting a critical eye at the Calvinist ethic. Finding it lacking, he sets out to redefine it.

On a typical day, he is up by 5:30 a.m.

He catches CNN, peruses the paper, works out on his Nordic Track exercise machine, breakfasts, shaves and showers, puts on a starched shirt and a suit (usually gray or brown), and is in his office by 7 a.m.

Sandwiched around his O.R. time—50 or 60 hours in an average week—are consultations, office visits, administrative conferences, meetings with colleagues and residents and residents-to-be, walking rounds, grand rounds, service rounds. Somehow, he finds time to keep current with the literature, to write, to dictate letters and review insurance claims, to oversee an office staff of six, to meet with his medical artist, to prepare lectures and edit film, and to tend to the affairs of his various medical societies.

Hendren used to drink eight or 10 cups of coffee a day, but in recent years, caffeine began to make his hands tremble ever so slightly. Now, he gets through the day with an occasional half cup of coffee, and sometimes a spot of tea.

The Hendrens' main residence is in Duxbury, on Boston's South Shore, about 45 minutes from Children's. It is a drive he rarely makes anymore on weeknights; nodding off behind the wheel doing 70 on Route 3 one night after an exhausting case persuaded him it's wiser to sleep at the apartment he and his wife keep a few blocks from the hospital. No matter what time he leaves Children's, and it's often after midnight, Eleanor has dinner waiting for him. She always has.

On the rare occasion he's home early, Hendren, son of a commercial filmmaker, delights in watching movies. Westerns and war films, particularly air combat, are among his favorites.

NOTHING IS WASTED

On April 30, 1990, Katie B. was back on the table.

She was 8 months old, as adorable as you please.

Hendren scoped her again and then opened her with a small incision across her lower abdomen.

By nature, Hendren is endlessly curious, and before he began the real work of getting down inside her bladder to relocate her strangely positioned ureter, he did some exploring. He's learned that you can never be too familiar with a patient's anatomy. If he were a young resident today, he'd stand a good chance of being criticized for moving too slowly.

What he discovered today was that Katie's unique insides included not one but two uteri. The first looked pretty good.

The second was pinched in the middle, creating in Hendren's mind an image he described as "like a 'wasp waist.'" He did not find a second vagina connected to it, but that didn't mean he wouldn't during the more extensive exploration that would accompany her reconstruction later in the year.

Moving the ureter went smoothly. Before he closed Katie up, Hendren removed a part he could confidently say she'd never need: her appendix. From now on, he could automatically rule out appendicitis should Katie ever have pain in that region, one of the busiest crossroads of human anatomy. Although he had a pretty good idea that second uterus was as useless as her appendix, he did not pluck that out, not today. A cardinal rule of the reconstructionist is that nothing is wasted, nothing gets damaged or thrown away, not until it has been absolutely proven there can never be a use for it.

After 5 hours and 10 minutes of anesthesia, less than half the time she'd be under the next time, Katie B. left the O.R.

RECHARGING HIS BATTERIES

Most Saturdays, Hendren works.

Come evening, he heads home.

He drives south toward Cape Cod, chatting on the cellular phone, as he does every week, to his 93-year-old mother. Mrs. W. Hardy Hendren Jr. still lives in Kansas City, Mo.—independent and alone since her husband, a lifelong smoker, died of lung cancer in 1978. Near Plymouth, the doctor son says goodbye. He leaves the highway, passing a cranberry bog on his way to Duxbury, a town that for centuries has been wedded to the sea.

"This is where I recharge the batteries," he says.

The Hendren house is white, with porches and alcoves and a patio and views across green lawn of the Atlantic Ocean. Hendren is not sure exactly how many rooms the place has, only that there are enough to comfortably sleep four sons, four daughters-in-law, seven grandchildren, two grandmothers, two dogs, and the ex-Catholic nun who lives there, minding the place during the week.

Home is the one place Hendren putters, sometimes for an entire day, which approaches the limits of how long he can last without getting itchy for work. He loves the water, loves to take the grandchildren on his powerboat or watch them comb the beach. At 65, he still water-skis. He has a BMW

750 motorcycle, and on good days, he likes to don helmet and gloves and take guests for rides. In his cellar, he has a woodworking shop. A skeletal hand scrounged from an autopsy years ago has been hung on the wall over his tool bench, along with a handwritten sign: "From a Careless Workman."

Upstairs are reminders of career. A grandfather clock a Dutch patient sent him. A picture of him in O.R. gear that Eleanor tacked to the refrigerator door. The bound reports of every operation he's ever done, all the way back to the first: an appendectomy he performed in July 1952, fresh from Harvard Med.

But family, not physician, is the dominant motif. A painting of a 19th-century forefather presides over the dining room, above a three-leaf table Hendren made at Dartmouth. Pictures of weddings and grandchildren crowd a baby grand. On the wall along the main stairway to the second floor, in ascending order of birth, are pastel portraits of the Hendrens' daughter and four sons. On the landing are annual photographs of a growing family.

The first is from 1947, when Sandy was a newborn and Hendren, 21, had yet to tie a knot.

DYING BY DEGREES

Eleanor noticed it first. Sandy, 7, wasn't herself.

She's urinating too often, she told her husband, who was a senior resident at Children's, training under Dr. Robert E. Gross. *She has an appetite but isn't gaining weight. She just doesn't look right, Hardy.*

Guessing that she had a urinary tract infection, an easy enough matter to treat, Hardy took a sample of her urine and examined it under a microscope in a Children's lab. Surely he would find an abundance of white blood cells, a telltale sign of infection. Surely this was no big deal.

Her urine was clean.

My God, Hardy thought. *I hope her urinary frequency is not based on spilling sugar.*

But it was. Sandy had juvenile diabetes. According to the medical texts, her life expectancy was 20

years. Toward the end, her kidneys might fail. She
might go blind. She might get gangrene, and the
best the doctors would be able to do then would be
amputate. Dying by diabetes, the young surgeon
knew, is dying by degrees.

*Her life's going to be as normal as we can make
it,* Hardy decided. *We're going to keep her out of
the hospital as long as we can.*

For years, more years than expected, a careful
diet and daily injections of insulin controlled her
disease. Sandy made it through grammar school,
high school, college. Despite weight gain and vision that was beginning to fail, she graduated from
Boston University with a degree in education.

And she sang. And played piano. And acted.
Like Eleanor, and like her grandmother, Hardy's
mom, Sandy was musically gifted. It was Sandy at
the keyboard leading holiday sing-alongs, Sandy
finding her way onto the amateur stage. She played
many roles over the years, but her most memorable
came well into adulthood, when she was Annie in
the musical of the same name.

*When I am stuck with a day that's gray and
lonely,* she sang, *I just stick up my chin and say:
Oh, the sun will come out tomorrow.*

A FINAL TRIP TO FRANCE

For a while after graduating from Boston University, Sandy taught first grade.

But medicine had a hold on Sissy, as it did on
three of her four brothers. Hardy convinced her that
becoming a doctor would be too grueling, what
with her failing health—but nursing might not. In
1980, at the age of 32, she graduated from B.U.
with her nursing degree. She was hired as an O.R.
nurse at the Massachusetts General Hospital, where
Hardy had his own department. On occasion, she
scrubbed in with her dad.

Sandy's last years were the worst. Her vision
continued to go. She lost three fingers and part of a
foot to gangrene. Her other leg was going bad
when, shortly before her death, Hardy learned he
was to receive an honorary degree at the University

of D'Aix-Marseilles, France. It was a huge honor, only the second time an American had been so selected.

I want to go, Daddy, Sandy said. *I want to be there when you get your medal.*

Sissy, he said, *we're going to take you.*

They did. Hardy filled a suitcase with gauze and antiseptic and some of his gold-plated instruments, and Eleanor packed their clothes, and the two of them took turns with Sandy's wheelchair as they brought her to Logan and onto a plane to Paris and onto another plane to Marseilles. Three times a day, Hardy treated Sandy's leg. Three times a day, he cleaned and bandaged, and Sandy, never complaining, gritted her teeth against the pain.

Sandy saw her father receive his degree. She was elated.

On the day after their return to Boston, her leg was amputated at the Mass. General Hospital, where she'd worked.

FACING A NEEDLE

On Nov. 1, 1990, three days before the sixth anniversary of Sandy's death, the Brinegars brought Katie, now 15 months of age, back to Children's Hospital. They were assigned to 8 West, which specializes in preschoolers.

Children's philosophy is that painful procedures should not ordinarily be performed in a patient's room, which is to be maintained as sanctuary in scary surroundings. And so, when it was time to get a line into Katie's veins and a tube down her nose, she was taken down the hall to a treatment room. To find a treatment room in a children's hospital, one need only follow the screams.

Jean couldn't bear to watch.

But Terry could. Terry didn't want his little girl facing anything like that alone. Terry wanted to keep his eye on things.

Terry held Katie B. as they came at her with the thing a child who's ever had a shot dreads most: a needle.

Observations and questions

1) Although the graphic shown below enhances understanding, it raises questions of taste. It focuses on a baby's buttocks and genitals. Is the art offensive in a daily newspaper? What guidelines would you use to decide on matters of taste in this story? Miller said the *Providence Journal-Bulletin* expected some calls complaining about the art, but didn't get them.

2) The WED concept of the unity of writing, editing, and design calls for early conferring among all parties needed for a story. "Working Wonders" was produced by a writer, editor, photographer, graphic editor, copyeditor, and others. Excellent journalism requires teamwork with early consultation.

3) Miller devotes quite a bit of space to the Orvar Swenson Medal ceremony. What does this vignette add to the story?

4) The award section ends on page 34 with a quote by Dr. Martin W. Abrams. What's the value of the kicker to this section?

Artwork provided by the *Providence Journal-Bulletin*

Working wonders: Day 4

NOVEMBER 20, 1991

As the first patients of the day are being sent to sleep in 16 nearby operating rooms, green-garbed doctors and nurses are beginning their day in a lounge at the Children's Hospital, Boston, at 7:30 a.m.

Some drink coffee. Some leaf through a *Boston Herald* that's making the rounds. Many scrutinize today's schedule, a computer-generated document two pages long.

They move through the schedule, stopping to circle a case or offer an opinion. The schedule lists each patient's name, age, procedure, surgeon, room, and an educated guess of how many units of blood might need to be transfused. The blood is a rough guide to the difficulty—and danger—of an operation.

Another measure is the surgeon's name.

Thirty-seven cases are on for today, Friday, Nov. 2, 1990. In Room 8, chief neurosurgeon Dr. Peter McL. Black is opening up a 7-year-old's brain to try to cure a seizure disorder. In Room 14, bone marrow is being harvested for a transplant a leukemia patient will undergo. There is some orthopedic work and rebuilding of a 5-year-old's deformed face, an implantation of an artificial testicle into a toddler, and a biopsy of an infant's tongue.

Brinegar, Katrin, cloacal reconstruction, another item on the schedule reads.

Two units of blood. A lot.

Hendren is the surgeon.

There's excitement today in Room 7, Dr. W. Hardy Hendren III's operating theater. What happens in this cramped, bright, stuffy space will determine a baby's whole life.

Hendren fastens his mask and enters his domain.

"Good morning," he says.

"Good morning, sir," the visitors reply, several

in accented English. Among today's observers are doctors from Poland, Mexico, and Brazil. Among the best and brightest surgeons their nations have to offer, none has ever tackled a cloaca.

Katie is already on the table, naked but warm under heat lamps. A ventilator breathes for her. Anesthesiologists put the final touches on the technology that will keep her alive: the intravenous lines, blood-pressure cuff, thermometer, EKG probes, and pulse oximeter. This simple electronic device, which fits the tiniest finger and monitors oxygen in the blood, has taken pediatric anesthesia from the realm of risky to the almost-always safe.

"This is a thinking case," Hendren says as he reviews his x-rays and notes and the sketch he made of Katie's anatomy.

"Nobody in his right mind does these."

A DIFFICULT NIGHT

Katie did not have an easy go of it the night before her reconstruction.

With Terry holding her, the nurses finally managed to get an IV started and a naso-gastric tube through her nose and down to her stomach. For surgery involving intestines, Hendren demands a thorough cleansing, and for that, the system must be flushed with a purgative: Go-Lytely, a clear, quick-acting liquid fed through the NG tube. Terry and Jean took turns emptying their daughter's colostomy bag.

After supper, anesthesiologists came by 8 West to have the obligatory permission forms signed. The Brinegars listened while the risks of putting a baby under were explained. Most severe, they were told, is death.

Katie eventually slept.

At 9, she awoke, crying and vomiting. Jean crawled into her crib to cuddle her. Around 11, Katie drifted off again. Jean slept at cribside, on a chair that converts into something almost describable as a bed.

Terry slept at Gardner House, where Children's rents rooms to eligible families for a pittance. He

was up at 5:30 a.m. He smoked one of the Marlboros his daughter's surgeon had beseeched him to
quit and was on 8 West by 6 a.m. with a cup of coffee for his wife. After three hours' sleep, Hendren's
residents were just beginning their morning rounds.

At around 7, Katie was brought down to Pre-op
Holding, where patients and parents play or read or
watch TV and try not to think of what lies through
the doors.

RECONSTRUCTION BEGINS

"Let's have the 10-scope and the nerve stimulator."

Hendren is handed both. The stimulator consists
of a battery-powered box, wires, and a disposable
probe that resembles a large blue pen. It activates
muscle tissue according to the same electrical principle high school biology students discover when
making frog legs twitch.

Katie is in stirrups. Hendren sits at the foot of the
table, impatient for yet another look. When he's
ready to go, he's ready to go.

"Room lights down, please," he says.

Dorothy Enos, Hendren's private scrub nurse
and full partner in all of his big cases, does not re-
spond as quickly as Hendren would like, which is
instantaneously.

"Dorothy? *Lights down.*"

The lights dim, but only when Enos gets around
to hitting the switch. Hendren gets a good long look
inside Katie, records a few minutes of videotape,
withdraws the scope, and touches the stimulator to
Katie's bottom.

"All right. Zap it."

Hendren zings here and there, searching for the
exact center of the sphincter and levator muscles,
which act as a thick clamp around the normal rectum. The margin of error is slim. A millimeter or
two off, and Katie's chances for continence will begin to plummet.

"That ought to be the anus right there. Can I have
a marker?"

Dr. Steve Stylianos, Hendren's first assistant to-

day, hands him a sterile felt pen. He marks the spot
with a blue cross.

"All right," he says, standing. "You can put away
the video."

As Enos does, Hendren apologizes to her for
snapping about the lights.

"I'm going to put on her headstone: 'With her
patience and understanding, she contributed great-
ly to our understanding of cloacas,'" he says.

"You can leave out the patience and understanding," Enos says. "I ran out."

Hendren looks to see if she's kidding.

This morning, she is.

'SAINT DOROTHY'

"Saint Dorothy" is the name Enos has jokingly
given herself. Hendren has bestowed another title:
WBSN, for World's Best Scrub Nurse.

Hendren's made such a big deal of WBSN that
Stylianos, his assistant chief resident for the 1990-
91 year, had a fake citation made up, not entirely as
a gag. Doctors who've seen Enos in action in the
O.R. marvel at her surgical sense, at the way Hendren in midoperation will turn to her for advice—at
how, almost invariably, he takes it. Hendren relies
so heavily on Enos that when she's on vacation, he
will not schedule a cloaca.

An accomplished gardener, fond of traveling and
collecting antiques, Enos, who has never married,
lives near Children's but spends a good deal of her
free time with the Hendrens.

Enos's father was a truck driver whose family,
who were fishermen, left the Azores for America at
the turn of the century. Her mother's people came
from England while John Winthrop, first governor
of the Massachusetts Bay Colony, was still alive.
Enos grew up near Boston and was enrolled at the
now-defunct Children's Hospital School of Nursing
when she met Hendren. He was a resident, already
making a name for himself, and not simply for his
skill with the blade. Even in the 1950s, Hendren
was extraordinarily confident—the personality of a
man who was shooting carrier landings at age 20.

Enos, who is in her early 50s, scrubbed with Hendren at Children's, where she was on staff, but as impressed as he was with her, he couldn't afford to employ her privately until 1962. He'd been at Mass. General for two years by then, and he was out straight building that larger hospital's first department of pediatric surgery.

"Help has arrived for us!" Hendren wrote in his calendar on March 12, 1962, the day she came to work for him. He's marked the anniversary ever since.

In the early '80s, when Hendren was being wooed back to Children's, the hospital administration balked on one point. He insisted on bringing Enos with him.

That might be the way they do it over at The General, but not here, Children's responded. *We don't have any private scrub nurses here.*

But this was Hardy Hendren. His response was simple: *I come as a package deal.* If they wanted him, and the patients he'd bring, they'd have to take his nurse—and three secretaries, too.

Children's did.

NO PREDICTIONS

Ordinarily on his biggest cases, where there is no certainty of outcome, Hendren will sit with parents and handwrite a customized "operative request." He deliberately does not label it a "permission" form, since that would imply that the surgeon somehow had initiated the proceedings. Hendren has parents—and a witness—sign his form.

"He has made it clear that there can be no guarantees about the function of the urinary tract, the bowel tract, or the genital tract, and that we must simply wait and see about all of these things," he wrote before an operation on a patient similar to Katie B. "We understand that if we are to improve our daughter's future, we must simply proceed with faith in the surgeon who is willing to try to help her."

Hendren has not drawn up a form for the Brinegars. He feels they understand the risks and uncertainty of outcome—and the fact that until he has their daughter opened up, he cannot predict precisely what he will do.

Terry had asked Hendren if he had any idea when he'd be done.

Yes, Hendren replied. "When the last stitch is in."

'IT'S PRETTY FANTASTIC'

Stylianos, 35, assistant chief surgical resident at the time of Katie B.'s reconstruction, is a man of boundless enthusiasm and humor. He settled on pediatric surgery when he was a third-year medical student.

"You get these babies with their insides all twisted, and you put them back together and send them on their way. It's pretty fantastic!"

Someday, Stylianos will head his own department, be invited to lecture at prestigious universities, have foreign visitors honored to be at his table. Even now, his responsibilities are enormous. When he's not in Room 7, Stylianos oversees many of the day-to-day activities of the Department of Surgery. He helps supervise the younger residents, schedules conferences, operates on his own patients virtually every day of the week.

In Room 7, he belongs to Hendren.

"Steve," the chief of surgery says, "we have to plan our attack."

He is talking about how he will get inside Katie, whether he will attempt the entire operation by cutting through her bottom and working from behind, or whether he'll need access through her abdomen, too.

"I think we ought to go in from above," Hendren says. "We can slip into the belly, mobilize the colon. Then we'll turn her over and go in through the bottom."

From an anesthesia point of view, turning a patient, even one as small as Katie, complicates matters: The risk of dangerously crimping or unplugging all those wires and hoses and tubes escalates. But there's no alternative; anatomy has the final say. There's just too much to do in too many far-flung parts of Katie B. to reach everything through a single opening.

Hendren asks Stylianos what he thinks of his plan.

Stylianos says it sounds fine.

WAR ON BACTERIA

In his four decades in surgery, Hendren has seen more than one patient breeze through a long, tricky operation, only to die later of massive infection—"complications" is the euphemism commonly used—that can be traced to the O.R., where stray germs invaded an open wound.

It's a senseless way to go, death from a speck of dust or a piece of lint. Unlike some other senior surgeons, who delegate the tedious work of preparation to the younger doctors, Hendren does it himself, rarely accepting help. Good preparation is good insurance against infection.

He is obsessed with hair.

His male residents are always clean-shaven, no matter how many hours they've gone without sleep. Hendren likes their hair as short as his, the female residents' hair not much longer.

"Bacteria jump off those things like rats off a sinking ship," he said to a bearded male nurse who visited Room 7 one day. The nurse came in with the standard cap and mask, inadequate for such a full growth. Hendren sent him to the locker room to change into more elaborate garb.

Worse than hairs are flies, which would be a disaster in an O.R. To get anywhere near the surgical suite at Children's, a fly would first have to get inside the hospital, no mean feat considering almost none of the windows open and the doors all automatically close. It would have to escape the Flintrol Insect Electrocutor. It would have to negotiate three flights of stairs, several corridors and corners and doors, all the while slipping past dozens of people with a profound professional interest in pest control.

Somehow, on the day of Katie's operation, one made it: a big, black, buzzing fly, separated from

Katie by but a single door.

Hendren spots it in the corridor outside Room 7 as he's on his way to his office to eat a bowl of fruit. He takes chase, swatting and shouting—half in Spanish, half in English—to two Hispanic attendants who happen to walk by.

"Fly! Fly! There's a fly loose in here! La mosca!"

Pam Spinney, whom Hendren recently hired to help with his medical writing, and who has come, with some trepidation, to see her first cloaca, joins the effort. Now four people are after the fly, running, swatting, closing fire doors, trying to isolate it, trying to head it off, shouting.

"La mosca! La mosca!" Hendren yells.

The fly escapes. At least they've shooed it away from the operating rooms and back toward the lounge, its probable point of entry.

EVERYTHING IN ITS PLACE

"Let me have a Q-Tip, please," Hendren says.

Stylianos hands him one from a sterile tray. Hendren dips it into Betadine, a syrupy substance lethal to germs. He cleans Katie's navel. Satisfied, he soaks a sponge in the Betadine. He paints Katie's abdomen, back and forth, up to her chin, down to her bottom, over and over until her skin is completely brown. He lifts a leg, paints it, wraps it in a sterile towel, then winds gauze around the towel. He does the same to her other leg.

Careful not to touch anything "dirty"—definition: anything not sterile—Hendren and Enos slowly bury Katie in blue towels and drapes, all cloth. Unlike other surgeons, Hendren doesn't like disposable paper drapes. Soon all that's left is the surgical field: Katie's bare belly and bottom.

The prep tray is wheeled into a corner. Hendren removes his gloves and glasses and puts on his Loupes, surgical spectacles that provide 3.5-power magnification—an absolute must for delicate work. His headlamp, which generates intense but cool illumination, fits above the Loupes. Hendren adjusts both, then leaves the room for the wash station, where he scrubs and scrubs.

Meticulously arranged atop Enos's sterile-draped carts and trays are instruments. Most doctors at Children's rely on house tools, which are held in common. Not Hendren. These are his, paid for out of his pocket. Mostly German, some virtually one-of-a-kind, a few designed by him, each is gold-plated and engraved with his name. Enos and Enos alone is entrusted with supervising their cleaning and sterilization.

She rolls them into place at the foot of the table. Stylianos—who, like Enos, is already scrubbed and dressed—positions himself to the right of Katie.

Hendren returns, his hands sudsy and dripping wet.

Enos gives him a towel, then assists him with gown and gloves: brown, size 8. He steps to the left-hand side of the table, adjacent to the ventilator. A nurse plugs in his headlamp cord. Enos slides into her customary spot to Hendren's right.

An Asian doctor who was visiting one day discovered the consequences of intruding on Enos's turf. As she was busily arranging her trays, the doctor, on his first visit to Hendren's room, innocently took her spot.

Hendren fixed him with one of his looks.

"That spot is sacred ground," the chief said, in a voice as dry as desert sand. "It's like a Shinto shrine. Dr. Choi would join his ancestors if he stood there too long."

Today, for Katie B., everything is in its natural order.

Hendren holds out his hand.

Enos places the correct knife in it.

Neither speaks.

Hendren makes the first cut, a long incision from chest to below the diaper area. Droplets of blood seep from tiny vessels. Hendren sets about burning them shut with the electric cautery machine and an insulated forceps called a Jake, which Hendren designed.

The Jake sizzles. Wisps of smoke rise toward the lights and a sweet smell, the smell of raw meat over hot charcoal, fills the nostrils.

A LONG WAIT FOR PARENTS

The Brinegars wait.

They play gin, make idle talk, watch the waiting-room TV. For a break, they go down to the cafeteria for coffee or outside for a smoke. Periodically, Doris Fina, the surgical liaison nurse, calls Room 7 for an update.

"Everything's fine," Hendren says. No matter what's going on in Room 7, that's always his response.

'NO PROBLEM AT ALL'

Hendren goes deeper.

Using a combination of cutting cautery, scissors, and blade, he proceeds through skin, fat, a layer of tissue called the rectus sheath, finally piercing the peritoneum, a thin but tough membrane that lines the abdominal cavity. There is no hesitation in his work, no false starts, not a single wasted motion. Hendren is as unflappable at his table as he was in a plane.

He places a metal ring around the wound and attaches several retractors to pry it wide open. He has to be able to get two hands and a multitude of instruments down in there.

Sometimes after an operation, the body in its mysterious ways grows spider-web-like scar tissues known as adhesions. They can entwine the intestines, strangling them in extreme cases, and taking them down can slow the surgeon to a maddening crawl. Katie, luckily, has pretty much escaped the curse of adhesions. Hendren begins to free up the rectum, slowly separating the tissues that hold it in its unnatural position, slicing them, Jaking the inevitable bleeders. When he turns Katie over, he'll have no trouble pulling the rectum through to the spot he's marked for an anus.

It's hard to remember that there is a living, breathing child underneath all this sterile cloth.

No legs are visible, no hands, not even a toe or one of Katie B.'s eyes. The anesthesiologist has taped those shut, and he's encased her head in a plastic bag to help retain warmth. Excessive fluid or heat loss during surgery can send a patient hurtling toward cardiac arrest.

Nowhere has nature duplicated the tints and textures found inside the human gut. Few but surgeons and pathologists and soldiers at war ever see them.

There are the small intestines, which range in color from plum to pink, depending on how blood is flowing to them. The large intestines are sturdy-looking, coiled like hawser and covered with capillaries. The bladder is small and smooth and shaped like a little girl's purse. Muscle is fibrous and stringy. Fat is yellow and globular, like fresh-killed chicken. And, of course, the ubiquitous blood: as brilliant as strawberries when fresh; gooey and the color of something dredged from a swamp when clotting.

"Plenty of bowel," Hendren says. "That's no problem at all."

INSIDE THE O.R.

On one wall of Room 7 is a *New Yorker* cartoon. It shows an operating room, a doctor, a nurse, and an octopuslike organ flying out of a patient into the air. Someone has written this caption:

"Whoa! Watch where that thing lands, Dorothy. We'll probably need it."

The sign on the opposite wall is not frivolous:

"If an operation is difficult, you are not doing it properly." This was the motto of another Children's surgeon, Dr. Robert E. Gross. When he was chief, the sign was in his room.

Gross retired in 1972. He died 16 years later, 83 years old and in a nursing home. By then, Hendren, his star pupil, had already trained dozens of his own surgeons. Today, many are chiefs of departments, full professors at prestigious medical schools, prominent in transplantation, urology, reconstruction, and open-heart work. One whose work has captured the popular imagination is Michael Harrison, the San Francisco doctor whose ground-breaking work in fetal surgery landed him in *People* magazine last year. Harrison was a resident with Hendren when Hendren separated his first pair of Siamese twins.

Hendren is fiercely protective of his top residents, who come to him with seven or more years' experience in surgery. He champions their research, their publications, their promotions. He buries them in the commodity they most covet, O.R. time. He lets them have their own patients, and while he's always available for advice, he's hardly ever looking over their shoulders.

Except when they're in Room 7.

There, he watches every move so intently that some have been known to sweat. The gospel according to Hendren is a lengthy book, but the first chapter contains the highest truth: Cutting and sewing and judgment remain the cornerstones of surgery, no matter how high-tech the age. Bad cuts and bad knots give bad results. There is no better recipe for a killer infection than a leak, even the tiniest leak, from an intestine improperly sewn.

IMPORTANCE OF STITCHING

No one escapes criticism for substandard stitching.

During one operation last year, a case that went 17-1/2 hours, Hendren was helped by a younger doctor. Through the morning and all afternoon, the doctor stood across the patient from Hendren, observing, admiring, holding retractors, picking the brain of the master himself with carefully rehearsed and intelligently posed questions.

As Hendren was closing up the boy's bladder, he asked the doctor if she would like to tie. Not only would she like to—she would consider it an honor. But hers was a nervous honor, and her hands shook. Struggling a bit, she managed to tie one knot. And two. And three.

On the fourth, Hendren cocked his head and said: "Who taught you how to tie?"

The younger doctor was mortified.

"That's an air knot," Hendren said. "You could fly an airplane through there." He beckoned to a nurse and said: "Air gauge, please."

The doctor was puzzled.

The nurse went to the cabinet and returned with

a sterile green package. Enos unwrapped it. Inside was a tiny plastic triplane, which Enos handed to Hendren. Imitating a sound he knows well, the sound of an airplane, the chief made several passes near the inferior knot.

"See? You could fly an airplane through that!"

UNSURPASSED TECHNIQUE

"Now let's see what we have here."

Hendren's gown is bloodstained. He's deep inside Katie B., exploring with retractors and forceps and the blunt edges of scissors and that most versatile of instruments, the surgeon's fingers. With them, he holds, pushes, joins, measures thickness, analyzes texture, clamps, traces a network of blood vessels to its source, isolates nerves he can't afford to sever.

All the while, thinking.

Hendren's greatest gift may be his ability to conceptualize—to look beyond the bloody wreckage of a deformed anatomy and imagine what it could look like, *should* look like. It is almost a four-dimensional ability, something that cannot be taught or gleaned from *Gray's Anatomy.* "His technique is second to none, but what's unique to Doctor Hendren is this vision," says Stylianos, who has studied under many masters.

"Hold this up here, Steve," the chief says. "Good. Thank you. Let me have a little retractor, Dorothy. Here's a Fallopian tube and a little uterus. This uterus—I don't think it goes anyplace. Now let me see the one on the other side. This one, I think, goes to a vagina. See, that's bladder."

As he cuts, Hendren is refining his mental blueprint.

Is the vagina properly sized?

Will we need colon to augment it?

Is there a second one hidden in here?

How's that blood supply?

Careful near that ureter. It's the only one she has.

"Look, Dorothy, look," Hendren says. "What the heck's this?"

Observations and questions

1) In the fourth day of the series, the writer turns to greater use of dialogue. Notice the difference in pace created by that change. Why might the writer decide to use more conversations at this point?

2) In the middle of a tense story on a little girl's operation, Miller presents the scene of a prominent doctor, his assistant, and two hospital attendants chasing a fly. What purposes are served by this section?

3) Writers use a number of techniques to capture a scene. One method is to let the writing imitate the mood of the scene. In the section "Everything in Its Place" beginning on page 49, Miller describes a meticulous medical procedure. Notice how the pace of the writing slows. How does the writer achieve this?

4) In the article "Five Frames to Support Your Articles," Jane Harrigan notes that Truman Capote mastered the technique of parallel narratives: two subjects moving along different paths to the same end. Miller has shifted between the doctor and the parents throughout the story, but notice how their paths intersect parallel on page 51. What is the effect of parallel narratives?

5) The ending of each story is especially important in a series. Each ending has to entice the reader to continue the story the next day. Study the ending to this story. Compare it to previous endings.

Working wonders: Day 5

NOVEMBER 21, 1991

Ben Trelease was full of the devil. His favorite mischief involved toy guns he built from coat hangers and wood. Ben sold his guns: the snub-nosed for a dime; bigger models, including the six-shooter, for a quarter or more. Ammunition was rubber bands.

But Ben liked to do more than sell his guns.

He liked to use them.

And he had no more cherished targets than the nurses at St. Luke's Hospital in Kansas City, Mo., where he was repeatedly admitted for a disease that eventually killed him—in 1939, the year the kid down the block, Hardy Hendren, graduated from grammar school.

Like Katie Brinegar, Ben Trelease had a defective urinary system.

He was a thin boy, with twinkling green eyes and blond hair. He loved reading *Popular Mechanics,* and he was good with his hands. With his father's help, he built boats. He put together a crystal radio. He assembled his own motor scooter from a kit, a feat that profoundly impressed his younger friend.

Hardy had an equally agile mind.

He was innately curious, and his parents helped satisfy that curiosity with an aquarium, an Erector set, American Flyer trains, the low-power microscope he'd asked Santa Claus to bring so that he might "see germs." Ben's sister Rosemary, who lives now in Rhode Island, was friends with Virginia Major, only daughter of Dr. Ralph H. Major, a prolific writer and professor at the University of Kansas School of Medicine. Virginia was Hardy's girlfriend.

All three families worshipped at St. Paul's Episcopal Church, where Ben's father was rector and Hardy's was warden, in charge of financial affairs. The two boys wound up in the choir. Hardy's attendance was near-perfect. Not Ben's. He was too sick for perfect attendance anywhere.

No one could figure out how to cure Ben.

He was in and out of the hospital, but nothing stopped the kidney failure that was fatally poisoning him. In the final months of his life, he was sent to California; there, a surgeon opened him up, got into his bladder, and left him with a tube.

Ben came home to Kansas City with a bag for his urine. Three decades later, his boyhood pal would write surgical history getting rid of colostomy bags.

On the day that Ben died, Hardy was with his friend's brother, Murray, who today is the rector of St. Paul's Episcopal Church. Murray was younger than Hardy. Murray was devastated. Hardy took him for a long ride on his Motoscoot, which he'd bought with the profits from selling subscriptions to magazines.

On and on through the Country Club district of Kansas City they rode, at one point swinging through Loose Park, where Hardy, who already dreamed of being a doctor, had dissected his very first specimen: a tadpole. Hardy tried to comfort Murray, tried to make sense of something so senseless.

Ben Trelease had had dreams of being a doctor.

IT STARTS WITH ANESTHESIA

"What the heck's this?"

Hendren is exploring Katie B.'s insides through the opening in her belly.

He feels around. It's a tiny organ, pinkish-white, soft, thin, something only the most experienced eye could identify.

"That's an extra vagina," he concludes.

As for what to do—whether to plug it or the other one in, or sew both together to make one, as he sometimes has to do—he'll deal with that later. For now, he's intent on turning his patient. He needs access to Katie's bottom, to begin putting her parts where they belong.

He packs her abdominal cavity with sponges, removes retractors and the ring, temporarily closes the wound with heavy black sutures, and gives the anesthesiologists—a second one has been called in—the signal to begin.

The development of anesthesia is one of the authentic miracles of modern medicine. Hendren and his nurse, Dorothy Enos, began surgery in an era when, sad as it might be, it was assumed a certain percentage of children would die on the O.R. table. Advances in technology and drugs, many made at Children's in Dr. Robert E. Gross's operating room, have enabled today's doctors to keep a baby under 24 hours or more—and bring her back, none the worse for wear and tear.

But turning remains risky.

Last fall, during a cloacal reconstruction not unlike Katie B.'s, the patient had just been turned, apparently successfully, when the anesthesiologist, a young resident, announced to Hendren:

"The patient's not ventilating."

As the anesthesiologist frantically checked wires and tubes and monitor displays, Hendren calmly removed the drapes, flipped his patient onto her back, and disconnected the hose joining the anesthesia machine to the endotracheal tube, which delivers air and anesthesia directly into the lungs. Still calm, Hendren pulled off his mask and began mouth-to-mouth resuscitation through the tube.

Meanwhile, help had been called. Senior anesthesiologists were almost immediately in the room, and they quickly discovered the problem: In turning, a hose had become unplugged. It was reconnected, with no harm whatsoever to the patient, who'd been without air no more than 20 or 30 seconds.

The resident anesthesiologist surely expected a reaming, but Hendren did not deliver it. Instead, he complimented everyone for their handling of the accident: the resident for promptly sounding the alarm, her superiors for immediate identification and correction of the problem, the entire room for remaining calm.

"As soon as people get excited," Hendren said, drawing the lesson of the day, "they don't work well. You can't think when there's bedlam going on."

WHAT LIES AHEAD?

Hendren props up Katie's midsection with a mound of folded towels. She's in the jackknife position, her sterile behind sticking into the air.

With the nerve stimulator, Hendren double-checks the location he chose for her anus; he's satisfied he can't do any better. Using an ordinary household toothpick dipped in green dye—toothpicks have finer points than felt pens—he draws a line where he wants the vagina.

"What do you think, Dorothy? How about there?"

Enos nods her assent.

Hendren cuts, along the line where the cleft of Katie's buttocks should have been. Absolute precision is essential in this cut, as are absolute vigilance and care. Not only do the organs that will be sewn into this space have to be perfectly aligned to function as God intended, but Hendren is getting into an area rich with vessels and nerves and, particularly with cloacas, quite conceivably a surprise or two.

"What you always have to be saying to yourself as a surgeon is: 'What tiger lies in the woods just beyond where I am?'" Hendren tells his residents.

As the wound deepens and opens, unfolding like the blossoming of a tropical flower, Hendren retracts the edges with rows of sutures and pronged, plierlike instruments called Weitlanders. At one point, he hits another vessel. He gets squirted, generously—just below his throat.

"The first time I saw surgery," he says, "I was pretty young. They opened up a lady's chest and a little bleeder hit me on my observer's gown. I wasn't at all sure I'd be able to handle that on a daily basis."

GROSS WROTE THE BOOK

Robert E. Gross was brilliant.

An operation he did at Children's in 1938 was the opening chapter in modern cardiac surgery; the

250-plus scientific papers he left demonstrate an extraordinary expertise in urology and general surgery as well. During a career that spanned 45 years, more than half as Children's chief surgeon, he won awards and honorary degrees. The textbook he single-handedly wrote, *The Surgery of Infancy and Childhood,* published in 1953 and translated into four languages, is still occasionally consulted. No pediatric surgeon worth his scalpel has not read it, at least as history.

Gross took chances no one else would. He got results no one else did. Untold thousands owe their lives to him and the generation of surgeons he trained.

But Gross could be unpredictable.

He took pride in bringing talented young surgeons along—but there came a point, at least for some, when Gross's support disappeared.

One morning early in July 1960, just days after he'd completed his chief residency—was finally fully trained—Hendren arrived in the O.R., ready for two operations he'd booked. In those days, the day's cases were written on a blackboard. Using red chalk, someone had drawn lines through Hendren's.

"Dr. Gross," Hendren was told.

The young doctor found the legendary one in his office.

"You're doing too much," Gross said. He advised Hendren to take an office down the street somewhere, maybe do some more lab work for a while.

Hendren was flabbergasted. Hendren was humiliated. Hendren immediately sought sanctuary with the Massachusetts General Hospital and a kinder mentor, Dr. Edward Churchill, who gave Hendren what he needed to build his own department of pediatric surgery. He would not return to Children's for 22 years.

THE MASS. GENERAL YEARS

Hendren's years at Massachusetts General were extraordinarily fruitful.

He invented instruments that today bear his name. He pioneered treatment of megaureter, a congenital defect of the upper urinary tract that had been a death sentence for many children. He began fixing cloacas, including the type that may be the worst congenital deformity a surgeon can correct: cloacal exstrophy. He made refinements in esophageal surgery and became intrigued with the sorts of problems that had killed his boyhood friend, Ben Trelease.

Until Hendren, the traditional view was that the best that could be done for children with certain severe urinary deformities—those like Ben's—was to give them colostomy bags. "Diversions," as such operations were called, often saved lives—but at a price. Hendren didn't think that price necessarily had to be paid.

He took kids with diversions and worked them up, memorized their strange anatomies, stayed up nights thinking about them. Then he took them into the O.R. to rebuild their insides—succeeding, in many cases, in not only getting rid of bags but restoring normal function. Some surgeons were initially skeptical of his results with these "hopeless" cases. One prominent physician went so far as to accuse him, behind his back, of falsifying his results.

But there they were, for all to see.

During his two decades at The General, Hendren founded a major research laboratory. He hired, encouraged, and promoted the person who succeeded him as chief of pediatric surgery: Dr. Patricia K. Donahoe, 54, one of a growing but still small number of female pediatric surgeons. Donahoe, who has written or co-written more than 130 scientific papers, including 19 of her first 25 with Hendren, was named one of *Ms.* magazine's Women of the Year in 1987.

Nothing captivated the public like Hendren's ground-breaking separation of Siamese twins, the first such operation in the long, rich history of Boston surgery. As a crowd including his wife and sons watched from the gallery that November day

in 1969—Sandy, his daughter, was there as a
nurse—Hendren, four surgeons, and four anes-
thetists separated the twins, who were joined from
bottom to chest.

The papers couldn't get their fill. Reports of the
12-hour operation went worldwide. There were interviews with Hendren, stories about Mr. and Mrs.
John Kobierski and their newborn girls, Maureen
Ann and Marie Elizabeth, who came through the operation with flying colors—and are alive and well
22 years later. Hendren assembled his team for a
photograph. He insisted that Enos, who'd scrubbed
on the case, sit with him in the front row.

Hendren even made one of his rare TV appearances: on *Garroway,* a morning variety show on
Boston's Channel 7. Hendren, brimming with detail about the historic surgery, arrived at the stu-
dio—and discovered that, in its infinite wisdom,
the programming department had selected Tiny
Tim as his fellow guest. Without skipping a beat,
Hendren said that was all right with him. Why,
even a renowned surgeon knew Tiny Tim's signature song, "Tiptoe Through the Tulips."

As a matter of fact, Hendren said, *once the camera's rolling I'll sing it for you.*

Just to prove he knew the tune, Hendren
launched into a falsetto rendition. Which, to the
producer's great relief, he did not repeat on-air.

LAWYERS ARE 'SCUMBAGS'

When it's going well, Hendren's loose.

A nurse often brings a boombox into Room 7,
and Hendren will allow the news or classical music, at low volume. He delights in telling stories and
jokes, especially stories about himself and jokes
about lawyers. Hendren doesn't hate all lawyers,
only those specializing in medical malpractice—
lawyers he describes, in more charitable moments,
as "societal leeches" and "scumbags."

Understandably, Hendren and his three oldest
sons, all surgeons, were taken a bit aback when
David, the youngest member of the family, decided
to make a career of corporate law. "If he'd have

gone into malpractice, he'd have had four people in line to castrate him," Hendren says. For an instant, you wonder if he's kidding.

There has never been a successful action against Hendren. Two suits have been filed, only one of which made it to trial, in early 1990. The mother of one of Hendren's patients claimed that while perhaps he'd saved her daughter's life in an operation, he'd left the girl with persistent diarrhea. The mother wanted millions. Hendren's lawyer, John Kiernan, a former prosecutor for Suffolk County, Mass., presented testimony showing that the diarrhea had been there all along. Hendren was acquitted in under two hours.

But the experience had profoundly offended him. He had to wipe weeks off his O.R. schedule. He had to sit, silent, while his name was publicly besmirched. It was an insult to have to be so intimately involved with people he considered liars and cheats.

"If you can't turn a rag into a quilt, they turn around and sue you," he says. Of malpractice law, he adds: "I view the present system as a cancer, which infiltrates and destroys those things in which it's involved."

So he jokes.

You're in a room with Saddam Hussein, a cobra ready to strike, and a lawyer. You have a revolver with just two bullets. What do you do?

Shoot the lawyer—twice, to make sure he's dead.
Or:

Have you heard the one about why they're using lawyers instead of rats now for laboratory experiments?

There are three reasons. One, lawyers are in such plentiful supply. Two, people tend to become fond of rats. And three, there are some things that rats just won't do.

INTENSE CONCENTRATION

Almost 5 p.m., some six hours into the operation.

Blood loss has been moderate but not insignificant. The anesthesiologist starts a transfusion.

Working from below, Hendren has cut clear through to the abdominal cavity he opened at the operation's start. If he wanted to, he could reach up through Katie B.'s bottom and see his fingers in her open belly.

"There's that extra vagina," Hendren says. "Remember we found that little vagina sitting in there? See it, Dorothy?"

Enos nods.

Hendren studies the two vaginas. There's really no comparison. The first is by far the more substantial of the two, of sufficient length to be pulled down and sewed where nature should have put it. It is connected to a normal uterus, Fallopian tube, and ovary, which means Katie B. may be able to have babies of her own someday. Although most of Hendren's cloaca patients have yet to enter their child-rearing years, or are just beginning to, two of the oldest ones already have had children.

Careful not to damage the inferior vagina, Hendren dissects it away from the urogenital sinus, which will become urethra. Then he removes the organ from Katie. Enos holds a tin specimen cup and Hendren drops it in. A nurse will package and label and send it to pathology for microscopic examination.

Next on the agenda is fashioning the urethra, a procedure requiring meticulous stitching with sutures as fine as hair. The tissues he uses come from the urogenital sinus, the cloaca.

Hendren falls silent.

During periods of intense concentration, the only movement is his hands, the occasional blink of his eyes, the shifting from one leg to another to keep the pins and needles at bay, the pulsing of the carotid artery, which delivers blood through the neck to the head. There is an occasional clink of instruments striking each other, the sound of the ventilator bellows, an electronic pulse, Enos's suctioning, but no words between scrub nurse and surgeon. Enos has been with him so long that she anticipates his every need, several steps ahead. No wonder that when she's on vacation, the less experienced nurses don't clamor to step in for her.

Hendren and Enos can go 12 hours or more without a break—without the hint of a hunger pang or the urge to use the bathroom or have a drink of water or a cup of tea. Hendren suspects their bodies undergo a fundamental metabolic transformation during such stretches, and he's offered to become a human guinea pig. He's asked the Anesthesiology Department to catheterize him, have his heart and brain monitored, have regular samples of his blood drawn to nail down exactly what's going on during a long case.

Hendren believes there's an excellent paper in it, but so far, no one has taken him up on his offer.

SPEED CAN LEAD TO ERRORS

In the days before ether, surgeons were much valued for their speed. People facing such procedures as, say, an amputation weren't in the market for someone who lollygagged around. The tradition is not altogether dead. Some surgeons still pride themselves on speed, in part because the quicker they are, the more cases they can do—and the more fees they can collect.

Not Hendren.

"Dorothy and I could set track records if we wanted to," he says. But speed increases the risk of errors.

By suppertime, Hendren has completed Katie B.'s urethra. With a delicate forceps, he examines the usable vagina, holds it this way and that until he has the exact position he wants. He begins stitching it into place.

Half an hour later, he's done. They turn Katie onto her back. Although her second, misshapen uterus would be useless for reproduction, it could cause serious mischief during puberty. Hendren takes it out, along with part of the Fallopian tube connected to it. He leaves both ovaries intact. Hormones produced by them will make Katie B. a woman someday.

"We're ready to bring the bowel down," he says.

"We want to be sure we don't twist it." A twisted intestine will lose blood supply and die.

The bowel doesn't go easily. Enos gives him some surgical lubricant. He greases the bowel and tries again.

"Now we're going to pull this through."

With one hand, Hendren reaches through Katie's bottom. His fingertips touch. He gets the bowel down in one smooth pull.

"See?" he says. There's nothing left to accomplish inside Katie's abdomen except make sure they haven't lost a sponge, which can cause intestinal obstruction, a sure prelude to trouble. After a correct count, every sponge present and accounted for, Hendren sews up Katie's belly with three layers of fine sutures. He sews several drains into her abdomen to handle fluids that accompany postoperative healing, turns her onto her stomach for the last time, and gives a final check with the nerve stimulator of the position of her anus. A-OK. He trims the bowel and begins sewing it into place.

Where once was nothing but featureless pink skin, a little girl's normal anatomy is starting to appear.

11 HOURS OF SURGERY

With the end of the operation in sight, Dr. Janusz Bohosiewicz, the Polish visitor, heads for the door.

"Where are you going, Janusz?" Hendren says from behind his mask.

"Home."

"Home. *Home?*"

"Is late."

"Late? What time is it?"

"Eight-fifteen," the anesthesiologist says.

"You're leaving before you see how we taper a rectum," Hendren says, a sparkle in his blue eyes. If you can't learn that, who knows how many Polish children won't be able to control their bowels right! Hendren says, not phrasing it exactly that way.

"OK. Will stay."

A few minutes later, the phone rings. It's Mrs. Hendren. She calls every night, wanting to know how her husband's doing. A nurse holds the phone to Hendren's ear. He takes calls during surgery, but only from a select few.

I'm closing, he tells Eleanor. *See you soon.*

As he cleans and bandages Katie B.—Hendren, not an assistant, performs those tasks—he admires his work.

"That looks pretty good, doesn't it?"

There is pride in Hendren's voice, enthusiasm and something else: an emotion that approaches surprise, as if, after 40 years of difficult cases, he's still the tiniest bit amazed at what can be accomplished.

Eleven hours and 20 minutes after entering the O.R., Katie B. leaves. Hendren looks for the Brinegars in the waiting room, but they've gone for more coffee. Hendren goes to the locker room and strips to his boxers and the support hosiery he wears to control swelling in his legs. The phone rings.

It's Terry. A nurse has tracked him down.

"Everything is fine," Hendren says. He gives a short synopsis of what he did, chats a moment about hunting, and says good night.

He removes his glasses and, with both hands, rubs his eyes red. His back aches. He's hungry. Tomorrow, he's going hunting with a friend. He'll be back home Sunday, the sixth anniversary of his daughter's death.

For Katie B., unconscious as they bring her to intensive care, tomorrow is the beginning of a long, painful recovery.

Observations and questions

1) In her article "Moving Readers With Ease," Sally-Jo Bowman lists several mechanical and structural transitions. She describes one form, the radical shift, as a transition in which the writer stops and turns in a distinctly new direction. Miller's lead in "Day 5" is a radical shift from the previous day. How does he help the reader follow this radical shift?

2) Consider the background of Ben Trelease's story. Miller went to Kansas City to interview Hendren's mother and see scenes from the doctor's youth. In guiding Miller around town, Mrs. Hendren stopped at St. Paul's Episcopal Church, and Miller met the Reverend Trelease. During their conversation, Trelease asked, "Has Hardy ever told you about Ben?" From there the story of an early influence in Hendren's life emerged. In digging deeper, the reporter found a rich source for readers.

3) On page 57, the story of Katie B.'s operation resumes at the exact point at which it ended on "Day 4." What is the effect of resuming the story with the same wording as in the previous ending?

4) Miller interrupts the report of the operation again. On page 59, another section on Hendren's background begins. What are the advantages and disadvantages of breaking the main story line?

5) The circular story is a favorite of many writers. That's one in which the writer starts the story at one point, and returns to that point in the kicker. In this case, Miller starts with a sick child who dies and ends with a sick child on the way to recovery. Explore other ties between the portrayals of Ben Trelease and Katie Brinegar.

Working wonders: Day 6

Katie Brinegar is tied to her crib, angry and con-fused at the terrible things being done to her. A week after her reconstruction and she can't eat. Her throat still hurts from anesthesia. Her bladder is in spasms. She's had spells of nausea. Medication helps, but it can't bring Katie B., 15 months old, home from hell.

Tubes and bandages get in the way of anything she attempts. The harness around her waist pre-vents her from rolling onto her belly, never mind escaping her steel bars. Doctors and nurses, strang-ers all, keep coming by.

One look at their rubber gloves and she's in tears.

At least she has Mommy and Daddy.

They can't pick her up—can't hug her, haven't brought Grover, her kitty, to visit—but they can kiss her, rub her back, hold her hand. They've packed her crib with stuffed animals and get-well cards and a mirror. She has her dolly, Vern, and a bouquet of balloons. She has her books.

Surgery heals the body—at the temporary ex-pense of the mind. The mind goes into retreat on the O.R. table, chased by chemicals that paralyze and block pain. After an 11-1/2-hour operation, it needs encouragement coming back.

"What's that?" Jean Brinegar says as she flips through the pages of one of Katie's favorite stories, which Mommy's cheerfully read over and over and over. "That's a pussycat. Yeah. And a sunflower."

"Kitty," her daughter says.

"Kitty. Yeah!"

Slowly, the real Katie B. is returning.

But her parents are only slipping deeper into "hospitalitis," depression born of monotony and loss of control.

Jean is beginning to wonder if they'll ever go

home. With Thanksgiving just around the corner, Vermont might as well be on the moon.

Her husband, whose natural instinct is to question authority, scrutinizes everything the staff does. Terry wants to know how long, how much, who ordered it and why. When he disagrees, he speaks his mind. The Brinegars are not winning popularity contests on 8 West. But they have made peace with activities therapist Nancy Majors and a few nurses, including Jeanne Flynn.

NO GUARANTEES

The pediatric surgeon's ally is youth. It's tissue that's "fresh and vibrant," in the words of Dr. Joseph P. Vacanti, the transplant surgeon who was Hardy Hendren's first chief resident at Children's.

"As a biological system," Vacanti says, "a child can handle stress better than an adult."

But nothing is guaranteed. When you're operating out where Hendren is, there is an unpleasant truth: Not every surgery succeeds.

Hendren is candid with families. They learn that surgery, even the best surgery, is not counted among the exact sciences—that often the surgeon must go back in and try something new, something again. Even the master can fail.

One of the worst deformities that surgery can correct is cloacal exstrophy: all of the problems Katie B. had, with the cruel complication of having been born with those mangled organs spilling out of a hole in the abdominal wall. Until recent years, cloacal exstrophy was a sure death.

The baby from New York had cloacal exstrophy.

She was sent to Hendren hours after birth, and through several surgeries he'd been able to move her organs back inside, close her belly, reconstruct a great deal of her insides. To try to make her continent, he'd sectioned off a piece of intestine, folded it back onto itself, and sewn the resultant creation into the bladder. Hendren invented the surgery. No one else in the world had ever made a "bowel nipple" and used it like this.

His next six nipples worked well. They made

their owners as dry as a bone, as Hendren is fond of saying.

His seventh nipple, inside the girl from New York, was a failure.

"Unfortunately, it looks as if we have probably lost the nipple," Hendren wrote after postoperatively scoping the girl. "We will let everything soften up, and probably next year will make another attempt to either make a nipple or do something else..."

THE NURSES' ROLE

Dorothy Mahoney, the registered nurse who manages 8 West, has handled Hendren patients since the 1950s, when she was a student and he was a resident at Massachusetts General Hospital. She came to Children's in 1981.

I thought I'd gotten rid of you! she joked to Hendren when, a year later, he was named the new chief of surgery.

Mahoney, a straightforward and evenhanded woman, runs a tight—if colorfully decorated—floor. She provides families leeway with visitors and overnight stays. She keeps a kitchen stocked with milk, juice, snacks, and baby formula. Most important to Hendren, her staff is skilled in an arcane art: nursing cloaca patients back to health.

They also have a sense of humor about the chief.

During the 1991 Department of Surgery end-of-year party, 8 West nurses put on their annual follies before an audience that included Hendren, his wife, Eleanor, and his scrub nurse, Dorothy Enos. Wizard Hendren was a character in the skit. Traipsing after him through the land of Oz was Dorothy, whose pet dog, Toto, was in desperate need of a cloacal repair.

The skit included a rap number:
My name is Jade,
I've got it made.
Now I can pee,
Because the wizard fixed me!

And this line, which drew laughter from everyone, even the chief:

I am the Wizard Hendren, the closest thing you can get to God!

'I KNOW HOW BUSY HE IS'

Early the morning of Nov. 16, Hendren ducks out of the O.R., where he's about to start an operation on a Saudi Arabian boy that will last until nearly midnight.

Two stairs at a time, he sprints from the third floor up to 8 West. Two weeks have elapsed since he rebuilt Katie B. Although he saw her in the intensive-care unit shortly after her operation, this is Hendren's first visit to her on the floor. He's been tracking her progress through his residents, who provide daily updates—customarily at night, or during surgery.

Hendren is occasionally criticized for not being bedside more often. Such complaints both irritate and hurt him. He sees only a simple equation: More O.R. time adds up to more patients benefiting from his true talent.

Most families, including the Brinegars, understand.

"I know how busy he is," says Terry.

"I don't care about the social aspects," says another patient's mother. "I just want him to fix my kid."

Hendren examines Katie and explains to her parents, in detail, what he did in his O.R. Everything is healing nicely and the chief is optimistic. There is no reason to think his little patient won't be normal in every respect.

"I'm really very satisfied," he says. "It really turned out quite well."

Terry has several questions. One concerns a piece of raw-looking tissue on Katie's bottom. Hendren says it may heal and pull back in on its own; if not, he'll be able to easily trim it.

"We can make a rectum," he says. "It's just not quite as good as God's."

HEADING HOME AT LAST

On Thanksgiving eve, 18 days after being admitted, the Brinegars go home. Katie B.'s organs are in the right place now, but she still has a colostomy bag.

Among those taking notice of their discharge is their private insurer.

"Based on the generally accepted criteria we employ for these reviews," the insurer had informed the Brinegars in a pre-admission letter, "we expect the length of stay will be four days."

The letter was a fraud. Hendren has yet to encounter an insurance company that knows what cloacal reconstruction is, never mind having developed "generally accepted criteria."

In his billing, Hendren encloses medical illustrations to explain what he's done. He also attempts to describe reconstruction in terms comprehensible to the insurance people, whose intelligence and integrity he does not hold in high esteem.

"This operation is equivalent in duration and difficulty to performing four open-heart operations one right after the other, or four total hip replacements, one right after the other," he wrote to an insurer after surgery almost identical in complexity and duration to Katie B.'s.

"The main difference is that there are many surgeons trained and qualified to do the heart procedures and total hip replacements, but very few who manage these difficult cloacal reconstructions."

ELEANOR RAISED CHILDREN

Hendren's family came of age during his Mass. General years.

Like his father, Hendren believed educating his children was the best investment he could make. All five attended private schools. Douglas, the eldest son, went on to Harvard College and Case Western Reserve medical school. William went to Dartmouth and Harvard Medical. Robbie did Dartmouth and Loyola University School of Medicine. David, the fourth Dartmouth man in the family, graduated from Northwestern University Law School.

Despite her diabetes, Sandy earned two diplomas: a bachelor's in education and a nursing degree, both from Boston University. Her last job was as a surgical scrub nurse at Mass. General, and on occasion, she worked with Dad. But her passion remained music. In her most memorable role, she played the lead in the musical *Annie,* staged by a popular Mass. General charity, the Vincent Club.

The job of raising the children fell to Eleanor, a woman of endless patience and good humor. It was Eleanor who fed the kids, Eleanor who got them off to school, Eleanor who chauffeured them around town, Eleanor who tucked them into bed at night, Eleanor who did the housework and accommodated the guests her husband was always inviting home and coordinated care of a daughter who was losing fingers and toes and eyesight as she slowly slipped away. Somehow, Eleanor managed to find time to start a clothing manufacturing business.

"Eleanor can do anything," Hardy says, paying his ultimate compliment.

Hendren wasn't hurting financially during this time. But with all those tuitions, he wasn't getting rich.

By 1975, when his children's educations were mostly done, the Hendrens left physician-infested Brookline for Duxbury, a small, affluent community on Boston's South Shore. On the occasion of David's graduation from law school, Hendren realized another dream: a powerboat.

He named it *Nomo*, as in "No More" tuition.

OUTSHINING HIS TEACHER

During his 22 years at Mass. General, Hendren had virtually no contact with Dr. Robert E. Gross, the mentor who'd made it impossible to stay at Children's. But the hurt never went away, not entirely.

"As I get to the end of an academic surgical career," Gross said in May 1974, when he was 68, "it has been a tremendous satisfaction to me on many occasions to find young men who have been through the residency training program and on our staff who have taken a new look at things…"

The occasion was the annual meeting of the American Surgical Association. Before a packed auditorium, Gross stood to comment on a paper that Hendren had just delivered. The paper was the first public account of a revolutionary surgery Hendren devised to make some extremely handicapped children normal—by getting rid of their bags.

"They have accomplished many things which we thought before were impossible," Gross went on. "As I reflect on these things, it is very appropriate to recall the words uttered so long ago by Leonardo da Vinci when he said: 'The brilliant pupil will certainly outshine his teacher.'"

Hendren was stunned.

As the audience stood to applaud, a doctor friend turned to him and said: "Hardy, that is your apology."

In 1981, Dr. Judah Folkman, who had succeeded Gross as chief of surgery at Children's Hospital, stepped down to devote more time to cancer research. Children's formed a national search committee for Folkman's replacement. Hendren was asked to serve on the committee. He accepted. One of his suggestions was to write to prominent surgeons asking whom they would recommend.

One name came back more than any other: W. Hardy Hendren III.

Hendren was asked if he would consider being a candidate. Well, yes, he would. He took himself off the committee while the decision was made.

Hendren was in Kansas City when it was disclosed.

Gross was the first to call with congratulations.

KATIE B. AT HOME

Christmas comes and goes. It snows. With her gardens slumbering, Jean waits tables at Chuckles, a restaurant in the middle of ski country. Terry commutes to a bridge job in New York. On weekends, when Jason's at his father's, Katie B. and Terry are home alone.

On this particular Saturday, he bundles his baby, loads her onto his back, and takes her cross-country skiing through the twilight woods. Back inside, he stokes the wood stove and throws supper on: Terry Brinegar's homemade spaghetti sauce, featuring Vermont-ripened tomatoes and spices Jean has grown.

The Brinegar residence was Jean's grandmother's before she died. It has two stories, is painted white, is filled with baskets and quilts and dried flowers and braided rugs, all Jean's handiwork. Down cellar, in a small shop, birdhouses and bat houses Terry makes are in various stages of construction.

As Terry's sauce simmers, Katie Beast lives up to her name. She's into magazines, her dad's boots, the pots and pans. She tries to eat paper and tear a page from one of her books. She picks up Grover the cat and gives her a hug. She smiles, blows kisses, says "Hi!" and "B!" She puts a bag over her head and prowls the kitchen, growling.

After supper, Terry lays her on a board placed across the kitchen sink. He undresses her, unrolls her bag, empties and rinses it, and rolls it back up. He gives her a new diaper. After a story, he kisses and tucks her into bed.

ANATOMICALLY CORRECT

On March 6, 1991, Katie B. is back at Children's.

In an operation lasting five hours, Hendren gets rid of her bag. He trims her rectum, which has not healed exactly as he wanted. "I think her outlook should be good," Hendren observes.

For the first time in her life, Katie is anatomically correct.

For the Brinegars, the full weight of that fact takes time to sink in.

"I feel that I'm afraid to relax because something else might come along," Jean says as she prepares to return home after an eight-day stay. "It's like I don't want to jinx it and say, 'Here's my perfect little baby,' and then have some kidney problem—since she only has one."

HE COULD WRITE A BOOK

Someday, Hendren plans to write a book.

He'll title it *Inside Number One,* and it will be a look at the great institutions he's seen intimately: Children's, the Harvard Medical School, Massachusetts General Hospital, the Hospital For Sick Children on Great Ormond Street in London, where Hendren was visiting surgeon for three months in 1962.

Some of the source material he'll use is in his second-floor study.

It is a comfortable room, with windows that invite the sea breeze on warm days like this. Shotgun shells share space with rare surgical texts on his bookshelves. A box containing his collection of human hearts, removed during autopsies and preserved in wax, is in his closet. Paintings of planes he's flown hang on one wall. On a shelf is a photograph of his daughter Sandy, sitting in a wheelchair; on her lap is the first Hendren grandchild, Sarah Grace Hendren, 10 now. In a file cabinet are report cards and old letters and photographs of his military days. Hendren has his Boy Scout merit badges and family Bibles and locks of his dead father's and daughter's hair.

"I guess I've been awfully fortunate," he says, "that I was born to a very good father who was a strong man, and to a super mother who was a very supportive mother. They raised us in a closely knit family of people who believed in the solidarity of family and religion and being motivated to do what's right—to be honest and hard-working and that sort of thing.

"And I think I was awfully lucky to meet the right person at a young age. You know, Eleanor is about the most solid human being you could ever look for. So nice and natural and unaffected. She's got the right sense of family and country and responsibility and accomplishment. She's a worker. She's always worked and accomplished."

Hendren goes to the window. Gulls are dive-bombing the ocean just to the right of his pier. Across the water, *NOMO* rides at her mooring.

"Eleanor and I were standing out there on the sea wall a couple of weeks ago, looking around and thinking how fortunate we were to be here and to have each other and to have a nice family and to have all of the grandchildren.

"And Eleanor said, 'You know, we have a lot, and we've done a lot, and we've never stepped on anybody else to get it.' And we never did.

"I think I've been very fortunate and I've been put in circumstances where I could work hard and do some things that other people haven't done before. Part of that is because of the talent that I've been given, part of it is by working hard.

"And you know, I don't think those are things you can really take credit for yourself. I don't think you should. I don't get up in the morning and say, 'Boy, am I hot!' I really don't. I recognize that there are things that I do better than others, but that's really not my doing, is it?

"I mean, I might have been crippled by diabetes."

SANDY'S BATTLE

By the last year of Sandy's life, her disease had taken fingers and toes and left her with a prosthetic leg. Her vision had deteriorated. Her music was in scrapbooks and posters now. Eleanor and private nurses took care of her in Duxbury in a bed set up in her father's first-floor library.

On the Friday before her 37th birthday, Sandy remembered that her license was expiring. *I need to renew it,* she told her mother. Eleanor drove her to the registry. The Hendrens' only daughter went in.

Those jerks! she said when she'd gone through the line. *They wanted to know if I had any handicaps and I said, 'Hell, no!'*

Writing with her left hand, which still had function, she'd filled out the forms. Squinting, taking her time, she'd passed her vision test.

And she'd gotten her license.

Sandy's birthday was Monday.

On Sunday, she had a party. A singing telegram was delivered. Family and friends from old shows came. Eleanor and Hardy had left for San Francisco for a surgeons' meeting. Sandy went to bed watching *Dallas,* her favorite show.

"A perfect end to a perfect day," she told her nurse.

"I can't wake Sandy," the nurse said when Hardy called the next morning at 9.

"She must have had an insulin reaction," Hardy said. "Quickly, go down to the refrigerator and get some glucagon and give her a shot."

It didn't work.

"Go get another one," Hardy said.

It didn't work.

Sandy was in irreversible coma. When two weeks had passed, when there was absolutely no hope Sandy would ever recover, her family gathered around her bed at the Massachusetts General Hospital, where she and her father had both worked. One by one, the people she loved spoke their private farewells. The 23rd Psalm was read:

The Lord is my shepherd; I shall not want.

He maketh me to lie down in green pastures: He leadeth me beside the still waters.

He restoreth my soul: He leadeth me in the paths of righteousness for his name's sake.

Yea, though I walk through the valley of the shadow of death, I will fear no evil...

Hardy disconnected his daughter from the machines and she died.

'LIKE IT NEVER HAPPENED'

A spring day in Vermont, 1991.

Katie B., going on 2 now, finishes her breakfast of cereal and banana. Jean changes her diaper, gets her into blue dress and bonnet, and spreads sunscreen across her face. Because of the medication she still takes to prevent infection, Katie B.'s skin is sensitive to sun.

Outside, a customer is waiting. Terry greets the woman and begins to show her around Jean's gardens, bursting with poppies and delphiniums and sweet Williams and foxglove and more than 100 other varieties of herbs and flowers.

Trowel and banana peel in hand, Katie B. follows her dad.

"My compost," she says, throwing her peel where it belongs.

"My fish," she says when she's over by the trout brook.

Terry makes the sale. He takes his coffee and sits on a rock within earshot of the brook. Tonight, he's going fishing.

"It's almost like it never happened..." he says. And in one sense, that's true.

But there's another sense.

"I mean," he continues, "it will always be there to remind me how lucky and fortunate that I am. I mean, I saw my little baby laid out with tubes going every which way and there was nothing I could do."

'A BRAVE GIRL'

Sandy's room is around the corner from her father's study.

It is a spacious and comfortable room, decorated in pinks and whites and blues. A portrait of Sandy as a girl is on a wall, along with her nursing diploma, earned in 1980, when she was 32. The Hendrens sometimes use Sandy's room as guest quarters, and a crib has been brought in, but little else has changed since the last day she was home.

"Sandy was a brave girl," Hendren says. "Sometimes I come in here and I can still hear her voice."

David Hendren, Sandy's youngest brother, a Boston lawyer, delivered her eulogy at a memorial service that filled a church to overflowing.

"Many will remember Sandy for her music, her favorite thing," David said. "Many of you who have been in our home know the familiar sight of Sandy at the piano, often with family and friends gathered around singing on holidays or weekends or any time the whole family was there.

"Away from home, Sandy participated in musical productions in New Hampshire, Boston, Plymouth, and Duxbury. I can't tell you how proud I was to be her little brother every time she set foot on-stage."

Outside the church was a cold and cloudy November day. Winter was in the air.

"I'd like to read the lyrics to one of Sandy's favorite songs," David concluded. "Anyone who knew Sandy would know that she believed in the meaning of these words—and believed that they had been written just for her."

The lyrics were from *Annie*.

The sun will come out tomorrow.
Bet your bottom dollar that
Tomorrow there will be sun.

As David spoke, the November sky opened and sunlight filled the church.

A SPECIAL PLACE

Today, a splendid Sunday in spring, is too beautiful to stay indoors.

Outside, Eleanor is tending her roses. Her husband compliments her, as he always does, then crosses the lawn to the boathouse, where he keeps the water-skis and the grandchildren's float toys and his motorcycle, a 20-year-old BMW.

"Let's go for a ride."

He hands a helmet to his guest. He puts on his helmet and gardening gloves, made of thick leather, and turns the key.

"OK. Hop on."

The sun is bright this afternoon, clear and strong and casting crisp shadows. Squinting, Hendren drives through his town, a historical old seaport still enchanted by the sea, waving to people he knows. He is a cautious driver, but when he has a good stretch of open road, he gives it the gas.

"This is a special place," he says, taking a left.

He parks next to an Episcopal church and walks around back to a pine grove. It is shadowy and cool, and the air has the faint scent of pitch.

Sandy's grave is marked with a stone bearing only her name and the dates of her birth and death. Hendren stands silently a moment, his head bowed, then stoops to examine the lily he and Eleanor placed a week ago, Easter Sunday.

Three of the four blossoms are gone by, and Hendren snips them.

He leaves the good one and turns to face the warmth and light of the sun.

Observations on non-deadline writing

I'm squeamish. Television appalls me with its gross close-ups of needle insertions and surgery in progress. So I didn't expect to finish reading G. Wayne Miller's book-length entry in the non-deadline writing category when he told me up-front it was going to be about the surgical reconstruction of a malformed infant.

I stuck around, though, and he led me through it with a taste and sensitivity that matched the narrative skill of a novelist. Miller wrote this series on a couple of levels and moved his complex characters and his masses of detail so deftly he made the difficult look easy. What began as a drama pitched to the struggle for the life of a grievously threatened baby became the biography of the extraordinary surgeon who willed his mind and hands to provide her with the physique that a cruel providence had denied. You will not forget Dr. Hardy Hendren.

True to the trend in feature journalism, Miller's reporting depth and writing sweep qualify this story to be a short book or a long *New Yorker* series more than the traditional newspaper take-out. Newspapers can be proud they've gained work of such power in their non-deadline columns. This is a celebration of an art form these winning writers have raised to new levels of excellence.

Paul Hendrickson's tender touch is just fine in his story of Hamlet, N.C., after a fire in the poultry factory killed 25. What a lesson in the literature of precise detail he teaches in such passages as this: "Everything is quiet. A dog, moving slow, crosses Hamlet Avenue. A boy on a porch blows on a cornet. Indian summer rises off the pavement in waves. The smell of fried chicken is already curling from Sunday pans."

Carol Morello's spirited scenes in Saudi Arabia before the battle come alive from the first take. Two soldiers sit on a cot kissing. They're husband and wife.

Evidence that the best writing has gravitated heavily to the non-deadline columns is present each year as the ASNE entries are parceled out to the judges, and the preponderance falls to the non-deadline panel. We're doing this category right.

Eugene Patterson, Editor Emeritus
St. Petersburg Times

A conversation with G. Wayne Miller

Digging deeper for readers

KAREN BROWN: Your winning story is about medical science. I understand that you once had thoughts about becoming a doctor.

G. WAYNE MILLER: Well, ironically, I had planned to be a pre-medical major when I entered Harvard. That lasted approximately one week.

Why were you interested in pre-med?

My big interest in medicine goes back to when I was in high school. My family was very friendly with another family whose youngest son died of a brain tumor at about age 6. He went through a very long, torturous, painful course until he died, and that involved our family intimately. I became quite interested in medicine at that time.

Did that aspect of your life affect your writing on Dr. Hardy Hendren's childhood friend who died?

Well, it did in the sense that I realized that the dramatic and impressionable events of childhood often influence you, and so the child's experiences relate very closely to the adult's.

What happened to your interest in medicine?

I said that my interest in medicine lasted

■ G. Wayne Miller, staff writer, *Providence Journal-Bulletin.*

■ **Born:** June 12, 1954, in Melrose, Mass.

■ **Personal:** Married to Alexis Magner Miller, a writer; two daughters: Rachel, 11, and Katherine, 7.

■ **Education:** Harvard College; graduated in 1976 with degree in English.

■ **Newspaper Experience:** *Wakefield Daily Item,* 1978; North Adams *Transcript,* 1978-79; *Cape Cod Times,* 1979-81; *Providence Journal-Bulletin,* 1981-present.

■ **Awards:** New England Associated Press News Executives Assn., third-place award in enterprise category for series "Children of Poverty," 1990. This series also won the National Journalism Award from Children's Express.

American Psychiatric Association, Robert T. Morse Writer's Award, for coverage of mental health, 1986.

New England Newspaper Assn., "Publick Occurrences" Award, 1991.

[EDITOR'S NOTE: I have edited these conversations for clarity and brevity, and, in some cases, recomposed the questions.]

about a week. Concurrent with an interest in medicine was my interest in writing, which was actually stronger and went back a lot further. When I got to Harvard there was a course called "English 70," an upper-level creative writing course. Just a small handful of freshmen in any given year were selected for that course. You had to submit samples of your writing, interview, and then, if you were lucky, you were selected. That course sounded very interesting to me, and I got in. Achieving that really reoriented me.

Were there writers in your family?

No, there were not. My parents are very strong newspaper readers. These are people who don't like to start their day without reading a newspaper. We had two newspapers: *The Boston Globe* and the *Wakefield Daily Item*. So that habit was there very early.

What were your early interests?

I played sports, lettered in track and played hockey. And in my senior year of high school, I was co-editor of *The Paper*, our school newspaper.

So you became interested in journalism early?

Well, no. I became interested in writing early. *The Paper* included a lot of literature: poetry and short stories. My interest was mainly fiction.

Let's go ahead through Harvard. What was your major, and what were the outstanding events in your life there?

I was an English major and graduated with honors. I continued to write. I don't think any of it was published because I had a bitter disappointment. I just absolutely wanted to be on the *Harvard Lampoon,* and I made three attempts. There's a competition to get on, and I failed. It was a profound disappointment. And from that I took a couple of lessons. One is that sometimes you fail and you have to learn how to live with failure. That's true in writing and in a personal sense as well.

The other lesson I learned is that I'm probably not a very good humor writer. And I thought I had been. In high school, I had written a couple of funny pieces; people laughed and thought they were really good. At Harvard, I realized how extraordinarily difficult humor writing is.

And so the lesson I learned, that I couldn't do it, was probably a good lesson, because if I'd tried to continue down that line, I think I would have been disappointed.

I've heard that one of the most difficult slots to fill at a newspaper is that of a humor columnist.

Yeah, one of my favorite writers is Dave Barry. He is one of the few people who makes me laugh out loud. To make someone laugh out loud who's sitting in a chair quietly, doing nothing but reading, is an awesome ability. And so the lesson I learned is, I don't have it. [Laughter]

You finished Harvard in 1976?

Yes, and I worked in a library and in a hospital emergency room to save money to go to Europe, which I did. Later I went to work for Delta Airlines. I was smashing bags, as they call it. I was on the ground crew. You see, I came out of Harvard not exactly sure what I was going to do. I thought I would do some writing, certainly, and I was interested to an extent in film, and so I hadn't really decided. I was doing fiction writing, short stories, throughout this whole time.

Were you selling any of your writing?

No, I wasn't even attempting to sell anything. I enjoy writing, and I have ever since I started doing it.

What about the discipline in writing? Did writing strike you as something that might become tedious?

No. Some people don't like the actual process of writing. We have a very fine investigative reporter at our newspaper, for example, who produces very fine work, but the part of the entire process that he likes the least is the writing. He likes the research, he likes the investigation, he likes the conferring with editors. When it comes to writing, he just doesn't like it. I'm not like that; I enjoy writing. Not that every minute of every day spent writing is enjoyable, but the majority is.

To answer your question about discipline, of course there's tremendous discipline in writing. I mean, I have a rule that I write something every day—whether it is strictly newspaper-related writing or whether it's non-newspaper writing. I do a lot of fiction writing. So one way or another, I like to write at least an hour a day.

How long have you done that?

Many, many years. As an inviolable rule, I would say I've done that for at least 10 years.

What do you get out of writing at least an hour each day?

I get a reminder to myself that despite whatever level of talent an individual may have, a lot of the creative process is discipline. It's actually doing it. It's work, hard work. You just have to remain at the top of your craft, and the way you do that is not by having brilliant inspirational bursts every couple of months. You get down and you just do it every day. A lot of it is scut work, you know; a lot of it is mundane and is not terribly flashy or even good. A lot of what you write, you discard up-front or in the editing process.

You said you published a novel and some articles. Tell me a little bit about those.

The novel is called *Thunder Rise*, published in 1989 by William Morrow. It's a mystery-horror-type novel.

What is it about?

It is about a fictitious town where children start getting mysteriously sick, and a Native American who thinks he has the answer to the sickness.

And how long were you on *The New York Times* best-seller list?

[Laughter] What a cruel thing to say! Well, I can tell you it was exactly zero weeks. But it was fun doing it, and it also came out in paperback in England.

I've had short stories in *Alfred Hitchcock's Mystery Magazine*, and I've had short stories in some anthologies, one of them called *Masques III*, published by St. Martin's Press. I've had a couple stories in the *Borderlands* anthology published by Avon, and a bunch of others.

These were basically published between what years?

The first *Alfred Hitchcock* piece was in, I believe, '85, so '85 to the present.

You did this while working full-time at the *Providence Journal-Bulletin*?

Yeah. This goes back to my one-hour-a-day thing, which, by the way, sometimes is four hours a day; it depends on the day.

Let's go back to your post-college days. At that time you were writing regularly, but not making a career of it.

Yes. In late '77, in fact, it began to occur to me that I better do something now with my life. After attempting to sell some articles and getting the dreaded rejection slips, I contacted my hometown newspaper, the *Wakefield Daily Item,* and was published. Later I published in *The Boston Globe* magazine.

You didn't go to journalism school. How did you get your education in newswriting?

In 1978, I started writing for the North Adams *Transcript,* working with an editor named Rod Doherty, who had a very profound influence on my career and my journalistic development. Rod was a very exacting and demanding person. Rod wanted things to be accurate. Rod did not like bullshit. Rod did like initiative. Rod told you bluntly and candidly what he thought of your writing, and he was a taskmaster. He's kind of a legend here in New England.

I spent about nine months at the *Transcript,* working with this very fine editor who was very demanding but very good, and in that nine months I learned the principles of accuracy. I learned how to construct a story, how to meet deadline, how to interview, how to re-interview. I learned how to do features.

You worked for the *Cape Cod Times*, then went to the *Providence Journal-Bulletin.* Is there a particular reason why you went to the *Journal*?

Yes. By that point in my career, meaning two or three years into journalism, I was recognizing good writing, bad writing, papers that fostered good writing, papers that weren't interested, and the *Journal* clearly was very interested in good writing. The *Journal* is a writer's paper.

You went in as a staff writer. What was your beat? And what's your route been during your 11 years there?

I started in bureaus. First Greenville, which was the more rural section of the state; then Newport, where the America's Cup races were. In 1983, Joel Rawson and Carol Young, who were running the

metro desk, were looking for someone to cover
corrections, the child welfare agency, and the mental health agency. Joel asked me if I'd be interested
in doing that, and I said yes. I did that for roughly
five years. During that time, I also did a couple of
major series, and that's pretty much what I do now.
I take about a year or so and look at an issue or an
individual or something that would combine good
writing with a subject or a person that would be of
great interest to our readers.

What I like to do with my series is go places
where readers and the media don't usually go. It
doesn't mean they never go, but they don't usually
go, and that was certainly true with the Hardy Hendren series.

**Let me ask a little bit more about the *Journal*,
and then I want to get into the story. You said it
is a writer's paper. What does a "writer's paper" mean to you?**

A writer's paper means that when I have a good
idea, I'm allowed to pursue it and then have it published, and that's fundamental to me. It implies that
a writer is valued, his or her ideas are valued, and
that what support is needed to take ideas and make
them into published pieces is there. So a writer's
newspaper encourages writing in the sense of seminars and having outside people come in, and having
inside people share their expertise. It means that
when I, as a staff writer, have a question, I can go to
a fellow writer and say, "Read this; what do you
think?" Also, that there is an editor that I can do that
with. In this case it was Joel.

**You are a project writer, but what about a three-
year reporter who's doing beat stories? Is it a
writer's paper for that person?**

Yes, I think it is. I mean, that person is an active
part of the culture. It really relates to the culture of
the newspaper. Is writing valued? Yes, it is. Are
there means to improve writing? Yes, there are.

When there is a good piece of writing, does it get the kind of display and graphics and photographic support it needs? Yes, it does. That isn't to say that every single story we produce is a gem, because some aren't. A lot of writing is still fairly mundane. But the culture for good writing is there.

Let's look at your story, "Working Wonders." And we'll start with the idea. How did the story come about?

The idea came about when I was looking for my next project. I had just done the "Children of Poverty" series, which was a look at the welfare system and one family living in that system. There was no apocalyptic moment in the sense that I woke up one day and said, "I've got to do the Children's Hospital," but here are the factors that went into the decision.

One is I'd written about children for quite a while here. I like writing about children. I've also done some medical writing on children. So I began to think, what could I write about that I haven't done before? Where could I take our readers where they haven't been or haven't been often or for a long time? It occurred to me that right up the road in Boston, which is some 40 miles from Providence, is a hospital that's used by many Rhode Islanders. Many think it's the best kids' hospital in the country.

I called the Children's Hospital with only a very vague idea of spending some time, telling some stories. I don't think they took the idea seriously. I asked them to send me their annual report because I find that catalogs and annual reports often have little nuggets of information that you might not glean in an interview.

Going over the annual report, I saw a list of leading staff people. Now, many staff people at the Children's Hospital are also professors at the Harvard Medical School. I came across the name of Hardy Hendren, chief of surgery. I had our librarian, Linda Henderson, run his name through databases for the popular literature. Linda is a very fine individual and enormously helpful. In doing anything like this, if you don't have a good relationship with librarians you're sunk. They're just an absolutely dynamite resource, and she's the best. She came back with a couple of clips. One of them was from 1969, when Hendren became the first surgeon in Boston to successfully separate Siamese twins. When I read that, I said, "That is an interesting individual. I've got to talk to this guy."

You got his name from the annual report. Some would think of that as a strange place to look for interesting stories. Then you said you saw his name in a list. What about his name stood out on the list of outstanding surgeons? Why pick him?

Well, because he was the chief of the department. I figured the chief had to be an accomplished person, because I knew the relationship with Harvard. After I called him but before I met him, I went back to Children's. They gave me his vita and two things leapt out at me. One was that he was an Eagle Scout and he put it on his vita, right at the top of his list of awards, and the second thing was that he had a daughter who was deceased. In fact, there was a third thing: that he had qualified as a naval aviator by landing on a carrier in World War II at the age of 20. So those three things together suggested that not only do we have an accomplished surgeon, but there is an interesting human being here as well.

How did you sell the story idea to your newspaper? Who did you talk to and how did you approach the story idea?

I went to Joel Rawson.

Is he your immediate editor?

Joel is the deputy executive editor now, but he maintains an interest in writing. And I've known Joel for a long time. I consider him a friend. So I went up to him and filled him in on my idea. I was telling him about Hardy Hendren and he was intrigued.

You asked me about a writer's relationship with an editor. A very important role an editor plays at the idea stage is to be a barometer, be a bellwether, somebody you bounce an idea off. The editor has to filter it, think about it, and tell you, yes, you're right on track here, or, no, you're not. Joel just said, yeah, you've got something good here. This is good, do it.

What else do you look for in an editor?

When I'm doing a project, I want somebody who is good and is in a position to make this a real project, to make this a serious piece of work. Somebody who can get this thing into print in a good fashion with photography and graphics. We have all seen stories in which you do a tremendous amount of work and it's either overedited, meaning too many people look at it, or it doesn't get the kind of play and graphics and photography support that it needs.

So the qualities you want in an editor are someone who understands good writing, who responds to an idea in a significant way, and who has the clout to see the project through.

And somebody who, having confirmed that in fact you have a good idea, can provide guidance at strategic points along the way.

Let's get back to "Working Wonders." As I looked at your story, I thought of what I'll broadly call two genres of stories. In 1990, the first story in *Best Newspaper Writing* **was about a baby with no brain. Last year, the first winning package included a story about Siamese twins who died as babies. So there's a genre of sick-baby stories.**

Then there's another type of story that your series brings to mind. I was reminded of Jon Franklin's Pulitzer Prize-winning story done at *The Baltimore Sun,* **"Mrs. Kelley's Monster,"**

about a doctor performing brain surgery on a woman. And I thought of Christopher Scanlon's story "Having a Baby," done at your newspaper. These are stories that take readers through medical procedures.

I wonder if these stories or others like them came to your mind as you crafted "Working Wonders." Also, what is the attraction of these types of stories to writers and to readers?

Well, the Franklin story came to mind. I don't think Scanlon's consciously came to mind, because although mine is a story about a sick child and about a hospital, it really is a portrait of Hardy Hendren. In that respect, it's a little bit different from your sick-baby story.

But is there a genre? There certainly is. And I think those kinds of stories have broad appeal to people because of what children are. Children are innocent, children are fresh, children are alive, children are full of energy, and children are immortal. So when deformity or disease interferes, there's a profound sense of unfair play. People are struck by that, and people are interested, and they hope that the child, having suffered, will then be made well. So there's almost an intrinsic appeal in that kind of story.

You also get into the appeal that any disease has to people, and that appeal is that it could happen to them, it could happen to you. This could be your tragedy. God forbid it should. In a sense that's why horror writing is appealing. You know these awful, terrible things happen, but you're reading about it in the safety of your home.

Let's talk about your reporting. How long did you spend actually reporting this story?

Let's see. Almost a year and a half.

How did you approach Katie Brinegar's parents, and what persuaded them to allow their daughter to be used as a subject here?

As we considered possible subjects, we wanted to show the people and use real names. Now, because of the kind of anatomical problem we're dealing with here, a lot of people said, "Forget it. What are you—crazy?" As I went along that fall and saw surgeries and met parents, those who said yes didn't have this complicated a problem. Then the Brinegars came along. They had exactly the kind of complicated problem that we wanted. Their reason for saying yes was they had been through hell. They had been through a long, tortuous set of problems with this baby, starting at birth, and they had learned many things along the way, and they wanted to share their experience with others who might be in that position.

I honestly think that part of what motivated them was they live in Vermont. They're not in the readership here. I think that was a factor as well.

You approached them at what point? Had the major surgery been completed?

Yes, as a matter of fact, I approached them after the surgery. I'd received their permission to view the surgery beforehand. But in terms of outlining all of what I wanted to do, I didn't do that until after.

What would you have said if it had been your daughter?

Would I have allowed this? Isn't that an interesting question! I can't give you—I can't tell you. I think I would lean toward probably not allowing it if I were living in this area. I'd lean toward no.

Even if the surgery had been completed and appeared to be successful?

Yeah, I think I'd lean toward no. What would motivate me toward saying yes, possibly, is what motivated them. So I have to give you a qualified no.

You said that you witnessed surgery extensively.

Would you talk a little bit more about the other reporting that you did? Who were some of the people you talked with? What other records did you use?

Bear in mind that I'm doing a book on this story. So there's more detail in the book, and I'm using a different patient in the book. Nevertheless, I did a tremendous amount of research. I found one problem I had never encountered before. Hardy Hendren has the closest thing to a photographic memory. It is a prodigious memory, and it was clear right from the beginning that this memory is pretty darn accurate. I would look into things that I could independently verify, and they all checked out. The problem then became, are you lulled into a sense of security? So as a journalist, I had to constantly remind myself that, as good as his memory is, somewhere along the line it's not going to be correct, so you've got to check everything.

To answer the question did I do a lot of research, yes, I did. Hendren has extensive files; he's a pack rat. He and the hospital, with written permission, gave me access to his records, and I spent a lot of time looking at operative notes, looking at results of tests, looking at personal histories, looking at insurance records.

I visited his mother, who is still alive and has a similarly prodigious memory, in Kansas City. I spent several days talking to boyhood friends, seeing where he went to school, looking at yearbooks. I visited his prep school in Virginia, and there I had access to school newspapers from the time he was there, yearbooks, school catalogs. I spent a lot of time at the Harvard Medical School and the Countway Library of Medicine doing the same thing. You can't do too much research. You really can't.

Let me question that. You fought against being lulled into not doing research, but can you do too much research? At what point do you tell yourself, I've learned enough; I don't need to get any more notes; I need to stop and move on?

Well, that's a good question, and there's no scientific answer. You reach a point where you begin to feel very confident about your material. You reach a point where you could almost write this thing off the top of your head, with the exception, of course, of quotations. Your editor helps in that. In addition, there were two or three colleagues, writers at the newspaper, with whom I was sharing this project. I trust their instincts and I value their judgment. They were very helpful in saying, all right, I think you're getting there; you really have it.

The key is immersion. You can't do this and do 20 other things. I realize that I'm very fortunate in being able to do this. Many writers don't have that freedom and that time. You can't do a project of this magnitude and do 30 other things along the way. Your thinking has to be primarily on that one project.

Let's talk about organization. How do you plan a project? How do you keep notes? What is your organizational process?

I start a project like this with a single slug called "Idea," or "Ideas." Into that I just brainstorm. As this thing takes shape, I just have an idea and I throw it in under "Ideas." I also carry around paper or a little notebook or something so when I'm driving or sitting on a bus or whatever, if I have an idea, I'll write it down, and then quite regularly enter that into the slug.

This story slug begins to grow in length, and it begins to fashion itself into something approaching a rough outline. Themes begin to suggest themselves. After a while my dominant themes begin to emerge. I break them out into their own slugs.

So the blocks of the story emerge as you go?

Yeah, some of that survives as almost finished prose, which I find very interesting.

I'm looking at organization as two things. One is the broad organization of the reporting. How do

you keep track of all the information? How do you keep track of your focus? But the second part I'm interested in is the organization of the story. The structure of your story relies on blocks. How do you select the neat segments?

Well, the first decision was how many voices did we want. You could have had a hospital voice, a Hardy Hendren voice, and then a Brinegar voice. I settled on a two-voice format, basically two alternating blocks, because we broke a lot of the hospital information out into sidebars.

The organizational technique of blocks allows you to tell mini-stories without major transitions. It also allows you to move backward and forward in time. You let the reader know that you can't depend on the story being chronological.

I play kind of fast and loose with time. I think if you are clear that you're changing tense and going back or going ahead, you can do that without confusing people. You just have to be honest about it. In the broad sense there's a chronological thread here.

You also use foreshadowing effectively. Early in the story, after you tell of the delivery, you write, "Jean dozed." Meanwhile doctors examine her newborn. Then you have, "Jean stirred." The short sentences and parallel structure build tension.

That's exactly what I was trying to do there, to put you on alert. One of the writers at the *Journal,* Brian Jones, said it's almost like the music in the movie *Jaws.* "Jean dozed." That implies sleeping, quiet, nice, everything is fine. "A crowd was assembling around Katie." I'm using details to tell you something bad. "A doctor opened a sterile package," "Jean stirred," here comes the shock, da-da da-da da-da (theme from *Jaws*). [Laughter] It's almost cinematic in that sense.

Did you feel that when you wrote it? Did you feel the cinematic qualities?

On some of these scenes I did, yeah. When I wrote about the P-47s at the beginning of "Day 2," I could almost picture myself being there.

Your first description of Katie's problems raises the issue of using medical terms. In the 11th paragraph of the story you say, "Where nature should have given Katie three openings down below, there was only one: what looked like, but could not be positively identified as, a urethra, which drains urine from the bladder."

What were the decisions you made about anatomical terms? You could have started by saying "the vagina," " the urinary tract," " the rectum," or you could have avoided those terms throughout. What type of concerns did you have about both the language that you used and the kind of references that you made?

We decided early on that if we're going to be writing about this, we're going to have to use the real terms, and throughout we do use terms like "vagina" and "rectum." I also felt that your average reading audience doesn't know all the technical terms here. So when we first used some words, we defined them, such as we do here with "urethra." We also had a glossary that we ran with the series.

After introducing Hendren by his professional credentials and listing the diseases that he combats, you follow with a strong paragraph. It begins: "Hendren has stationed himself on the leading edge of science and surgery, where nature's worst mistakes taunt medicine's best minds." I'm interested in the turn of a phrase at the end of the sentence. Did that emerge in your early drafts, or did you create that in editing?

That was one of the phrases from my notes that suggested itself to me during one of the operations.

In watching the surgeries, then, you weren't just gathering factual information.

No. When I'm reporting, I always think in terms of the larger meaning. Phrases come to me and some of them end up in the finished prose.

It's interesting that you would point to that paragraph, because some of that, but not nearly that much, was in my first draft. Brian Jones, my colleague, read it and said, "Right there you've got to tell us who this guy really is. You've got to work on that paragraph."

This is a very strong paragraph. It is enhanced by the repetition: "Nothing is too weird for Hendren. Nothing is too hopeless. No one is refused." And there's a strong ending to the paragraph: "If surgery were law, Hendren's operating room would be the court of last appeal."

Right. Much of that came on rewrite.

The second day's story begins with the vivid description of a scene that took place half a century ago. There are no attributions. What are your guidelines on how much authority you can use in a story?

I think if you've spent a year watching someone, and if you really know what the hell you're talking about, you can use an extreme degree. And I think that's part of the power of good writing. Part of the power is the trust that a reader has in the writer. The reader has to know early on: Folks, we're reading something by somebody who knows what he's talking about. I think that's absolutely critical.

Some reporters are following the trend of the writer being more authoritative, instead of using many attributions. Problems come about when the writer's statements are not supported by thorough reporting.

That's important. Now the caveat is you don't bull-shit people. Don't try this if you don't know what you're talking about. The solution is to put in time and learn what you're talking about.

Sandy, the deceased daughter, keeps emerging in the story. Why did she emerge in several places?

It was actually Joel's suggestion that we have her as a theme throughout because she really was such an important part of Hendren's life. Rather than doing her entire story at the end, when you visit the grave, we spread it out a little bit, so that as you read and as you head toward what looks like a successful conclusion to the Brinegar story, in the back of your mind you have the idea that there is not always success with sick children.

There's a natural "kicker," or ending, with the visit to Vermont in 1991. It's a spring day and Katie is tagging after her mother and father. She seems to be a normal little girl, destined for a normal life. But that's not the end of the story. Why did you decide to have the strong emphasis on Sandy at the end?

As a reminder that not every story has a happy ending. Now some people would quibble with this ending. The editor for the book that I'm doing on this subject doesn't want the visit to the grave as an ending. He thinks it's too much of a downer, and I think there's some validity to that. But I used that ending for this series because I want you to know that not every story has a happy ending. Katie Brinegar's did and Sandy's didn't, and that, I guess philosophically, is the way life is.

Another reason for ending the story that way is at the very end Hendren visits the grave and sees the Easter lily they had put there the week before, and he instinctively trims the bad blossoms. There he is, the surgeon right to the very end. He is instinctively and innately a surgeon, always trying to improve.

You've talked about the amount of detail necessary for a story like this. What's your advice for a good writer who's at a newspaper that can't afford to send a reporter to Kansas City and can't give the space or won't give the space that you have here?

My advice is that if you have a good idea and are willing to fight for it, you usually can get the space and the time. You may have to juggle your schedule and you may have to work a little harder. When I started in my career, I obviously wasn't doing this kind of stuff. But what I did was make time for stories that I wanted to put a little more of my heart and soul into, that lent themselves more toward quality writing. As for the space, if you tell a story well, people will read it.

That's a good way of looking at journalism.

This was an unusual project. It's not the kind of thing we do every day, certainly, and I think it goes back to my prime interest in this kind of a series. That is, let's go somewhere where you haven't been and let's learn something about the people we write about, but let's learn something about ourselves as well.

Paul Hendrickson

Finalist, Non-Deadline Writing

Paul Hendrickson joined *The Washington Post* in 1977, and is now a staff reporter for the Style section. Previously he worked for *The National Observer*, the *Detroit Free Press*, and *Holiday* magazine. In 1980, he used an Alicia Patterson Foundation fellowship to write a book, *Seminary: A Search,* published in 1983. He also wrote *Looking for the Light: The Life and Hidden Art of Marion Post Wolcott,* published in 1992, and his work is anthologized in the 1976 and 1980 editions of *Best American Sports Stories.*

Hendrickson is a graduate of St. Louis University, and has a master's degree from Pennsylvania State University. His awards include Penney-Missouri awards, the Lyndhurst Foundation Fellowship's three-year award, an Associated Press award, and *Playboy* magazine's Nonfiction Prize. His ASNE finalist story portrays a small town struggling with grief and the weight of national attention.

Reverberations of a town's tragedy

OCTOBER 22, 1991

HAMLET, N.C.—The first of the 25 bodies brought out of the poultry factory that morning was Peggy Fairley Anderson's. Everybody in town seemed to know her. Most people spoke of her as just Peggy Fairley. She was 50 and she was much loved in the small community of 6,200, and so at her wake, Nelson Funeral Service—which is on the same street, Bridges Street, as the poultry processing plant itself—was packed with mourners.

At the Family Hour, one of Peggy's daughters, a small woman of perhaps no more than 80 pounds, started to address the body: "Wake up, Momma." Her brothers and sisters and others in the family tried to console her. She was not to be consoled. "Wake up, Momma," a grown daughter kept saying. Before anyone could stop her, she managed to get her arms under the body and had begun to lift it out of the casket. She seemed to be trying to bring her mother to her bosom. One of her brothers and one of the funeral directors managed to get her down onto the floor and hold her there, telling her it would be all right.

Harvey Knotts is relating this. He's one of the proprietors of Nelson Funeral Service, which is in one of the black sections of Hamlet, just down from the old rattling Seaboard Air Line Railway, which long before poultry processors ever showed up was so vital to the economic life and psychological well-being of this town. Nelson mortuary service handled the burials of four Imperial Food Products workers who died on Sept. 3 in an almost unimaginably grotesque early-morning flash fire that, for a moment anyway, put a little Carolina Sandhills burg smack onto Page One of the world.

"You're asking the extent of this whole thing on us as a community?" Knotts says. He's shaking his head. "Well, I witnessed that scene. I've directed lots of funerals in Hamlet. I began to lose it myself that night.... It was the unnecessariness of it all, if that's a word.... It's not like getting over the death of an elderly parent. There was an unnatural air about it. That's what the shock is about."

And in a way, that's what this story is about. Not the first waves of shock, from which the whole country seemed to reel a little after reading about padlocked doors and blocked exits and $5.50-an-hour employees clawing at them from the inside. But the aftershock, the smaller waves, the almost hidden ones, from which a town still trembles, though perhaps not at first look.

It's about a place and a people not as they were then, in the first hours, but as they are now, weeks later, alone again—or mostly so—with their pain. Which is okay by them, the alone part. The larger world has moved on to new grotesqueries, but Hamlet is still...Hamlet.

* * *

It's 75 miles southeast of Charlotte. The land is sandy and piney, with some pitch and roll. John Coltrane was born here. Tom Wicker of *The New York Times* was raised here. It was founded in 1873 by an Englishman who wanted to build a mill and send woolens abroad. He told three of his friends that in his native England a clot of houses was called a hamlet. Fine, they said, let that be the name.

What seems so different here? The illusion is that nothing's wrong. There's a Hardee's and a Burger King. There's a Betty's Bingo and a Food Lion in the small shopping strip on the way to Rockingham. Churches sit on nearly every other corner. Essentially these are segregated congregations: black houses of worship, white houses of worship. Some have wondrous names: the Rock of Faith Temple Miracles Church of God in Christ. That name's in blue lettering on a white sign hanging from a metal pole on Pine Street. The music that drifts out from inside is wondrous too.

Across town, on Entwistle, up by the town's two water tanks, are fine old Victorians, with wicker on the rambling porches and long-needle pines shading the patchy lawns.

The fireball struck that Tuesday about 8:20 a.m. in an odd-rigged, 33,000-square-foot windowless assortment of adjoining brick boxes hard by the railroad tracks. In effect, the plant, which is sealed off now, is a maze of large rooms separated by movable walls. Once it was the home of the Buttercup Ice Cream company. So a building's history went from ice to fire.

After it happened, somebody from New York sent stamps—it's what she had.

Campbell Soup donated 300 cases.

Stanley Hand Tools in Charlotte gave $2,500.

The town library became the Victims' Assistance Center.

For 11 years chicken parts got processed in this non-union and just-above-minimum-wage workplace. They got processed for fast-food restaurants, up North and other places. The workers, who came from all over Richmond County, would move through the plant in a kind of assembly line of fowl: cutting, cleaning, trimming, cooking, packaging, freezing. It's an old story in the hard-used and labor-intensive rural South: Out-of-town employer comes in and sops up whatever cheap labor is at hand—gladly at hand, because there's so little else. Imperial Food Products is headquartered in Atlanta.

Eighteen of the dead were women, many of them young single mothers.

At least 11 school-age children lost a mother or father.

There was no sprinkler system. The place had never had a state inspection.

Twenty-five died, yes, but there were also more than 50 injuries, some of them critical. Which is to say that of the approximately 90 workers in the plant at the time of the fire, it was the destiny of fewer than a dozen to come out unscathed.

In the days following, there were signs all over town, outside churches and graveyards, that said: *SLOW. FUNERAL.*

A SURVIVOR, TALKING

Her name is Sylvia Ann Martin, although newspapers kept identifying her as "Sylvia Chambers." For three days she lay unconscious at Duke Medical Center in Durham. This is her third day back home.

"Doctor says my brain has blocked it all," she says. "I just can't remember anything about from where I was working to where they found me."

She's got on pink pajamas with lacy cuffs. She's got on red socks. There's a huge white bandage on her throat. She points to it. "It's where they did the tracheotomy."

She comes from a family of 18. Above her head is a poster: "Welcome Home Sylvia. We missed you! We love you!"

The television is on. It's Saturday-morning cartoons. Three or four other people are in the room. One is her older sister, Rosa Lee Capel. Rosa Lee says, "We tried to keep it away from her." She means talk of the accident. "She asked me some things yesterday. I wouldn't tell her."

Sylvia: "They told me I was in for my blood. I kept asking questions. Later they told me, 'No, the plant exploded.'"

Her small tight body has begun to rock.

Her sister gets up and goes to another room and brings back a dampened pink washcloth. She gives it to Sylvia. The younger sister folds it into fours, holds it at her mouth in the way of people sick at their stomach.

"So hard to sleep," the survivor says.

Rosa Lee says, "I noticed just yesterday when somebody came in and mentioned it, her hands started going like this." She is moving her fists up and down.

"Six different kinds of medicine," the survivor says.

"Never gonna go back in that place," the survivor says.

A little later, out in the parking lot of this government-subsidized housing development, Sylvia Martin's boyfriend, Ray Von Chambers, who took off from his job at a textile mill to help tend her in the hospital, who drove her home to Richmond County, who's been with her for 11 years, says: "For a week straight I slept on chairs in the waiting room at the Duke hospital. Just moved them together. Didn't want to be anywhere else. They weren't really sure she'd ever talk again. I think she's coming out of it."

A minute later: "I noticed when we were driving along in the car on Thursday, when I was bringing her home, every time we'd see another car, well, she'd start to draw up beside me."

APOCALYPSE THEN

It's a burn whose outer layer has scabbed over. The real damage is below the surface.

But how did it happen? A ruptured fuel line near a huge deep-fat fryer. The purely technical answer —provided by state investigators in a report three days afterward—is that a hydraulic line five feet above the plant's concrete floor broke, spewing oil in several directions but most lethally toward a gas-fueled cooker. The oil spewed at a pressure of about 800 pounds per square inch. Which is why the term "fireball" is not at all hyperbolic.

But it was smoke inhalation, not so much the flames, that killed the workers.

"It was like closing your eyes and putting your hands over your face," one of the wire services quoted a firefighter as saying in the first hours. Another from-the-scene dispatch said: "Others died as they groped, gasping in the dark for escape."

Helicopters (they were carrying the injured to Charlotte and Chapel Hill and Durham as well as to a burn unit in Winston-Salem) made Bridges Street seem like the middle of the Vietnam War. It was the upswirl of dust and wind, it was the acrid smell, it was the menacing THUNK of rotary blades.

Investigators said in the preliminary report that approximately 40 of the 90 workers initially tried to escape through a door secured by dead bolts on the outside. "They could not have gotten through that door with a battering ram," Tim Bradley, deputy commissioner of the fire and rescue division of the state insurance department, was quoted as saying in *The Washington Post.* The state report found that at least two fire-exit doors in the plant were locked, and in addition a loading dock was blocked by a truck and a dumpster. The report concluded that if doors had not been locked or blocked, some of the 25 victims could have survived.

There were descriptions, almost too lurid to read, about a worker whose *head* was outside the building, sticking through a kicked-open slit, but whose body was still inside. That worker's name is Mattie Fairley. She's the daughter-in-law of Peggy Fairley Anderson. She has survived.

Her mother-in-law had eight children, 17 grandchildren. Peggy Fairley Anderson lies now in Green Chapel Cemetery. Her husband, Alforence, who's been at home since the funeral, is about to resume his job at a heavy-equipment company in Charlotte. He gets up for work at 4 a.m. "They treat you with more respect in Charlotte," he says.

Two weeks ago those who survived, and the 125 or so others who weren't at work on that shift, were informed by letter that the company will not reopen the Hamlet plant. Additionally, a sister plant in Georgia has now been closed. Imperial Food Products is facing bankruptcy. Court records in Atlanta indicate the owners are millions of dollars in debt to a bank in Pennsylvania. There's been much talk in Carolina about the filing of criminal-negligence charges against the owners, but to date this hasn't happened.

Authorities are awaiting a full report from the State Bureau of Investigation (SBI) and other agencies. Questions of locked doors and blocked exits, of negligent maintenance, of shoddy fire-prevention practices will be key elements in the report, which is due soon. The SBI is known to be interviewing all first-shift survivors. Some Carolina legal experts have said that the most likely charge would be involuntary manslaughter. Some victims' families have called that an outrage; industrial murder is what it really was, they say. If Imperial does seek protection from its creditors under bankruptcy laws, this almost certainly will delay, maybe permanently, any legal settlements to the families of victims. Several suits have been filed; others are expected.

Why were some of the exit doors locked in the first place? That is still not entirely clear. But scores in Hamlet will tell you that the reason they were locked is because the plant managers absolutely believed their employees were stealing them blind —not money but chicken parts.

THE CRUELTY OF CHANCE

A man named Phil Dawkins died. He was 49. He belonged to Pine Grove Baptist Church in East Rockingham. His wife works at Hamlet City Hall. Phil Dawkins wasn't a poultry worker, he was a Lance Peanut man whose job was servicing vending machines in Richmond County plants and mills. Imperial Foods was one of the regular stops on his route. People say he was supposed to have been at the factory Monday. But of course *that* Monday was Labor Day.

Phil Dawkins's son, who works in a Richmond County paper mill, is a member of the Cordova Volunteer Fire Department. He helped fight the fire. He didn't know his father was in the building.

"I will explain it to you, and then you'll have it," Phil Dawkins Jr. says in steady tones. "There was an inside team, bringing them to the loading dock, which is where the majority of the victims were placed. My team was the outside team. Our job was loading them. We loaded them onto backboards, covered them with sheets, put them on stretchers, then rolled them to the doctor. There were doctors on the scene. I didn't know he was in there till the guys I was working with told me. They said, 'Phil, your father.'

"And so that's how I found out about my daddy."

ILLUSIONS AND REALITIES

The Silver Star rolls through at 8:46 p.m. It's on its way from New York to the sunny climes of

Florida. In the Sandhills night, one or two passengers detrain.

Last year Hollywood came to Hamlet to film parts of *Billy Bathgate*. The moviemakers made Main Street over to look like a town in upstate New York in 1935. Afterward Hamlet decided it would keep parts of its movie set intact. So an out-of-towner walks along the upsloping Main Street today and sees walls and windows painted with the name "Onondaga." Except that in the window of Hollywood's supposed Mohawk Diner are notices for "The Disaster Relief Headquarters."

California illusions, Hamlet realities.

Last year Hamlet got an "All-America City" designation in a national competition in Arizona. The town won the prize along with Coeur d'Alene and Harrisburg and Sioux City and some others. Hamlet was terribly proud.

These days, in the lobby of the town's handsome city hall, which is only a few blocks up from the fire site, there are some tacked-up condolence cards. They're a fraction of what's come in. The cards are usually addressed to "The Town of Hamlet" or "The People of Hamlet." They come from strangers who aren't strangers. One sympathy card, sent from New York, arrived with a neatly scissored Associated Press clipping, cut from the *Syracuse Herald-Journal*, as if the sender was struggling to let Hamlet know just what the shock was like to somebody living so far away: *Screaming workers pounded and kicked locked exit doors as fire swept a chicken processing plant here yesterday...*

These condolence cards contain messages like: "I just wanted to let you know I'm sorry. Please take care of yourselves."

THEIR TOWN

Norva Jernigan's talking about outsiders, especially press outsiders, who come in for 10 minutes and think they understand the place. She's the library supervisor. It's a new library, built mostly with local funds. She's on the Fourth of July parade

board, she's on the Seaboard Festival board, she
went to Arizona last year to help sell the town and
get the All-America award.

"They come in for a while and that's all they
see—the terrible conditions in that plant, the $5.50
an hour, the sealed doors," she says. "They don't
know how we take care of our own. We all know
each other. If we don't know you, we know your
sister. I had a reporter from up North, I think it was
Baltimore, asking me if I really didn't think it
wasn't hurting a lot of the people because the ones
who died were poor black people from the wrong
side of the tracks. I think the implication was if they
were mostly black who died, we somehow wouldn't
care."

Richard Moore, another library worker, is listening. "We had to watch the ambulances flash by here
all day," he says. "They came right up Main. I think
the biggest shock to me was to hear three were
dead. That was the first report. That was a disaster.
But 25 dead?"

Jernigan: "I tell you there was a gloom settled
over this town. No one smiled. It went for days."

This Saturday, Hamlet will hold its annual
Seaboard Festival. It's always on the fourth Saturday in October. It's a day of music, crafts, food.

"I said the other day, 'This festival might be the
thing that pulls us out,'" says Moore.

"We'll be reaching back once again to our roots,
the railroad," says Jernigan.

"Get past it," says Moore.

"Well, maybe not past it, but move ahead," says
Jernigan.

SUNDAY MORNING COMING DOWN

Almost everybody's in church. Services start at
11. Everything is quiet. A dog, moving slow, crosses Hamlet Avenue. A boy on a porch blows on a
cornet. Indian summer rises off the pavement in
waves. The smell of fried chicken is already curling
from Sunday pans.

Over on Bridges Street there's still yellow police
tape wound around the outside of the Imperial

Foods building. A fireman's slicker slung over a railing. A discarded hard hat. Flies swarming atop some gelatinous extinguisher foam on the gravel by the loading dock. A dozen overturned rubber waste cans, with this on them: "Inedible. Carolina By-Products."

There's a scent of something charred.

At 425 West Ave., William Rush, pastor of St. Stephen AME Zion, is taking his text from Matthew 5, verses 11 and 12. He's preaching on a theme of "It's going to be all right, after a while."

The pastor's voice is swelling and falling, full of that strange violent Southern holiness. Rush says over and over, "If you can just hold on a little longer. It's going to be all right after a while." Part of the brilliance of his sermon is that he never once mentions Sept. 3 or the fire.

The day before, in his parsonage, the pastor had said: "I think it's still a nightmare.... We're just a little hamlet. I think that's what really troubles us. That it happened here, in a place as small as this, in a county as compact as Richmond. My people have asked me, 'Why Hamlet?' 'Why me?' But turn it around. 'Why not Hamlet?' The people of Hamlet are no better than the people of Chicago or Pittsburgh. If these 25 had not died, then these foul and hazardous work conditions might never have come to light. One lady asked me, 'Reverend, do you feel this is the will of God?' It's such a hard question to answer. I'm trying to lead them away from it now."

THE SOUTH AS A LAYERED PLACE

On the day following the fire, one of the photographs carried by newspapers across the country was of the son of the owner of the company at a press conference with the fire chief and mayor. That son's name is Brad Roe. He was the 26-year-old operations manager of the Hamlet plant. He was known to have worked at the plant every summer since his 13th birthday. He stood up at the 3 o'clock press conference on Sept. 3 in a sleeveless jersey. Twenty-five had just died, had just been brought out on litters, their deaths owed at least in part to the way the company had operated its plant—and the son of the owner hadn't even bothered to put a real shirt on?

In the weeks since the fire, the Roe family of Atlanta—which has generally refused all comment to the press—has been painted in some accounts as a family of Simon Legrees. The Roe family could not be reached for this story, and others at the small company refused to speak for the record.

Abbie Covington is talking. She's the mayor. She's an eloquent spokeswoman for Hamlet. She's hurting for her town and she feels what happened was inexcusable. She thinks the healing process is going to go on much longer than anyone realizes.

"The fact that [several] doors were locked is a terrible thing," she says. "That's it. They're going to have to be punished for it. I don't back up from it a minute. But I am satisfied in my own mind that they never, ever in a million years thought that something like this would happen. I could never believe the owners thought to themselves, 'These doors are going to be locked to keep these people from stealing chicken parts, and if there's a fire, and they die, tough.' The fact is, Brad is the one who raced to the Fire Department. You know why he had an undershirt on? I'll tell you. Because he'd been helping get people out. He was half crazy about it. His outer shirt was covered with soot and char. The truth is, I don't think there's anything they can ever do to him he won't do to himself. It's killing him, that's what I believe."

The Philadelphia Inquirer

Carol Morello

Finalist, Non-Deadline Writing

Carol Morello has been a reporter for *The Philadelphia Inquirer* since 1983. Previously, she worked for newspapers in Mount Clemens, Midland, and Lansing, Michigan, and in Rochester, New York. She graduated from Michigan State University and was a fellow at the University of Southern California's Center for International Journalism, where she studied Latin America. As part of the program, she spent a summer at the Colegio de Mexico in Mexico City. She also wrote stories for the *Inquirer* from Mexico. More recently, her stories have come from the Middle East, where she is a foreign reporter for the *Inquirer*.

Her editors described her Persian Gulf War reporting as follows: "While others were writing of the American military's combat will, Morello was writing of the struggle by individual soldiers to write wills. She wrote of the empathy in a Graves Registration Unit whose men could not look at photos of loved ones in wallets of the dead. She wrote of the false bravado of carrier pilots 'catapulted into the sky, fully expecting someone would die.' This is not the work of a sentimentalist. This is the work of a keen-eyed writer who doesn't miss a thing."

As the ground war nears, troops' talk turns profound

FEBRUARY 21, 1991

[This article was subjected to U.S. military censorship.]

NORTHERN SAUDI ARABIA—With the prospect of battle at hand, it was a day for friends and lovers to say quiet goodbyes.

It was a day for saying things that had been put off while time had been abundant. Now time seemed preciously short.

In a tent at the front line two soldiers sat on a cot and embraced, their kisses interrupted by soldiers tromping through.

Brian and Diana Laskey are members of the Army's 467th Engineer Platoon, but when their unit moves forward in the attack, regulations require that she be left behind.

Their conversation the other morning was not casual chat. "We have risk factors in the States," Brian Laskey said. "Well, I figure the risk factor just jumped up 10 times here for us. It's time we talk about it."

"Death scenarios," he called them—how to break the news to their three children if one of them does not come home.

If one of them dies, he told her gently, the other should remarry, for the sake of the children. Diana shook her head in disagreement.

"You should get married again, for the sake of an income," he pressed on. "We have to think of the kids first. In my situation, it wouldn't be for the income, it would be to have a mother for them."

But Diana was hearing none of it.

"You'd better come back, you'd better come back," she scolded playfully, one hand resting on his shoulder and the other waving a finger at him. "And when you do, you'd better come find me first."

Later, after they had parted, she revealed more profound emotions.

"I don't know why he said what he did," she said. "I thought about all that a month ago."

And then she put her head in her hands and wept.

* * *

The members of the 467th are firefighters from a reserve unit based in Garden City, Kan. They have been together since their unit was called up early in December.

But in the shadow of the Iraqi border, the two women, Sgt. Diana Laskey and Spec. Sharon Marquez, are required to remain a five-minute drive to the rear of the unit.

It had rained the day before, and as dawn broke bright and clear, tiny sprigs of clover poked their heads through the desert floor. On this sunny morning, with a sense that the ground war was imminent, they prepared for what they feared might be a final visit with their buddies before the fighting began in earnest.

After breakfast, they returned to their tent to shave their legs, spray their necks with perfume, and don a little eyeliner.

Specs. Gordon Morton and Larry Coltharp arrived to pick them up, throwing their flak jackets on the women's cots and plopping to wait.

"Everyone's a lot more scared and terrified," Coltharp said. "I just tell them, 'Let the Lord take care of you, and you do your soldiering.'"

Morton pulled out a wallet photograph of his wife, Brenda, and 3-year-old son, who wait in Kansas.

"Last night, I was thinking of my son drooling, looking up at me," he said, his eyes lingering on the photo. "I've told my wife, 'Be ready to have another baby when I get home.'"

The theme of getting home dominated conversation along the drive up to the 467th's encampment. Parties were planned, as casually as if the soldiers were on a Kansas hayride instead of bouncing down a desert road flanked by a sea of tanks and camouflage tents.

They found the camp bustling with men pack-
ing, smearing a half-inch of mud on their lime-yel-
low fire trucks, and washing their clothes in bar-
rels. It was at this point that Diana Laskey greeted
her husband, and they had their conversation about
death, about their family's future.

Sharon Marquez wandered through the camp
like the proverbial earth mother, as the soldiers
who consider her a sister and confidante called out
her nickname.

"Hey, Munchie, c'mere," they beckoned to her
affectionately. She's called Munchie, short for
Munchkin, for her diminutive stature.

She listened as, one by one, they poured their
hearts out. She seemed older and wiser than a 20-
year-old who crosses off the days on a rose-colored
calendar by her cot and falls asleep clutching a teddy bear.

Sgt. Gilbert Cruz, a 20-year-old Colorado State
student, was the first to get her attention.

He and his two older brothers—Jonas, 21, and
Philip, 23—came to Saudi Arabia in the same unit.
They had grown up together, they made a decision
to go to war together.

Now they hoped to go home together.

In fact, the Army agreed to separate them to
make sure that at least one of Jenny Cruz's three
children would come home alive.

"I went to Mass, and the priest rubbed oil on our
hands," Gilbert Cruz said. "It's something they do
only for baptisms, confirmations, and the terribly
sick. When the priest said, 'See you next Sunday,'
it was with a tone of voice that I haven't heard since
my mom said to us, 'Be careful.' The priest made
me real apprehensive.

"When I got back, I went on guard duty and
watched the sunset. All I could think of was, it's
pretty cut and dry. Either we live or we die. You see
the boom-boom, the lights, and every day it gets
closer and closer. And one day, they're going to tell
you to go in. You want to get it over with, but you
don't. You don't know what will happen.

"Sunday was a bad day for me. I'm real apprehensive about the decision Phil and Jonas and I made."

* * *

As lunchtime rolled around, Capt. Bryan Page of Wichita, Kan., pulled out the Danish ham and the mustard and the chocolate-chip cookies his wife had mailed him and invited Sharon Marquez to join him.

Page had been going to the men in his unit, one by one, coaxing out their thoughts. Some chats have lasted only 25 minutes; others more than four hours.

When Page needs someone to talk to, he said, "I talk to Sharon."

He told Marquez he had advised the men to write last letters home. He mailed a letter for his wife, Bunny, to his father, with instructions not to pass it on unless he dies.

"If I come back, I don't want anyone to know what's in that letter, not even Bunny," he said. "My fondest wish is that she never gets to read it. I want to go back and be able to destroy it."

Over the last three months, Page said, the men of the 467th had grown closer than they ever were during their monthly weekends of training. "We sit around at night out here in the desert and talk about how beautiful the sky is, and the sunsets," he said. "If we talked like that back in the States, we'd all laugh and snicker. Being here brings everybody close, real close.

"In fact, if this was a prolonged conflict, I think I'd be scared of that closeness. Losing friends, I feel such a responsibility for them. I worry about that, how I'll handle it if I lose some.

"That's my biggest fear. Not going up, not being in Iraq. My biggest fear is losing someone. What if something happens to one of the Cruz brothers? What if something happens to Brian? If it does, I don't want anybody else to tell Diana. Yet I realize it would be somebody else, if we're up forward."

* * *

As the afternoon wore on, Marquez wandered over to Spec. Ken Fresquez, 26, of Denver. He carries a little stuffed bunny she gave him in his helmet for good luck. This day she gave him a rosary that she had not taken off since her boyfriend gave it to her two years ago.

"Someone I care for very much gave this to me," she said, "and now I want to give it to someone I care for."

"My mother mailed me some Noxema here," Fresquez said, "and I gave it to a woman I met on Valentine's Day who was sad because she hadn't received any Valentines. She was so happy she almost hugged me. I guess little things mean a lot here."

He paused, then leaned over to pat Marquez's boot.

"Like friends," he said.

After the desert night settled in, the soldiers of the 467th stood in a circle, holding hands while Gilbert Cruz said a prayer about coming home. The men to either side of Marquez gripped her hands so tightly that they turned numb.

And just beyond the camp perimeter, a line of tanks roared past.

Colin Nickerson
Deadline Writing

A newspaper pressroom was Colin Nickerson's entrée to newswriting. As a college junior with no clear career interests, he responded to a small newspaper ad for someone to bundle, load, and deliver newspapers. "The job interview was in the City Room," Nickerson said. "I watched the editor give out assignments. There'd been a wreck and he'd point and say, 'You go cover that.' It struck me as interesting. All of a sudden, I badly wanted to work there, even though I knew I would just be bundling up newspapers and throwing them onto trucks."

The experience led him to pursue a career in journalism. He worked as a reporter for several small newspapers before joining *The Boston Globe* in 1980, where he eventually became a foreign correspondent. Ironically, the interview that led to a career didn't land him a job. "The kicker is I didn't get the job I was seeking," Nickerson said. "I didn't get that job at all."

With fire far away, ground troops settle in

JANUARY 23, 1991

IN EASTERN SAUDI ARABIA—Nearly a week into the war with Iraq, Cpl. Christopher Flaherty, 25, of Holbrook, crouched in his foxhole after all-night sentry duty and watched dawn bleed across the horizon. His eyes were red from wind-driven sand and his lips were blue with cold.

All through the darkness he had listened to low-flying fighter-bombers hitting targets somewhere across the Kuwaiti border to the north. By now, the whump of distant detonations had lost much of its terrifying strangeness, even from this front-row vantage point.

"It seems real and unreal all jumbled together," said the Marine infantryman. "We hear the bangs, we see all those jets, but the battle isn't ours yet. You think of the chemicals and the missiles and you feel in danger, but you also feel like a spectator."

Although a few Marine units have come under intermittent artillery fire, and some reconnaissance patrols have engaged in brief small-arms skirmishes with Iraqi squads, the vast bulk of infantry, armored, and other ground forces massing near the border have had no tangles with an enemy entrenched not too many miles away. The war, for grunts like Flaherty, has settled into a routine of waiting for the half-dreaded, half-yearned-for order into combat.

"It scrapes on your nerves, living in your fighting holes and waiting for the real fight to start," said Cpl. Brian James, 21, of Gulf Breeze, Fla. "We've got past the point where we sit around talking about how tough and leatherneck-mean we are. We have got to the point where we know the day is coming when we'll have to prove it."

Meanwhile, near-constant training for battle continues on the bitter cold desert flats stretching toward Kuwait.

"All right, you gentlemen, listen up!" 1st Sgt. Philip Woll of Atlanta bawled to a circle of Marines in combat gear. "When the gas hits, you've got 15 seconds to get that mask on. You can't see nerve agent, you can't taste nerve agent, you can't smell nerve agent. So what are you going to do when the nerve agent hits? Now!"

Sgt. Woll roared off the seconds as the Marines fumbled frantically with their mask kits while trying not to drop their weapons, a cardinal offense for an infantryman: "13, 14, 15..." Perhaps half the 30 or so Marines had their masks on. "...31, 32, 33..." Many still had not completed what might become a life-or-death task if Iraq employs its chemical arsenal.

"One minute...and you, you, you, and you are dead," Woll singled out the Marines still struggling with the goggle-eyed devices.

"OK, gentlemen, let's try again."

From the distance sounded the muffled boom, boom of exploding shells.

"The gas has everyone kind of on edge," James said. "It doesn't make sense, but twitching from gas seems a million times worse than twitching from a bullet wound. It is the fear of the unknown."

Spectators, so far, at their own war, the Marines get the news from BBC Radio broadcasts and sometimes wildly inaccurate word of mouth.

"I hear Israeli commandos caught Saddam Hussein last night—that true?" a young sentry at a desert supply compound asks a reporter.

Informed it was not true, at least as far as the reporter knew, the Marine shook his head. "I guess there aren't going to be any miracles out here. I guess we are going to have to win this one the hard way."

Observations and questions

1) One of the classic rules of good writing is to use active verbs. Notice the strong, picturesque verbs in Nickerson's lead: "...Cpl. Christopher Flaherty, 25, of Holbrook, crouched in his foxhole after all-night sentry duty and watched dawn bleed across the horizon." Look for other strong verbs that move the piece.

2) Nickerson quotes four characters in this story. Consider how the characters are staged. They enter and leave the story without unduly overlapping each other and confusing the reader. Box the name of each on first reference and notice how each is presented.

3) A four-paragraph incident on page 123 conveys the urgency of precautions in war. What elements enable Nickerson to preserve the drama of the exercise?

4) A lively quotation can crystallize feeling in a concise statement. Cpl. James's comment is an example of that type of quotation. He says, "The gas has everyone kind of on edge...It doesn't make sense, but twitching from gas seems a million times worse than twitching from a bullet wound. It is the fear of the unknown." What are some other characteristics of lively quotations?

Shells, prayers in dead of night

JANUARY 29, 1991

NORTHEASTERN SAUDI ARABIA—It was 11:55 p.m, close to the Kuwaiti border. With a purr of hydraulics, automatic loaders inserted the 200-pound anti-armor projectiles into the breeches of the hulking 203mm mobile howitzers of the U.S. Marine raiding party.

On Gun No. 3, with the improbable nickname "Peace Maker" daubed on its cannon, Cpl. Tobias Rios, 27, of Elizabeth, N.J., rammed home an "eight-charge"—80 pounds of black powder trussed in a canvas satchel.

Nearby, teeth chattering with cold, Pvt. Douglas J. Hanneken, 24, of Winchester, Mass., prepared to relay fresh loads. Like his fellow artillery forces, his charged "high" was equal parts adrenalin and fear. Enemy batteries and missile launchers were near, too near.

"This is what we've been training for," Hanneken said. "This is the moment we've been dreaming of and dreading."

At 11:57 p.m. the breech locks clicked shut. Hydraulics growled as the long guns adjusted for target, an Iraqi military supply depot located a few miles across the border.

The wind was bitter cold, numbing the faces and hands of the howitzer crews, bringing tears streaming from unsorrowful eyes.

"Better them than me," grunted Staff Sgt. Robert Vasquez, 30, of Waterbury, Conn. "Better them, period."

At 11:59 came the order: Stand by!

Then, almost instantly, the command: Fire!

The howitzers boomed. Tongues of flame licked the blackness. The tremendous recoil of the weapons jolted the desert floor. A rank wash of cordite fouled the air, briefly blotting the moon. The gun crews feverishly reloaded, firing at will.

This morning's 2nd Marine Division artillery raid was the largest ground attack so far launched against Iraqis positioned in Kuwait. Basically a hit-and-run strike, it involved two fast-moving Marine batteries—one of 155mm guns—backed by mobile rocket launchers and a screening force of amphibious assault vehicles and infantry.

"The purpose is to harm and harass the enemy, to keep him on his toes, then knock him on his butt," said Capt. Mark Murphy, commander of the 203mm battery. "We move in quick, hit hard, and then boogie out of Dodge. By the time he hits back, we ain't there."

Each battery fired 36 rounds in a matter of minutes.

The outgoing shells whistle-whooped through the air, the sound fading, fading...then came a flash on the horizon. Dozens of deadly glimmers reflected off the clouds—followed by the muffled thunder of impacting rounds.

"Dropping a load dead on target is a damn complicated science," said Cpl. Matthew Speese, 27, of Jacksonville, N.C., whose job is to jerk the firing lanyard on Gun No. 3, the so-called Peace Maker. "You've got to factor in a hundred variables, from the temperature of the powder to the velocity of the wind. But believe me, we can drop these babies dead center into a trash can more than 10 klicks away." *Klick* is military slang for "kilometer."

Of the howitzer's nickname, Vasquez said: "It is not meant to be funny. Saddam Hussein has created a situation where the only way the world is going to find peace is by blasting him and his war machine to kingdom come. It is sad, it is tragic. No one is laughing out here."

The daring close-to-the-border raid was mounted and fired in about 15 minutes.

Prop-driven OV-10 Bronco spotter planes swooped near the targets, calling in coordinates, confirming "secondary" explosions that signify a hit.

The 203s fired "dual purpose" rounds, equally lethal to men and machines. The shells, basically bombs carrying more bombs, explode before hitting earth, flinging out scores of bomblets whose bursts of shrapnel can lay waste to structures, punch holes through light armor, and generally wreak havoc upon enemy mechanized units or fixed installations. They can take out an artillery battery or missile launcher, and transform a light tank or troop carrier into something looking very much like Swiss cheese.

"It is the deadliest round this battery packs," Hanneken said. "It lays down a wicked pattern of metal spray."

The 155mm howitzer battery blasted Iraqi positions with white phosphorous incendiary rounds, followed by salvos of shells containing "bouncing Betty" anti-personnel grenades. These hit the ground, jump into the air, and explode at about stomach level. Gut rippers, they are called, the scourge of infantrymen.

"Jesus God," muttered Cpl. Lee Welverton, 22, of Enterprise, Ala., as the howitzers barked, the orange flames plumed, and the whump-boom of impacting rounds rolled back to the ears of the young men who had fired them. "Jesus God have pity on their souls."

Observations and questions

Nickerson's job was to take readers to the scene of the battle. Consider the devices he uses.

1) He shows readers how the weather feels in the battle: "The wind was bitter cold, numbing the faces and hands of the howitzer crews, bringing tears streaming from unsorrowful eyes."

2) He lets us see what is happening: "Tongues of flame licked the blackness. The tremendous recoil of the weapons jolted the desert floor. A rank wash of cordite fouled the air, briefly blotting the moon."

3) He explains the action with a colorful quotation: "We move in quick, hit hard, and then boogie out of Dodge. By the time he hits back, we ain't there."

4) He lets us hear the action using onomatopoeia: "The outgoing shells whistle-whooped through the air, the sound fading, fading…"

5) He forms the picture by using comparisons, including metaphors and similes: "They can take out an artillery battery or a missile launcher, and transform a light tank or troop carrier into something looking very much like Swiss cheese."

Look for other examples of techniques Nickerson uses to make the scene vivid.

Close call leaves two Marines 'Lucky as Hell'—and ready

FEBRUARY 23, 1991

NEAR KUWAIT BORDER—With a red pen and shaky hand, Marine Lance Cpl. Robert Grady, 21, of Madison, N.C., last night inscribed a new nickname on his battle helmet: "Lucky as Hell."

His partner, Lance Cpl. William Noland, 25, of Memphis, also scrawled a new nickname on his camouflaged Kevlar headgear: "Lucky as Hell II."

The two were the only occupants of a Humvee all-terrain vehicle accompanying a large Marine reconnaissance foray into the bitterly contested no man's land between Saudi Arabia and Kuwait when an Iraqi advance force opened fire with artillery, mortars, and small arms at about 11:50 a.m. Thursday, Saudi time.

"We saw mortar rounds exploding in front of us, one, two, three," said Grady, who was riding gun seat while Noland drove the vehicle loaded with Stinger anti-aircraft missiles.

"The fourth round nailed the Hummer in the rear. There was a loud boom, we were thrown up against the windshield, then we shoved out and were running for cover," Grady said. "Lucky to be alive, I guess."

Neither man was injured.

"All we want is another vehicle so we can get in action for some payback," Noland said.

Fierce fighting between light-armored infantry units of the Marines 2nd Division and Iraqi forward troops continued Thursday night and into yesterday morning. Howitzers boomed, counterbattery missiles streaked across the sky, and Harrier jump jets flew low-level strikes against enemy forces probing American lines.

In this stretch of the front, two Marines were wounded and evacuated to medical units in the rear, while it appeared numerous Iraqi soldiers were killed in action, according to Lt. Col. Jan

Huly of the 2nd Division and accounts given to the Marines by enemy prisoners.

"The Iraqis are becoming more aggressive as we screen closer to their positions," Huly said.

The fighting was the heaviest ground engagement in the sector controlled by 2nd Marines so far in the gulf war. It came as Marines made final preparations for a massive assault on heavily fortified Iraqi positions in Kuwait. If diplomacy fails, these troops say they are ready to move.

IRAQIS SURRENDER, RESIST

"Clearly the Iraqis have not lost their will to resist," Huly said. "We see that some will surrender without putting up much fight. But others will battle to the bitter end."

The back-and-forth fighting occurred on a featureless swath of desert marking the border. At times, Marine units were engaged in Kuwait, but no attempt was made to hold territory.

At least 81 Iraqi infantrymen surrendered in this sector as Marines pummeled enemy tanks with round after round of 155mm artillery fire and aerial bombs. Two Iraqi tanks and five ammunition supply trucks were destroyed. Another "four to five enemy tanks are probable kills, but we cannot confirm them while the contact continues," Huly said.

An Iraqi artillery battery reportedly was destroyed by a Marine Harrier fighter-bomber.

As this dispatch was being written near the front, the ground reverberated to the constant boom of artillery from both enemy incoming shells and friendly outgoing rounds. Helicopter blades sliced the air as Cobra gunships skimmed off in search of Iraqi targets. The wind carried thick smoke and the heavy odor of cordite from high explosives.

Meanwhile, Marines and the reporters accompanying them were told this morning to begin taking pills intended to slow the effect of poison gas and other chemical weapons that may be employed by the Iraqis against an assault. The instruction was yet another sign of the preparation for an imminent ground push into Kuwait and Iraq while efforts continue for a settlement on diplomatic fronts.

ONE VEHICLE DESTROYED

Combat engineers continued to bulldoze passages through the immense sand berm that hugs the Saudi border for the length of Kuwait. If an assault is launched, the cuts will serve as avenues into no man's land for American tanks, armored vehicles, and infantry when the long-anticipated ground attack begins, possibly within a few days.

Gouts of flame and long, red rocket trails illuminated the northeastern front into the dark early hours yesterday. At 10:45 a.m. the artillery duel appeared to be intensifying with blasts ripping across the desolate flats where Marines have taken up assault positions.

The battle began when a Marine tactical convoy —a spread-out formation of armored reconnaissance vehicles and Humvees—came out amid small-arms and mortar fire at 11:50 Thursday morning. The American force took cover, then counterattacked about an hour later.

The only Marine vehicle destroyed in the fighting was the military utility vehicle, or Humvee, containing Noland and Grady. It was struck by a mortar burst in the opening minutes of the engagement.

The all-purpose vehicle was loaded with six Stinger missiles. The job of the two Marines was to defend the patrolling formation with the shoulder-fired weapons in the unlikely event of an Iraqi air attack.

"We were several miles in when all of a sudden there were random shell hits and smoke and noise," Grady said.

'LUCKY SHOT'

The blast that destroyed the rear of their vehicle ignited the fuel loads in two of the rockets.

"The Iraqis aren't very accurate. It was a lucky shot," joked Noland. "But it was a very good lucky shot."

Neither man seemed fazed by the experience,

their first taste of combat. Both were complaining that they had not received another vehicle in which to rejoin their battalion, still fighting with Iraqi forces.

They were upset at losing all their personal possessions when the Humvee was struck. "I lost my dental floss, a snapshot of my girlfriend, and a picture of my father when he was in the Marine Corps," Grady said.

Noland said: "I guess the Iraqis aren't as wimpy as maybe everyone thought. They fight pretty hard. But we Americans are kind of like swamp alligators—you can hit us pretty hard and we still come back snapping."

Observations and questions

1) The first seven paragraphs of the story tell of an adventure of two Marines. What do you learn about the two? What assumptions do you make about them? How does Nickerson develop the character of each?

2) Think of the story the way a cinematographer would. The first section is a close-up of two men charged up from a near-death experience. The next scene is an overview of the war. The last scene returns to the two Marines. How does the writing and the type of information given change with each scene?

3) Cutler Andrews presents a study of war correspondents in his book *The South Reports the War.* Andrews includes one of the most colorful writers of the Civil War, Felix Gregor de Fontaine, who wrote for the *Charleston Courier* under the name Personne. Here's an example of his writing: "I look around me and see men barefooted and ragged, bearing only their muskets and a single blanket each, yet all inspired by the hope of another battle." Compare the tone of this 19th-century dispatch to that set by Nickerson.

4) It's difficult for a reporter in a war to avoid including himself or herself in the action. Compare Personne's approach above to Nickerson's in the last two paragraphs on page 130. Which of these techniques, or others, best serve the reader?

For Marines, swift advance on city

FEBRUARY 28, 1991

WITH 2ND MARINE DIVISION, Kuwait— Fierce but sporadic fighting continued in drenching rains outside Kuwait City early yesterday morning, but for every Iraqi unit still holding out against the allied onslaught there were many more eager to abandon their tanks or fling aside their AK-47 rifles and surrender. Thousands of Iraqi troops had already quietly slipped from Kuwait, even as their president was still vowing to fight "the mother of all battles."

"Turned out to be more like the fourth cousin of all battles," joked Sgt. Paul Lanclos, 24, of Opelousas, La., whose infantry unit was among the first waves to smash through Iraqi minefields and bunkered positions, encountering heavy but wildly inaccurate shelling.

Across Kuwait, the sandy terrain was strewn with white cluster-bomb casings and angled remains of Iraqi vehicles, along with the homely artifacts of the dug-in Iraqi troops' day-to-day lives— encrusted cook pots, items of clothing, a tattered mattress at the bottom of a fighting hole, ammunition crates employed as makeshift furniture, and tin pots for washing clothes.

Like leaves in the wind, tens of thousands of American "surrender or die" leaflets, dropped by bombers in the days before the ground invasion, swirled in the air and formed drifts against crude bunkers.

Four days after surging across the border from Saudi Arabia in the largest armor, air, and infantry assault since World War II, U.S. Marines closed in from the west and southwest of Kuwait City. Sporadic fire fights and the crash of artillery boomed on the outskirts of the city as Marines mopped up pockets of Iraqi resistance.

"The military machine of Saddam Hussein is dead," said Lt. Gen. Walter Boomer, commander of all Marine forces in the battle for Kuwait, as an Iraqi tank exploded less than a mile away, sending trails of white smoke and chunks of metal through the air. "Iraq had the men, the materials, and even the training to put up a harder fight. But in the end, most didn't want to die for the 19th province."

Saddam Hussein, after invading the oil-rich emirate last August, declared Kuwait to be Iraq's 19th province, a claim Iraq only yesterday appeared to renounce at the United Nations.

MORE THAN THEY HOPED FOR

As many as 3,000 Iraqi military vehicles were abandoned or destroyed in and around Kuwait City, according to Maj. Gen. William "Pit Bull" Keys, commander of the 2nd Division, whose Marines were the first to reach the suburbs of the city following a swift advance up the length of Kuwait.

"We've accomplished everything we hoped for and a little bit more," said Keys, his face grimed by battle, adding that Marines "won't shoot anyone who wants to surrender.

"We want to stop as many of them from retreating as possible and destroy as much enemy equipment as possible," Keys said in an interview.

There was no exact tally of Marine losses last night, but one field commander characterized casualties as "almost unbelievably light." The 2nd Division, which a *Boston Globe* reporter accompanied on the drive to Kuwait, lost four men killed in action. About 40 Marines were wounded.

The push across the mine-strewn desert involved hundreds of military vehicles—from sophisticated M1-A1 main battle tanks to Korean War vintage Jeeps with missing windshields and rust-rotted floor plates—churning through a moonscape pocked by allied bombs and scarred by elaborate Iraqi trenches from which shredded white flags of surrender fluttered.

Helicopter gunships skittered low over Marine convoys winding for miles over dunes and across arid flats under skies stained black by the smoke from burning oil fields and enemy vehicles.

In the rapid advance, which brought Marines to strategic "phase points" hours and sometimes a day ahead of schedule, truck-drawn artillery crews were hard-pressed to keep up with the tanks and mechanized infantry. The gunners would stop, hastily unlimber their howitzers, fire a few ear-cracking volleys, then rehitch the weapons and barrel north to new covering positions.

Shuffling columns of Iraqi soldiers who had abandoned their weapons plodded among the dunes. Often their pleas to surrender formally were brushed aside by the onward-rushing Marines. One bedraggled bunch approached Marine unit after unit, waggling their hands over their heads and crying, "No fight! No fight!"

Hundreds were rounded up and transported to internment camps, but as their numbers swelled and Marine transport trucks ran short, the Iraqis were simply given cold rations and instructed to keep marching south where military police awaited them near the Saudi border.

"They are coming out of the woodwork," said a colonel with a tank battalion. "The phrase 'Take no prisoners' is assuming a whole new, if less sinister, meaning. We want to help these poor bastards out, but we are overwhelmed—they have to find their own way to POW camps."

MEETING THE INFIDELS

After many weeks under intensive American aerial bombardment, many Iraqi troops seemed weirdly elated to meet at last the "infidel enemy," as Saddam Hussein has characterized the U.S.-led military alliance. And American troops seemed startled to find many of the enemy were far less ferocious than billed.

"We are supposed to be at war with these guys," said Pvt. Edward Love, 20, of Cleveland. "But when I went up to take their pictures they started smiling and waving at me."

But not all Iraqis gave up so easily.

Artillery and tank duels raged as the Marines closed in on a vast quarry and landfill just a few miles from Kuwait City. Tongues of flame belched from M-60 tank muzzles. Shells hit enemy tanks with such force that the hulls were ripped from the vehicles. Burning flesh tainted the damp air.

For reasons that Marine commanders were unable to explain, Iraqi tank and artillery fire, although often intense, was almost invariably inaccurate. The 6th Armored Regiment, roaring down on a dug-in Iraqi tank battalion, destroyed scores of the fighting vehicles without taking a single disabling hit in return.

BLACK SMOKE, RED SKY

Guttering fires from these fast, furious encounters cast reddish reflections against the night sky, and at daybreak burning fuel formed hundreds of pillars of black smoke while ammunition exploded.

Boomer was ebullient about the progress of the conflict even after spending the night in a marooned armored convoy shaken, but undamaged, by constant blasts of incoming artillery rounds impacting nearby.

"It has gone incredibly well," he said. "If this makes military history, it will be as the first military plan that has gone exactly as planned."

By their fourth day of combat, young Marines had been transformed into wary-eyed warriors eager to finish the battle and get on home. During lulls in the fighting, they would crawl into muddy foxholes for an hour or so of rest, wolf down cold field rations, or take snapshots of each other beside destroyed Iraqi vehicles or bunkers. Despite warnings about booby traps, many scrounged for souvenirs. Iraqi officers' insignia were particularly prized, as were enemy bayonets, medical kits bearing red crescents, and other bits of abandoned military gear.

Enemy prisoners were treated kindly, if not with a great deal of respect.

"They ain't very good fighters," said 19-year-old Lance Cpl. Jason Benko of Elyria, Neb. "I only hope they are good lovers, like the joke goes, so at least they got something going for them."

Observations and questions

1) Nickerson sets up a powerful lead much as a good comedi-an sets up a joke. The end of the first paragraph creates a frame for Lanclos's joke in the second paragraph. Experiment with changing the sentence order in the first two paragraphs and no-tice the difference in the effect.

2) The third paragraph is strengthened by the use of adjec-tives. Underline the adjectives. How would the section read without them? What guidelines would you set for the use of adjectives?

3) Near the top of page 137 we read: "Shells hit enemy tanks with such force that the hulls were ripped from the vehicles. Burning flesh tainted the damp air." Nickerson touches on the horror of war without going into graphic details. How much should readers see of the grotesque acts of war?

4) What level of respect does the enemy deserve in a war sto-ry? Is that level achieved here?

5) Lively writing can disguise the hard work of searching out facts for a story. What are some of the details in this story that go beyond observation?

War diary: From chaos and fear, a victory

MARCH 3, 1991

WITH 2ND MARINE DIVISION, Kuwait—
Smoke from blazing oil fields and Iraqi tanks blotted the dawn. The 2nd Marines, having charged so far so fast that their western flank was wide open to enemy counterattack, had spent a shivery, sleepless night in hastily scooped fighting holes, intermittently lashed by icy rain and the hot wind of high explosives.

The Marine fighting and command convoy with which we—four reporters from *The Boston Globe, New York Newsday,* and the Associated Press and Reuters—were traveling last week had been more or less marooned on the edge of a minefield since our second night out as tank and howitzer duels raged all around.

With both enemy and friendly units on the prowl, with visibility approaching nil and communications not much better, the convoy commander had called a halt and positioned the 62 vehicles into a defensive laager.

The artillery still crashed as the blackness of night gave way to the battle-smogged twilight of day.

Rising stiffly from their troughs, the grunts gave vent to the obscenities that are the Marine infantryman's equivalent of a rooster's cock-a-doodle-doo. A ritual salute to the morning.

"If I can hear myself cussing, I reckon I'm still alive and kicking," said Sgt. Francis Goodline, 21, of Middletown, N.J.

Nearby, Col. Sepp Ramsberger boomed gloomy verse in a cheerful voice:

"Beneath this bowl we call the sky,
Whereunder crawling cooped we live and die,
Do not raise your arms to it for help,
For it, as impotently as you and I, rolls on...."

The grunts shook their heads. Sooty rain dripped

from their battle helmets.

"Omar Khayyam," the colonel said of his rendering of lines from "The Rubaiyat."

"That's, uh, great, sir," a goggle-eyed corporal said. "Real inspirational."

It was Tuesday, barely 74 hours since the 2nd Marines had breached the first line of enemy minefields and entrenchments. Today they would push on to Kuwait City.

* * *

Three days earlier, on Sunday, Feb. 24, at 5 a.m., the division's 6th Regiment was about to go in.

For hours, the Marines had waited anxiously, suited up in chemical-protection gear of filtering charcoal between two layers of rubbery material. The suits were at once hot for lack of ventilation and clammy from the cold sweat of fear. Some Marines dry-retched in their anxiety. Most simply sat in their assault vehicles, staring stonily ahead. Lots of jokes; little laughter.

The air cracked to the sound of heavy bombing by B-52s and fighter jets. Cobra gunships hovered, ready to fly close air support. Heavy artillery thundered. The world was consumed by horrific sound.

The assault assembly point was in no man's land, a few hundred yards beyond the enormous sand berm marking the Saudi border. The Marines began crossing the line of departure at 5:30 a.m. sharp, with combat engineers leading the way.

The first minefields were encountered at 6 a.m., a few miles inside Kuwait. Under sporadic shelling, engineers fired "line charges"—long ropes of high explosive capable of blasting a path through the deadly sands.

Then came tanks with three fanglike plows that gave them the appearance of gruesome metal sharks. A mine exploded under one tank, blowing its treads and leaving it stranded. The crew survived.

At least some of the mines were loaded with chemical agents, probably mustard gas, according to Marine accounts. But the deadly fumes quickly dissipated.

Faster now, faster. There were six breach points,

and the Marines tackling the four on the eastern
flank were taking heavy artillery and mortar hits
from Iraqi positions, now within sight.

By 7 a.m. the Marines had broken through two
breach points to the west and were fanning out behind the first enemy lines in light armored vehicles.

Lt. Mike Haggerty of Pittsburgh and the troops
with him were pinned down by intense artillery and
small-arms fire. "We were taking all this incoming
and you lie there thinking, 'Oh, God, make this my
lucky day. Roll sevens, dear God, roll those lucky
seven dice.'"

Nearby, Sgt. Rick Bowman, 28, of Logan, Ohio,
was blazing away with a Mark-19 40mm grenade
launcher attached to the turret of his Humvee all-
terrain vehicle. Sgt. Paul Lanclos, 24, of Opelousas,
La., was at the wheel, jerking it madly left and right
as concussion waves from artillery blasts rocked
the vehicle.

Sgt. Larry Dozier, 31, of Brockton, Mass., was
in the rear seat perched on a crate of orange juice, a
stash for thirsty times ahead. He was clutching his
M-16 carbine and wondering how things could
possibly get worse.

It was then that the mine exploded beneath the
rear wheel, blowing the tire off 100 yards and sending sharp metal shards upward directly toward
Dozier. The orange juice was the Brockton man's
salvation. The cans absorbed the shrapnel, but the
impact sent his assault rifle and helmet flying from
the vehicle.

Then he was on the ground, panicked to find
himself unarmed.

"I need my rifle! Where's my rifle?" he cried
above the din.

By late morning, all six breach lines were clear
and Marines were marking the three main lanes of
attack north with red, blue, and green garbage cans
weighted with sand. Harriers and A-6 attack jets
were swooping in front of the mechanized infantry
surge, zeroing in on enemy armor.

* * *

Monday. Feb. 25. The 2nd Marines were pushing rapidly past a series of "phase points" named for animals—phase points Fox, Elk, Moose, Panther were behind them, with Horse still ahead.

By late afternoon, most of the division had passed through the first lines of Iraqi entrenchments. "We've got full combat power forward," said Lt. Col. Jan Huly, a bit miffed that his proposal that the final phase point be called "Anteater" had been rejected as unmilitary sounding.

So far, in the largest Marine assault since World War II, the 2nd had suffered three infantrymen killed in action and 11 wounded.

Strangely, the low numbers were somehow crueler than a larger casualty count. "Hundreds dead is anonymous, unless one happens to be your buddy," mused Cpl. Scott Fuller. "But when three guys get popped, well, you find yourself wondering about them as people, men with wives, children."

Greasy black smoke from hundreds of flaming oil heads billowed like hurricane thunderheads to the northeast. The flame trails of surface-to-surface missiles were swallowed by the towering mass. Our convoy was bouncing at a rapid clip along a trail carved by tank treads. In the distance, shell bursts winked and sparked like land-bound stars. Geysers of earth rose from the nearer hits.

We stopped to gobble cold field rations beside an abandoned Iraqi bunker fortified with sandbags. The roof was tin sheeting covered with sand. There were an Igloo water cooler, an empty box of laundry soap, a pot containing cooked rice, and a pair of socks dangling from a loop of string attached to the wall.

The socks were still damp; the bunker's occupants had fled recently.

* * *

Night of Feb. 25. Maverick missiles unloosed by night fighters flying close air support for advancing Marines scored solid kills on the trio of Iraqi T-62 tanks lurking in ambush. Stabs of flame as the rockets left the tubes, then the orange bursts of impact.

Rack up three points for the fly-boys.

But there were no cheers from the grunts in the column of military vehicles wending its way through an artillery duel with no clear idea of who was firing at whom. Their mood darkened when word got back that the jets had also dropped dud cluster bombs whose canisters had popped apart in midair, as designed, but whose hundreds of "bomblets" had failed to explode.

The ground ahead was strewn with hundreds of pieces of live ordinance.

No turning back. Artillery rounds were crashing behind.

"Forward the Light Brigade," sighed Col. Roger McElraft, tossing his holstered .45-caliber Colt pistol onto the seat of his Humvee and inserting an unlit cigar between his teeth.

Outside the Humvee, the colonel dropped to his knees. Master Gunnery Sgt. Jerry Dale dropped beside him. The two Marines began creeping through the bomb debris, navigating by compass and feeling out a safe track by hand.

"This isn't what colonels are supposed to do," muttered McElraft.

"This isn't what master gunnery sergeants are supposed to do," growled Dale. "Sir."

Sixty-two light-armored infantry carriers, Humvees, command vehicles, and supply trucks followed the two crawling point men.

Inch by inch, the column threaded its way past the ruined Iraqi tanks, demolished enemy bunkers, and the widely scattered bomblets.

Just as the pair reached clear ground, a TOW gunner in the Humvee just behind caught movement through his thermal sights. "Uh, Sir, got dismounted infantry ahead," he urgently whispered. "Don't think they are friendlies."

The Iraqis numbered 16, and some still carried weapons.

They ambled toward the Marines shouting, "Salaam! Salaam!"

A peace greeting, a cry of surrender.

But to Col. McElraft's ears it sounded like "Saddam! Saddam!"

"I thought, my God, Iraqi kamikazes," he said later.

He reached for his side arm, remembering, too late, that he had left it on the front seat. So he yelled: "Hands up!"—like some town-taming marshal in a movie Western. "'They just sat down, docile as sheep."

* * *

Tuesday. Feb. 26. Black rain wept from the heavens, droplets of crude oil that tarred vehicles and streaked faces with a gooey film.

Overhead, heavy-lift helicopters with enormous water containers slung beneath flew missions of mercy to Iraqi soldiers surrendering by the tens of thousands.

On the radio, the BBC was reporting that Saddam Hussein's legions were fleeing Kuwait City and that the dictator had formally renounced claim to the "19th province."

"It ain't over till it's over," said Maj. Gen. William (Pit Bull) Keys, the commander of the 2nd Marines. "We want to try to stop the withdrawal. We want to destroy as much enemy equipment as possible."

The Marine mechanized columns roared north, passing thousands of Iraqi soldiers shuffling south. The Iraqis surrounded vehicles, begging to surrender formally, but there were neither extra trucks to transport them nor Marines to spare for guards. Instead, the Marines tossed them packets of field rations and spare blankets, then ordered them to step aside.

Onward then, onward. Tattered white shirts, strips of cloth, even underpants fluttered from makeshift poles atop hundreds of Iraqi bunkers and entrenchments as symbols of surrender.

It was as if every light garment had been pressed into service as a symbol of surrender.

From high vantages, the desert seemed aswarm with military men and machines: Marine M-60 and M1-A1 battle tanks; fast-moving light-armored infantry carriers; Humvees and 5-ton transports; the insectile cargo carriers called Dragon Wagons; bulldozers, heavy forklifts, ammunition trucks, diesel tankers; mobile howitzers that would pull into firing position, blast off volleys, then rejoin the mechanized surge.

"Schwarzkopf! Schwarzkopf!" defeated Iraqis chanted the name of the American commander. "No gun! No gun!"

But not all Iraqi troops had laid down their weapons.

Outside a vast landfill and gravel quarry near Kuwait City, Marine M-60s ran smack into entrenched battalions of T-62 and advanced T-72 tanks backed by armored fighting vehicles. Flames spouted from cannon muzzles, shells whistle-whooshed down range.

It was over in less than an hour. Scores of Iraqi tanks were reduced to shredded metal, blazing coffins for their crews. The stench of burning flesh tainted the wind. The skies howled with low-flying Cobra attack helicopters and twisting, jinking Harrier and A-10 armor-killing jets.

* * *

Wednesday. Feb. 27. The crack-rattle of small-arms fire echoed from the shantytown suburbs and junkyard bunkers where isolated Iraqi troops were making a final stand.

"We don't want to be killing anyone anymore; it's just senseless. The war's over, the thing is won," said Col. Larry Livingston.

There was a fire fight sputtering beyond a rise a few hundred yards away, but Livingston, like many Marines, was sick of the slaughter. "Send over a psych-ops team with loudspeakers. Try to talk those guys into giving up."

Nearby, Maj. Richard Moore, an intelligence officer, was poring over some literature seized from an Iraqi bunker, among it a document on trench warfare and a manual on Soviet artillery tactics.

"I suppose they wanted to fight by the book, but they were reading the wrong books," he said.

"When we fought in a way they didn't expect, they just collapsed. It wasn't that they lacked courage, they just couldn't adapt."

Naval Corpsman Jesus Juarez was down at a jury-rigged first-aid tent, tending to an Iraqi officer with a gaping flesh wound in his leg. The burly 26-year-old medic from Lawrence, Mass., applied compresses and bandages with a tender touch, all the while murmuring assurances to the officer, who seemed terrified.

"It's OK, man, it's over, you are going to be OK," said Juarez.

The muffled boom of artillery sounded from the east. The killing and the destruction went on. But it was mopping-up action, the dirty work of a winding-down war.

"You know, my big fear going in was I'd be overwhelmed by casualties among my own guys. I'd lie up nights worrying that I'd let my Marines down," said Juarez, moving on to the next wounded Iraqi. "But mostly I've been patching up enemy troops.

"Doesn't make no difference to me. We're all God's children, aren't we? All God's children gone insane," he said with a sigh. "I figure this war was as righteous as a war can be. But that isn't saying much. I don't see a whole lot of glory in it."

The fourth and final night of the ground war was descending. The flickerings from hundreds of fires cavorted like red demons all around the rim of a ruined land.

Observations on deadline writing

I had read *The Adventures of Tom Sawyer* to my 10-year-old just before going to St. Petersburg to help choose the ASNE writing award winners whose stories are reprinted in this book. It occurred to me in retrospect what a remarkable likeness there is between the elements of Mark Twain's storytelling and the elements of good deadline writing.

When a violent thunderstorm blows up one night on the Mississippi River island where Tom, Huck, and Joe Harper are hiding after faking their own deaths, Twain covers it as a good newspaper reporter might. He doesn't *tell* you the storm's coming; he *shows* you. When it comes, you feel its full might through his close attention to detail. This detail and the confidence with which he gives names to the natural phenomena around the boys give his voice authority. The storm is an event that happens in time—it has a beginning, a middle, and an end. That is how Twain describes it. You experience it with the boys, feeling relief when it has passed.

So there you have it, the elements of good deadline writing: detail, chronology, and the authority to tell the story. Through these a writer is able to put the reader at the scene.

The last—authority—is perhaps the trickiest. In Twain's case, you can deduce from the writing that he knows Mississippi River thunderstorms from experience. That is what gives his description such authority. The authority in the voices of Colin Nickerson and Paul McEnroe depends on their closeness to the action.

Doug O'Harra's story about the Iditarod Sled Dog Race derives its authority from another source. From beginning to end, you could tell you were reading someone who knew the game, knew the course, knew the players.

One more thing: You can't win the deadline writing contest unless you are where the story is. In a war, at the sudden death of a great racehorse, during the overthrow of Marcos, in a brush with the Tontons Macoutes—the only thing between the reader and the event is a great storyteller.

C. Michael Pride, Editor
Concord (N.H.) *Monitor*

A conversation with Colin Nickerson
Dispatches from a distance

KAREN BROWN: In 1976, you were the only reporter at a small weekly. Four years later, you were a reporter for *The Boston Globe*. Four years after that, you were a foreign correspondent for the *Globe*. Did you have the sense that you were advancing rapidly?

COLIN NICKERSON: Well, I was very interested in getting overseas. I was willing to work hard.

What did you learn about writing when you worked at the small newspapers?

I learned that writing was a lot tougher than I'd ever expected it to be. I learned that writing takes a lot of thought and a lot of effort. That the whole difference between a bad newspaper story and a good newspaper story has nothing to do with what the story's about. You can write a good newspaper story about a selectmen's meeting in a little Vermont town of 200 people, and you can write a bad newspaper story about some dramatic calamity or disaster that affects thousands of people. The difference is usually the amount of thought and effort that the reporter, and then later his or her editors, are willing to put into it.

Talk a little more about how you learned that the type of story doesn't dictate the quality of the writing.

I believe you take every story you're given and try to make it come alive for the readers.
When I was writing for *The Chronicle* in

■ Colin Nickerson, Asia bureau chief, *The Boston Globe*.

■ **Born:** May 29, 1950, in Cambridge, Mass.

■ **Personal:** Married to Nancy Devries, a psychiatric nurse.

■ **Education:** Marlboro College, Vt.; graduated in 1974 with degree in English.

■ **Newspaper Experience:** Sole staff reporter for *The Chronicle*, a weekly in Barton, Vt., 1976-78; staff reporter, *Rutland* (Vt.) *Herald*, 1978-80; *The Boston Globe*, 1980-present.

■ **Awards:** Overseas Press Club Award for coverage of the Ethiopian War.

Overseas Press Club Citation for Excellence for coverage of Persian Gulf War.

Barton, Vermont, one of my jobs was to cover the courts. I'd look for the most offbeat kind of crime. We once had a crime involving somebody who went around and stole several hundred house plants. It was an inexplicable, bizarre crime. I led with it, and I made it interesting. I'm not saying that all you want to do is make news stories sing. Sometimes the most important thing to do is to convey the most important information. But there is no reason not to work hard, think hard, and try to write the best story you can.

What kind of editing did you get when you reached the *Globe*?

Gerry O'Neill was my editor. He was a great editor. I wouldn't say he was terrific with words, with writing. Generally when he'd rewrite a sentence or paragraph of mine, I'd want to write it back the way it was. But he was terrific with placement, with where the lead should be, where the "nut graph" or the summary paragraph should be. I sometimes put the summary too low in a story. His ideas about story structure were always terrific.

I've been lucky in the editors I've had. When I joined the foreign staff, Kathryn Tolbert was my editor for a very long time. Now she is the Washington editor. She had a way, as Gerry had, of looking at a story and saying, well, maybe this would be better here. And it usually made sense to me. She was instructive, positive. There are some editors in this world who are a little bit like dogs. They like to pee on every story just to show they've been there.

But the changes your editors made were primarily organizational?

Yes, primarily. Nobody had problems with my writing, except for the very justifiable charge that I occasionally overwrite. And I don't remember having huge problems with my structure. But I guess the most common criticisms I've had are that I write too long and I tend to put the news peg or the what-it-all-means paragraph too low. I've had a lot of help with that from editors.

You started in the northern New England bureau, and soon became a roving feature writer, then a foreign correspondent. Most of this time you were working independently of close editing, and you were moving farther and farther away from Boston. How do you keep a sense of the reader?

I think the Boston reader is impossible to define. A profile of the Boston reader is going to include affluent Brahmins, Cambridge academic types, and blue-collar workers from South Boston and Dorchester. It's going to include the whole middle-class medley of Americana living in the suburbs, all races, all economic strata. So you really don't have to think of one reader. Once you get overseas, you begin thinking more in terms of what would be a generally interesting story for readers of a big American newspaper.

You became a roving correspondent in Africa in 1984. What were the parameters of your work there?

Oh, everything from covering coups in Uganda to covering developmental issues, social issues, environmental issues. Of course, the big ongoing story while I was there was the anti-apartheid movement in South Africa.

What other stories did you cover?

A lot of coverage was frantic, like joining up with the Tigre Peoples Liberation Front guerrillas as they fought the Cubans and the Russian advisers in the Ethiopian army. But there was also a lot of time to poke around countries where not much was happening and write about people, in Malawi, or Mali, or up in the east central area. I wrote about Tuareg tribesmen. I found a town where slavery still exists.

I spent three days with a farmer in Mozambique and wrote an article about what his problems were, what his income was, how the government wasn't helping him a bit, how the guy had never heard of the programs that were supposed to help farmers. But he was getting along. He had himself a few pigs, and he was growing himself some corn. He was a smart, savvy guy. And he was getting by. He was able to grow enough food to sell it. So he had enough money to send his kids to school. It was one tiny little success story in Africa.

After covering Africa, you became Asia bureau chief in 1988. Since then, you've done some of the most important stories in the news. That includes Tiananmen Square and U.S.–Japanese trade relations. Would you talk about some of the stories that were most important to you, and some of the ones that were most challenging?

The big story in '88 was the Afghanistan War. It had clearly become a Vietnam for the Soviets, and they were getting pummeled. I went in with the muja-heddin in '88, spent a long time traveling to Afghanistan covering that war, which was really at its most vicious state. Like everybody else in Afghanistan, we were bombed, strafed, attacked daily, hourly. Kind of extraordinary.

Let's talk about getting to the scene of the action. And let's do that by looking at your winning stories. Few reporters really got close to the action of the Persian Gulf War. How did you manage to get there?

Well, I was part of a combat correspondent pool with the 2nd Marine Division from a few days before the war started until the end. So I was out living in foxholes from mid-January until the beginning of March.

I know some correspondents have a lot of problems with the Army in terms of access to the troops and stuff like that, but the Marines were pretty good about it. They took us on several combat missions before the invasion of Kuwait. We accompanied them on the invasion, too. I had a pretty free hand to go around and talk to whomever I wanted.

About how many press representatives were with the group?

There were six at the outset, and it expanded to eight. There were four writers, Jeff Franks from the Reuters news agency, Denis Gray from the AP, Susan Sachs from *Newsday,* and me. And then there was an ABC crew of three people led by Linda Pattillo, a camera man, and Sadayuki Mikami, an AP photographer based in Tokyo.

Did the *Globe* have other reporters in the Persian Gulf?

Oh, yes. We had reporters in Dhahran, where the troops were disembarking from planes, and in Riyadh, which was the base of the military central command.

So your job was to present the color of the war.

Yes, I was covering the combat and, to a large extent, the color. The correspondent in Dhahran would also do some of the color stories, back in the rear echelons where the Scud missiles were falling. Those reporters carried a lot of weight on the day-to-day coverage of the war. The ground war was going on long before the U.S. actually invaded. There were lots of skirmishes, a lot of attacks back and forth across the border. But there was also a lot of "down" time, in which essentially you would write color stories. This first story in my package is an example. We could see the bombing. We could hear the planes flying overhead. We were in the middle of a war, but as for the Marines, the combatants, they weren't really a part of it.

In a sense, the soldiers were observers, like you.

Right. They were watching the bombs go off and worrying. One of the most important things in journalism is to talk to people. You've got to talk and talk and talk to people. You don't just come in and whip off a few questions. You sit down and split a chocolate bar or something with a Marine, and ask questions about his life, have a conversation, spend a half-hour or 45 minutes, an hour, with the guy.

You don't seem to be shy about talking to people. How would you describe your personality?

[Laughter] I don't know—uh, quietly aggressive. I like to go after stories, but I don't bluster. I don't like to go in screaming about the rights of the press. My approach to dealing with idiots in the military who are trying to restrict the press is either to go around them or to talk to them a bit and say, "Look, I'm here simply to tell people at home what's going on. I don't see why you feel threatened by that." I guess I like to be the observer. I don't like to be part of the story.

You start your first story, "With Fire Far Away, Ground Troops Settle In," by setting a scene in the first three paragraphs. And then the fourth paragraph is a "nut graph." You say that the battle is far away and explain that these people are waiting for things to happen. And then you have another block, about the drill with the gas masks. The story ends with the block indicating that for these soldiers now, the war is really in the media. So the format seems to be in blocks, with the "nut graph" around the fourth paragraph. Did you think of it that way when you wrote it? Did you see the story in blocks?

I tend not to conceive of the whole story. I went into the story knowing I wanted to say something about these young guys in their foxholes. I'd been struck by what Cpl. Flaherty had said to me about the reality and unreality of it all, and I wanted to get that up high. And so I kind of wrote the story paragraph by paragraph. I didn't have any idea of where it was going to end. I just wanted to set a tone, create a feeling, give the reader an impression of the strangeness of sitting out there waiting for a war that is raging.

Do you go back and edit, or do you just write straight through and file?

When I'm out in the desert writing with a typewriter, I write one draft. And then I may pen in a few corrections, a few new words. When I have the luxury of writing with a computer, I don't redraft a whole story, but I might spend a lot of time drafting and redrafting some paragraphs until I feel they're just right. Sometimes it's easy to say what you want to say. Obviously, when you have the perfect quote, the quote that sums it up, you don't have to do any work at all. You just plug in that quote.

You have a number of excellent quotations in your stories.

But you have to work to get quotes. The quotes are not dropped in your lap. I've heard so many reporters complain that they don't get good quotes. If I had simply gone in and asked two or three questions, they'd have given me the usual gung-ho nonsense: "Well, we're proud to be here. We are ready to do our job. We just want to do what we're told to do." It's when you sit down with them, and maybe share water from a canteen, and just chat, that finally they'll open up and say what's really on their minds.

Many reporters feel that they don't have the time to get to know sources and make them feel comfortable. They've got to get the story and get out of there.

Well, in the Persian Gulf, it was deadline writing. I wrote this first story four hours after I started reporting it. I had two or three good interviews. You can spend time. When I say "time," it might be a half-

hour, or it might be 15 minutes. You need to show
that you care about their story. You're not interested
in the responses that they give either under instruction or to hide their own fear and confusion. You are
interested in what they're thinking; you are curious
about them as people.

**Does the paper ask you for a particular length,
or in this case did you just write to the length
that seemed necessary?**

I write to the length necessary. You have to understand that for a whole month and a half out there, I
was totally out of communication with the *Globe*. I
was filing these stories back, and they were being
used by pool reporters. I had no way of contacting
my editors and my editors had no way of contacting me during this entire period.

So I couldn't write to length. I couldn't even do
stories they might think I should be doing. I decided entirely what stories to write, and they had no
choice but to accept what I filed. [Laughter]

**You said that you tended to write long, but these
stories are pretty concise.**

I suspect this one has been trimmed. I overwrite. It is
a weakness, and I have counted on editors like
O'Neill, Tolbert, Tom Ashbrook, Victor Lewis, John
Yemma, and Louisa Williams to yank my leash.

**Let's go to "Shells, Prayers in Dead of Night."
This story stands out to me because of the roll
call of soldiers. There's something in the names—
it's almost like reading the Vietnam Veterans
Memorial. You get a sense of different ethnic
groups, different places, different people. Was
that your intent in using the names here?**

I was with an AP photographer and a Reuters writer.
And I knew the Reuters writer was going to write a
story something like, "Marines yesterday launched
the largest ground skirmish against Iraqi forces en-

trenched in Kuwait so far this war." So I wanted to do something different. I wanted to describe the mission. I wanted to get the kind of tension and the feeling of a military raid, a small-scale military action.

But I wanted to show it isn't only these machines. That there were guys there from all over, like that corporal from Alabama. There were also the swaggerers. That staff sergeant, Vasquez, giving me the macho kind of stuff. But he was saying it honestly. I just wanted to interpose the machinery, the weaponry of war, with what the people who were sending these shells were thinking.

At one place in the story, a corporal says, "But believe me, we can drop these babies dead center into a trash can more than 10 klicks away." And then you write, "*Klick* is military slang for 'kilometer.'" How much does the reader need to know about terms and equipment?

Generally speaking, not much. I wanted to explain that a dual-purpose round is a particularly vicious type of shell. It's an anti-personnel shell, meaning it's meant to kill people. But it is also meant to destroy machines, tanks, anything. And I wanted to convey the feeling that you've got these ordinary young men out there doing something very violent.

Okay. You start the story in the middle of a scene: "It was 11:55 p.m., close to the Kuwaiti border. With a purr of hydraulics, automatic loaders inserted the 200-pound anti-armor projectiles into the breeches of the hulking 203mm mobile howitzers of the U.S. Marine raiding party."
The action continues. It is not until the 11th paragraph that you say, "This morning's 2nd Marine Division artillery raid was the largest ground attack so far launched against Iraqi positions in Kuwait...." I would say that's your "nut graph."

Yes, you could say that's the nut graph. But for this story, I didn't think a nut graph was that important.

I just approached this as a pure feature.

That was a good move, but it's interesting to me that you don't feel compelled to have a "nut graph" by the third or fourth paragraph, as is often the case in stories.

No, not for this kind of story. For this kind of story, the drama is the contrast of human beings versus deadly machines.

In some ways, the next story is more dramatic. It's titled "Close Call Leaves Two Marines 'Lucky as Hell'—and Ready." You start with the two Marines, Robert Grady and William Noland, setting the scene and talking about why they were so lucky. The third paragraph is sort of a "nut graph": "The two were the only occupants of a Humvee all-terrain vehicle accompanying a large Marine reconnaissance foray into the bitterly contested no man's land between Saudi Arabia and Kuwait when an Iraqi advance force opened fire..."
After you give more details about the accident, paragraphs eight through 11 give a different type of summary. They are about the larger war. Then you go back to the two Marines. Tell me your thoughts on the organization of this story.

Well, there were a lot of things I wanted to write about. These were people I did not have a lot of time to talk to. I came across them, and somebody told me their story. I jumped into the back of the other Humvee that was carrying them. And as it was bouncing them along back to a place where they were going to get a medical checkup, I had time to ask them a few questions. They were obviously jazzed, high. They'd had a terrifying experience, a very close call. They were all cranked up with adrenaline. I wanted their story to be my lead and to be part of the story. But I also had a battle to describe. I had to get the news in. So I started with these people because I thought this was the most interesting thing I'd seen. And then I got into a summary about what had happened in that sector that day. But I thought I could build a hard news story about the war around this incident involving these two young Marines.

You usually quote the foot soldiers, but in "For Marines, Swift Advance on City," you quote officers, including Lt. Gen. Walter Boomer. His quotations are noticeably less colorful than those of his troops.

Officers are real careful about reporters and what they say to them.

The story ends with a quotation by a 19-year-old who says, "They ain't very good fighters. I only hope they are good lovers, like the joke goes, so at least they got something going for them." This Marine is the one of the few people quoted who uses colloquial expression or dialogue. He says "ain't," for example.

Do you generally clean up quotations to standard English, or do you quote most people exactly the way they speak?

I try to quote everyone in fairly standard English. I don't like making people sound illiterate. You've got to think of what your purpose is. There is little point in making somebody sound like a jerk, like an uneducated fool. But I don't think the use of "ain't" does that.

The other thing is that when you are dealing with young Marines, if you are going to quote everything, there would be a lot of ellipses where you take out profanity, which is every other word out of a Marine's mouth.

You addressed that at one point. In the fifth paragraph of "War Diary," you wrote: "Rising stiffly from their troughs, the grunts gave vent to the obscenities that are the Marine infantryman's equivalent of a rooster's cock-a-doodle-

doo. A ritual salute to the morning." You indicated there that you weren't quoting the profanity you heard.

Well, you can't. I never in my life heard people swear like these people swear. Sometimes you will talk to somebody who says three or four expletives for every two words. And maybe there is some sense in there. But it's usually better to paraphrase the statement. I have no ethical problems with taking the profanity out of a quote.

"War Diary" is a summing up of the war. What did you want to get across to the readers?

Well, I wanted to convey some of the strangeness, some of the weirdness, and some of the themes that had stuck in my mind but I hadn't found a way to write about before. Like we were squatting out there in the middle of a minefield with shells from both sides blasting all around our perimeter, and suddenly this colonel, a very high-ranking officer, begins booming out quotes from "Omar Khayyam." I hadn't had a way to put that in before.

So this story wrapped up a lot of pieces for you, and for the reader.

Yeah. There was a lot of string, and I used it in this piece. The war was over. The big-picture people in Washington and in Riyadh for the *Globe* had done the big stories about what it all meant, and I was doing a page-one story, not so much on what it all meant, but what it all felt like, what you heard, and what you saw out there.

Sometimes I think that one reason a lot of reporters have stress is because they never get to tell the real stories that they see, whether it's a war or a city council meeting. They save string internally, and they never get to get it out. The public loses too.
I have a couple more questions. A couple

means more than two.

Okay.

What does it take to be a foreign correspondent? You were out there in danger, in the middle of bombings, getting to know people and telling stories quickly.

What it takes to be a foreign correspondent, and not just a war correspondent, is the ability to work independently, to work without direction, to understand that, even when you get the direction, sitting in Boston is very different from sitting in Afghanistan or somewhere. You've got to have the ability to say, "Well, look, what you are suggesting really isn't the story." This isn't meant as a criticism of my foreign editors. I have terrific foreign editors. Oftentimes in the Third World you will go for days, even weeks, with no contact at all with the desk. And you have got to decide, how am I spending my time? What are the stories I am going to write?

A lot of people find it hard to work outside of that newsroom environment. A lot of times I think they find it hard for professional reasons. They feel if they go off and disappear for four or eight years, they are going to be forgotten, and maybe they will never become managing editors of the paper. But I think that all I have ever wanted to be, as long as I have been a journalist, is a foreign correspondent.

You sometimes miss the camaraderie of the newsroom, of working closely with and seeing the editors you work with, knowing the other reporters. I have been overseas so long that I hardly recognize half the bylines in *The Boston Globe* anymore, and that saddens me.

What about the opportunity to bounce stories off other reporters? Are you able to find other journalists to bounce things off, or do you write without connection with colleagues?

No, you've got to do without that, because the people out here are your friends, but they also are your competitors. The reporters I know in the countries I work in are from *The New York Times, The Washington Post, The Philadelphia Inquirer.* Sure, we talk and trust each other in a way that we wouldn't if we were covering Washington. But on the other hand, if I have a great story idea, I am probably not going to bounce it off my very dear friend David Sanger at *The New York Times.* There is still a feeling of competitiveness.

How do you cope with the danger?

It's hard. You're frightened. I am always frightened. The Persian Gulf War was an easier war, and a safer war, than some I've covered, like those in Afghanistan, Sri Lanka, Angola. But I guess you've got to have a feeling that it's worthwhile journalistically, that the readers are not served just by some guy in the State Department saying he thinks this is what's going on. That is not very helpful. And the only people really able to go in, scope out what is going on, and communicate what they see are journalists.

As a U.S. foreign correspondent, you write to an audience that is known to have very little knowledge about geography or foreign affairs. How do you adjust to that in your coverage?

It's frustrating. You hope you're fighting the good fight, to make Americans more aware that there are other countries out there that are inhabited by real people with real lives. And these people can be interesting. But Americans can be so bloody indifferent to the rest of the world. Most of the time I'm writing out of China or Bangkok or Calcutta or Kabul, and I don't know if people are reading or not. People sometimes assume that reporters are deluged with letters from readers saying, "Thank you for explaining it to me." Usually the only time you hear from a reader is when somebody is saying, "You misspelled some word in Japanese. What a fool you are. You don't deserve to be the Asia correspondent."

So you can only hope that if you try hard and look for the stories that are going to be of the most interest, people will read them and become more interested.

With the type of stories that you do and the hectic nature of your beat, what do you do to get away? How do you relax?

[Laughter] I don't know. I'm not good at relaxing. One of the bad things about being a foreign correspondent is it tends to be a kind of seven-day-a-week, 14-hour-a-day job. I guess I relax by reading, when I have a chance. When I take a vacation, I take a real vacation. I go back to my home in Vermont, go up to a cabin I rent in Quebec's Gaspé Peninsula, and really tune the news out of my mind. Well, except I listen to the BBC every evening.

The last question is on your future. What do you see as your future?

Personally, I want to stay overseas as long as I can and as long as I can still do a good job. I don't want to end up like some foreign correspondents who kind of lose their legs and end up just sitting in capitals reporting from capitals. That's no way to be a foreign correspondent. You have got to get out there, get out to the provinces, get out to the villages. There comes a time in your life when it just gets harder and harder to do that. Then I guess I'd want to come back. But for now, I want to remain a correspondent. I love it.

Paul McEnroe

Finalist, Deadline Writing

Paul McEnroe is a national correspondent at the Minneapolis *Star Tribune*, where he has worked for 12 years. Before that, he worked at *The Ann Arbor* (Mich.) *News*. He graduated from Northern Michigan University, and received his master's degree from Michigan State University. He said that when he's not in the newsroom, he receives lessons from his 5-year-old daughter on how to fish for walleyes, observe the Minnesota Twins through her eyes, and grow flowers, tomatoes, and hot peppers.

McEnroe worked independently of the press pool in covering the Persian Gulf War. He worked along the northern Saudi Arabian border with a *Star Tribune* photographer and two reporters from other dailies.

On last night of war, death had last word

MARCH 3, 1991

KUWAIT CITY, Kuwait—The boots of Mayden Saddam Ammer were half-filled with his blood. Set under the operating cot where the Iraqi soldier lay, the boots leaked, staining the ground red.

A chunk of shrapnel was wedged into his brain just above the bridge of his nose. A large-caliber bullet had gone into the back of his right thigh, tearing out through his right buttock. He had three other wounds from small-arms fire. Ammer had been wounded as he was about to fire a rocket at a U.S. tank. An Army medical team was trying to save him.

A few kilometers away, a company of tanks commanded by Capt. Frans Barends waited for more enemy tanks or vehicles to enter their "kill sack"—the tankers' talk for an area where they do their best to destroy anything that moves. The brigade had taken down 25 tanks in the afternoon. Barends's company had been fighting for 20 hours. Now under a full moon, their patrol would continue until dawn.

Sixty miles to the east, Sgt. Paul Thomas bedded down with Egyptian commandos. After five months of living with them in the desert, the Los Angeles native had a feeling something would be different by morning. Tomorrow, there'd be a celebration.

"When I got in this U.S. Army back in '75, the United States soldier was looked upon as scum," said Thomas, a Special Forces trooper. "But now, whether you were back in Dhahran cooking chow or popping caps up at the front with the bad guys, we're all gonna be stinking heroes when we get home."

It was just past midnight Wednesday, the eve of Kuwait's liberation. The night was a mix of death and jubilation, fear and futility. And the war was almost over.

166

***

At an Iraqi bunker complex behind the front lines overrun by the Egyptians, Thomas, and other Special Forces troopers, dozens of pairs of black boots littered the ground. The soldiers were so desperate to get away that they went shoeless.

In the trenches that ran 20 yards from bunker to bunker, flies swarmed over fresh piles of excrement. The Iraqis were so afraid of the bombardment that they were unable to relieve themselves in privacy.

Inside the bunkers, crates overflowed with ammunition. Shipping labels stapled underneath the wooden lids showed the munitions had been manufactured—predictably—in the Soviet Union, Yemen, and Jordan. But there were just as many crates showing other places of origin: Some crates were stenciled "1980, United States." Nearby were boxes of bullets from Saudi Arabia. So two coalition forces had sent their troops against enemy ammunition made in their own countries.

Two soldiers were still in the bunker, tired, afraid, and hungry. They'd had a bellyful of war, all eight years of it, against Iran. They had no stomach for more. They were so starved that they couldn't wait for water to boil. So they swallowed dry, instant coffee and chased it with salt.

Shahoz Sleman, 48, had lived in these trenches for months with his friend, Klefa Adb Al-Salmo, 55. Their fingers were cracked open from exposure. They were clothed in tatters and stooped hopelessly.

"We were dug in so well the bombing didn't hurt us too bad," said Salmo, father of eight, married three times. He was conscripted, forced into the bunkers.

"At night, I'd just put cotton in my ears and sleep. But I have no fight left in me anymore," he said. "I fought in the Iran-Iraq War. I always felt Iraq and Kuwait were one people, brother and sister, cousins. Why should I die if that is the case?"

When Sleman was asked what he thought of Saddam Hussein, he swept his hands from his shoulders down to his legs as if he wanted to be rid of his wretched body. His answer: "Just look at me."

***

When the invasion began at 4 a.m. Sunday, Capt. Bob Jones swung his Humvee into a column of Egyptian armor and raced through a cut in a 20-foot-high berm of sand and entered Kuwait.

"You do wind up in strange places," said Jones, an honors graduate in forestry from Oregon State University, now a Special Forces adviser with the Egyptian Army's 4th Tank Division.

A loudspeaker on one of the vehicles blared the Egyptian national anthem. Colonels stood to the side and saluted their troops. The tanks were painted with yellow leaping lions. It was raining and muddy, "infantryman's weather."

This was where the U.S. command feared their "nightmare scenario": allied troops hung up amid flaming oil-filled trenches, barbed wire, and mines, bombarded by chemical weapons. It never happened. Under fire, Egyptian commandos stormed ahead to shut off the valves that fed diesel fuel into the trenches.

The advance halted when the Egyptians came under Iraqi artillery fire 20 miles into Kuwait. From 9 a.m. until 2 p.m., the Egyptians unleashed a continuous barrage of howitzer shells and rockets while Jones called in air support.

From the rocket launchers came orange flashers, then a whacking sound as the Soviet-made rockets streaked toward Iraqi positions. They exploded five seconds later.

By noon, troops in the rear stood around smoking cigarettes, as if on weekend National Guard duty. By 2 p.m. a jeep pulled up to the front with a loudspeaker blaring pleas in Arabic from the Egyptians, calling for their brothers to surrender.

By 4:30 p.m. the sky was nearly black, darkened by smoke that belched from the big guns and hundreds of burning oil wells.

With no wounded Egyptians to treat, Lt. Muhammad Mustafa, a doctor, took a detail of soldiers into the bunkers to pull out the bodies. He spent the afternoon helping bury Iraqis in shallow graves. When he had finished, Mustafa walked away to be by himself.

Before he went to sleep among the Egyptian commandos, Sgt. Paul Thomas listened to an A-10 Warthog making a bombing run nearby. "Hope they got good grid 'cause we don't need any fratricide," he said with a sigh, thinking about being killed by "friendly fire."

The night was a safe one for Thomas and the Egyptians, but about 100 miles away, British soldiers were forced to fire at another Warthog as it strafed them, killing nine. Finally, after repeated radio pleas for the plane to cease firing, the British shot it down, killing the pilot.

In an Air Force medical evacuation unit near the Saudi Arabian city of Hafer al Batin, Specialist Michael Muller was helping to carry more than 50 wounded U.S. soldiers onto C-130 transport planes. They had been caught in a fierce tank battle in southern Iraq. Many were blinded and horribly wounded.

"One man's lips are burned off," Muller said. "Another can't see. Shrapnel wounds all over these guys. One is on oxygen and can't swallow. You look at them and know it wasn't an easy deal for all of our side, believe me."

***

On their way to Kuwait City, four journalists found out why tankers call it a "kill sack."

It was 10 p.m. "It's six klicks south through the desert 'til you hit the dirt road, take a left, and go three or four more 'til you hit the blacktop," said a U.S. major, an intelligence officer with the Egyptian commandos. "Then you're on the way to Kuwait City, 50 or 60 klicks out. You should be all right, but remember the Marines just took the air base. They get nervous at night."

Was there a password? "Yeah," the major said. "It's called 'Americans! Don't shoot!'"

Five kilometers onto the blacktop was an abandoned Iraqi munitions carrier loaded with 5-foot-long artillery shells. Just beyond, an Iraqi tank was afire, sparks spitting from it. There had been a huge fight here. The first reports of a cakewalk weren't true. But going back would be as risky as going ahead.

Just past the burning tank, a long form moved across the road median and approached with his hands outstretched into the headlights. He pointed across the road: Seven more shadows were moving the same way. They wanted to surrender. But there was no room in the Land Rover, crammed with four journalists and gear.

I told him in sign language to go back to his men, cupped my hands and put my head on them and made a snoring sound: "Go to sleep." He smiled. "Thank you very much," he said in English, hurrying back, grateful his men would not be harmed. Half a mile farther on, a blue light flickered on and off. It came from an Iraqi armored personnel carrier. The area was full of fleeing soldiers signaling to each other, most of them afraid of being shot if they tried to surrender in the dark of night.

At one junction, a decision had to be made which way to go. Someone shouted from about 50 yards away. Moments later, a rumbling sound came from behind. There was nowhere to go. A low-flying Warthog searching for targets was overhead. We came to a fence and jumped out of the Land Rover. We tried to become part of the desert floor, dropping flat in the sand on our stomachs. Behind, at the top of the rise, a tank appeared. Four soldiers fanned out from both sides of it. It was impossible to tell if they were allied or Iraqi.

If they were Iraqis, it was obvious what would happen. If they were Americans, we could only hope they'd hear us before they fired. We shouted: "American! American! Minnesota! Minnesota! U.S.A.! Minnesota! American!"

"Stop, stop, stop, hands higher, hands higher," they screamed—in English.

"What in the hell are you doing here?" demanded Specialist John Edwards.

We didn't have a good answer.

"Any farther and you stood a good chance of being dead," said Capt. Barends, a company commander in the 2nd Armored Division.

"This area around Kuwait City is still far from secure. They're fighting all over the place, and intelligence says there's about 100 Iraqi tanks and trucks around here trying to get out. I'm under orders to shoot anything moving.

"The only reason your car got this far was it was a low-grade target and it had the inverted V (the allied symbol to differentiate from enemy vehicles). We spotted it about four klicks back, figured our guys in the next kill sack could pick it up. Good thing you didn't know which way to go because a quarter mile more and you'd be..."

An hour later, a tank in the kill sack destroyed a white pickup truck. No one knew who was in it.

***

"It took out the femur in his right leg and bone fragments shot out his ass—4 centimeters in diameter. Then he took a chunk of shrapnel in the skull. So much blood lost, his veins are depressed and difficult to get blood into him. Previous fractures, looks like old tank injuries. When they found him, he was covered with blood from the waist down. See his boots, full of blood. Lost at least six pints of blood. Lose five and you can die from shock."

Chief Warrant Officer Charles Russell was checking on his patient, Mayden Saddam Ammer. A 19-year veteran and physician's assistant, Russell had spent two hours trying to stabilize Ammer, since just past midnight Wednesday. The patient, covered by a foil thermal blanket, was slipping in and out of consciousness. Beside him lay two more wounded Iraqis.

Abruptly, Ammer rose up, his right arm raised and spastic. He opened his mouth and tried to speak, making only a weak guttural sound.

"Kaz, Kaz, he's seizing!" cried Russell, 35, calling for Capt. Yamamoto Kazunori, the doctor. Kazunori, 31, rushed over. The soldier's head slumped, and Russell clamped an oxygen mask over his face while Kazunori pushed on his chest, trying to keep the heart going.

The ground was strewn with gauze packages. Medics dug through kit boxes for syringes. Only one small light was on in the tent. Outside, tanks idled, sending the smell of diesel fumes into the tent. Kazunori and Russell talked quietly to themselves over the hissing of the oxygen. Kazunori ordered three shots of a drug to counter a possible morphine reaction. "I want a higher flow," he ordered. A medic turned the oxygen up a notch. Five more minutes. Russell kept shaking his head.

"Come on, come on," he urged the Iraqi soldier.

Kazunori ordered the tank outside the tent to be shut down so he could hear better through his stethoscope.

The soldier's bowels released, the smell filling the tent. Five minutes more. "The heartbeat is almost nonexistent," Kazunori said.

The oxygen mask was removed. Thirty seconds later, Russell walked out, shaken. Kazunori pulled the blanket over Ammer's head.

A medic, Specialist Raymon Gonzo, 22, dropped to his knees at the head of the cot, bent his head in prayer, and made the sign of the cross. Five more minutes. Everyone waited outside until Gonzo came out.

Gonzo finally emerged from the tent. "Take him out of there and take him to A-Lot until we figure what to do with him," Russell said.

He finished a cigarette. His hands shook. "All you saw was his brain response at the end," he said. "We got his heart going, but his brain just couldn't keep up with it. I didn't think he'd live that long, but by the time they come here, they're human beings—not just the enemy."

Mayden Saddam Ammer was buried in an unmarked grave next to a troop truck.

Anchorage Daily News

Doug O'Harra

Finalist, Deadline Writing

He was born in Columbus, Ohio, but Doug O'Harra has spent the last decade in Montana and Alaska as a sawyer, tree planter, bartender, and reporter. He attended Ohio State University before leaving to go west. After a stint working in the woods, he returned to school and graduated from the University of Montana. Later he earned a master's degree in English and fine arts from Montana and taught creative writing at the University of Arizona. Graduate studies and teaching interrupted his work as a reporter for the *Missoulian,* then the *Anchorage Daily News.*

O'Harra's reporting on the Iditarod Trail Sled Dog Race offered a test of journalistic ingenuity and enthusiasm, as well as deadline writing. He had to sleep in drafty school gyms, make sure his portable computer didn't freeze, locate phones in villages along the way, and coax interviews from mushers intent on finishing the race.

[EDITOR'S NOTE: O'Harra is outfitted for reporting in sub-zero temperatures in the above photo.]

Swenson 'wasn't going to give up'

MARCH 16, 1991

NOME—In the swirling eye of a blizzard, with no sign of another musher anywhere, Rick Swenson trudged blindly into the wind, leading his dogs step by step toward the finish of the 19th Iditarod Trail Sled Dog Race.

The four-time champ—eclipsed for a decade by the four spectacular wins of Susan Butcher—wondered about his rival. Was she close? Was she ahead? Where could she be in this whiteout?

The wind battered him and could swallow all sign of trail. But Swenson intended to reach Nome even if he walked every step.

Maybe even if it killed him.

"I just kept going forward," he said later on. "I wasn't going to give up. I was going to Nome."

After driving and walking 77 miles in about 23 hours, Swenson seized his fifth Iditarod championship Friday as hundreds of people hooted and cheered along the frigid streets of Nome.

In a race of extremes—from swift, icy trails to slow, wallowing slogs—Swenson mushed the 1,100 miles from Anchorage to Nome in 12 days, 16 hours, 35 minutes, the longest race since Libby Riddles took 18 days to win in 1985.

Martin Buser was two hours back, and Butcher, driving a swift team thought certain to win a day earlier, was third at 6:59 a.m. Tim Osmar was fourth, and 1989 champ Joe Runyan was fifth, three minutes behind Osmar.

Swenson said his victory "demonstrates that there's still room to outrun the fastest, most well-financed, and slickest operation.

"I really think it boils down to this: I had the determination to get here, and Susan gave me the opportunity to get here first."

Swenson's decisive run began at 2:38 a.m. Thursday in White Mountain. His mandatory six-hour layover over, Swenson drove out on the frozen Fish River an hour behind Butcher. Cold and blowing on the river, it got worse when he turned for the hills.

"As soon as I got around that turn, it was brutal," he said. "I could see it was going to be serious."

For a few miles, Swenson slowly followed the trail markers—reflecting orange in his headlight's beam. Then, to his surprise, he came upon Butcher and her team, parked across the trail. She was in the sled in a sleeping bag.

"I yelled: 'Hey, come on, Susan. Get out of that goddamn bag and let's have a race!'"

A few hundred yards farther, the blizzard thickened. Suddenly Swenson's headlight burned out. He stopped, and as he struggled to replace the bulb and get the light working, his bare hands began to freeze.

Moments later, Butcher pulled up and helped Swenson get the lamp fixed.

"My hands were really cold," Swenson said. "I was glad she was there."

For the next hour or so, the two four-time Iditarod champs shared the task of searching for trail markers—one at a time. It was painstaking work: One would stay with the teams while the other would go ahead, turning the lamp back and forth like a floodlight, hoping to glimpse the next trail marker.

There was nothing unusual in the two rivals helping each other, Swenson said. "We've known each other for a long time. I have a lot of respect for Susan."

Swenson took his turn out front at one point, assuming Butcher was behind. But the two teams had veered apart in the whiteout.

Swenson never saw her again.

He pressed on, picking his way marker by marker.

"I had no idea" she wasn't out there, he said. "All I knew was I was moving forward.... It was so bad out there, if you were standing on your sled, you couldn't see your leaders."

Finally, Swenson reached a place he recognized,

about 12 miles out of White Mountain. Ahead lay Topkok Hill, where the wind always blows hardest.

Swenson adjusted the harnesses, shortened the gangline. He knew he had enough food for three feedings and the gear to survive the weather.

"As long as I stayed on the trail, I wasn't going to die," he said. "The key was—you had to stay on the trail, or no rescue party would find you."

Then, to make sure his dogs didn't lead him astray, Swenson rigged up a line in front and started leading the team himself.

It was often slow going, always frustrating. On hills, the sled would overtake the dogs and tangle the lines. Over and over, Swenson had to unsnarl his dogs. But he kept moving.

"I think that's what made the difference, because the dogs were more than willing to go with me," he said. "It was like: 'You want to go? Well, come along.' They were really good about it."

After walking and mushing for hours, Swenson arrived at the shelter cabin at Topkok, on the Nome side of the hills, about 11 a.m. Thursday. Inside was a White Mountain schoolteacher with a broken snowmachine and a blazing fire. Less than 50 miles remained.

Swenson rested five hours and fed his dogs half of his food while the ground blizzard thickened. About 4 p.m., he resumed the march to Nome. "That was the worst part of the whole trip," he said.

Suddenly, about 5 p.m., a snowmachiner roared out of the whiteout.

"What are you doing?" Swenson said.

"I'm going to Nome," came the reply.

"Is this the trail?" Swenson asked.

"Yep," the man said. "There's the marker."

The snowmachiner told him what happened to his rivals—that Butcher, Osmar, and Runyan had turned back—but Swenson still assumed that Butcher was somewhere behind him, driving hard. "When he said they turned back, I thought he meant Runyan, Osmar, and Buser."

Only when he reached Safety three hours later did Swenson learn the truth.

"I thought I was going to win the Iditarod," he said.

Five hours later, he did. The first five-time champion won $50,000 and a new diesel pickup truck.

"I never worked so hard for anything in my life," he said.

For a half-hour or so, Swenson stood in the bitter cold and posed, talked, smiled, waved to the shouting crowd. After they backed in the truck and gave him the keys, the orgy of public relations and ceremony ended. People scattered for the bars, and Swenson strode down the street, looking for a place to warm his feet.

Several people ushered him to the Nugget Inn, where Hugh O'Brian—who played Wyatt Earp in a television series—emerged into the 50-degree-below-zero chill factor in an Old West marshal's get-up, a black cowboy hat and a .44 Magnum revolver in his holster.

Swenson was taken aback when O'Brian presented him with the pistol. "This isn't loaded, right?" he said as he grasped the pistol in his fingerless gloves.

The wind whipped by and O'Brian's exposed ears whitened in the cold while Swenson admired the pistol. Finally, he'd had enough of that. "Let's go in for a drink," he said.

Swenson strode into the bar, where people yelled and clapped. He ordered a Black Jack and Coke, then settled in with Wyatt Earp at his elbow.

"Hey Rick," a drunk man called out. "Alaska: where men are men—and the women turn back!"

But Swenson, known for his brashness, sipped the drink and answered like a statesman. "Hey, Runyan and Timmy are men. They all turned back."

When told that the others had considered the weather deadly, Swenson said maybe it was. But he would have gone through almost anything to shut up "those guys in Fairbanks" who always razz him on the street with, "Hey Rick, why can't you beat that woman?"

"What's my life worth anyway," he added, the

bar bursting into laughter, "if I had to go back and listen to that crap 365 days a year?"

After talking with reporters and bantering with the patrons of the bar, Swenson downed the last of his drink and stood up to leave.

But his fire wasn't out yet: "Alaska," he said, grinning, wrinkles cutting deep into raw skin around his eyes. "Where men are men—and the others turn back."

Russell Eshleman Jr.
Short Newswriting

Russell Eshleman's days are spent following the course of Pennsylvania state government. For nearly seven years, he's matched politicians' proclamations to their voting records and expense accounts. He translates "legalese" into language that encourages citizens to read. His goal in writing is to explain tough issues and tell taxpayers what their public servants are doing.

But the statehouse is not home for Eshleman. Away from Harrisburg, he spends time with his family, coaches baseball for youth programs, volunteers as a basketball referee, and is active in his church. For him, home lies in the beauty of the southeastern Pennsylvania area where he was born and grew up. Eshleman covers the beat that interests him most, for the newspaper that he's always admired, in the region that he loves.

Even for trees, age could have its privileges

MARCH 12, 1991

HARRISBURG—Everybody complains about deadwood in state government, but a Montgomery County legislator wants to do something about it.

The Senate Environmental Resources and Energy Committee is considering a proposal that's enough to make a lumberjack wince—a bill requiring anyone who wants to chop down a 200-year-old tree to get a permit.

It's called the Historic Tree Act, and the sponsor is—as you might suspect—Sen. Stewart J. *Greenleaf.*

The proposal would require the Bureau of Forestry to establish and maintain a state register of historic trees. Besides 200-year-old trees, qualifying timbers would include historically significant trees chosen with the help of the Pennsylvania Historical and Museum Commission.

Trees on the list would be protected from destruction or defacing unless the person felling the tree obtained a permit from the state. Permits would be issued only to protect the public health, surrounding property, or the tree itself or for a compelling public reason. Violators would be subject to fines up to $500 or imprisonment up to six months.

At a time when lawmakers wish they could make money grow on trees since they're far from out of the woods yet on important budgetary matters, Greenleaf's proposal might be just the sort of diversion that could make its way through the legislative thicket.

It does, after all, enjoy the backing of a Bucks County Republican who is a key member of the environmental committee—Sen. James C. *Greenwood.*

Observations and questions

1) Eshleman sets the mood of the story in the lead with the casual, all-embracing phrase "Everybody complains..." What other words and phrases help maintain that mood?

2) In this story, Eshleman refers to the Senate Environmental Resources and Energy Committee, the Historic Tree Act, the Bureau of Forestry, and the Pennsylvania Historical and Museum Commission, yet the story isn't weighed down by these proper names and bureaucratic labels. How does Eshleman manage to keep a smooth flow in spite of these lengthy proper names?

3) The sixth paragraph reads: "At a time when lawmakers wish they could make money grow on trees since they're far from out of the woods yet on important budgetary matters, Greenleaf's proposal might be just the sort of diversion that could make its way through the legislative thicket." Underline the references to trees. Try brainstorming another topic to see if you can write similar puns.

4) Eshleman builds his story on a fairly light topic. What suggestions would you make about when to use puns with serious topics?

Domino's bites back at tax

JUNE 13, 1991

HARRISBURG—Hold the anchovies, the green peppers…and the taxes.

That message was being delivered at the Capitol yesterday by the folks from Domino's Pizza, who are involved in a lobbying campaign.

Lobbyists for the pizza-maker distributed hundreds of pepperoni-size pins with the words "pizza tax" and a bar drawn through them to legislative offices. Their goal is to kill what they believe is a half-baked idea by Gov. Casey to eliminate a tax exemption they now enjoy.

"When we talk to our customers, they're surprised and disappointed by the proposal to tax pizza," said Bob Deak of State College, who owns seven Domino's franchises and is leading the no-pizza-tax campaign. "We don't think taxing food is a direction the state should be heading in."

Casey, as part of a $2.74 billion tax package, has proposed language that would reverse a 1989 state Supreme Court decision that said pizza, when it is either delivered or picked up to be eaten at home, is not subject to the sales tax.

The Casey administration estimated that the exemption cost the state $10 million a year.

Not surprisingly, the Casey administration is panning the no-pizza-tax pins.

"If the product is delivered ready to eat, there's no reason it should not be taxed the same as restaurant food," said Revenue Department spokesman Rod Snyder. "It's considered a luxury item."

But Deak doesn't buy that proposition. He said the proposal would generate just $4 million for the state and is simply the result of an angry Revenue Department trying to "get even" for the 1989 Domino's court decision.

"The reality of today's society is that having pizza delivered to your home is not a luxury," Deak said.

Observations and questions

1) In the editorial flow of stories, headlines are written after the stories. Yet readers get to the headlines first, and often use them to make decisions about reading stories. Notice how the headline "Domino's Bites Back at Tax" captures the essence of the story in mood and fact. Consider other headlines for the story.

2) The structure of this story is common for legislative debates. The writer states the problem, presents a speaker arguing for one side, gives some background, presents testimony for the other side, and allows a rebuttal. It's a standard format that works in a short story. How is Eshleman able to keep the debate short?

3) One source of humor in this story is the use of serious men with serious titles making semiponderous statements that sound ridiculous. Read the quotations in isolation. Why are they amusing?

4) A more subtle form of humor comes from alliteration. The second paragraph says, "...the pizza-maker distributed hundreds of pepperoni-size pins with the words 'pizza tax'..." Look for further examples of alliteration and other means by which the writer builds humor into the story.

Legislator buckles down on jet instead

AUGUST 17, 1991

HARRISBURG—Leaving Harrisburg during the budget crisis, he said, would be "entirely inappropriate and irresponsible."

"The General Assembly should remain in session until a budget is hammered out," he continued.

"We know the taxpayers of Pennsylvania are looking to us for leadership during this fiscal nightmare."

So what did Rep. Fred C. Noye (R-Perry) do after uttering those words last month?

He went to Alaska.

"It's time to buckle down and go to work until a budget is in place," Noye said in a news release July 3.

But on July 28, with a budget still not in place—and hundreds of angry state workers protesting in the Capitol because they were not getting paychecks—Noye took a respite.

He flew to Alaska for three days compliments of the American Petroleum Institute and the Alaska Oil and Gas Association, which wanted to show Noye and legislators from other states potential oil and gas exploration sites on Alaska's North Slope.

Noye, the House Republican caucus chairman, said this week that he saw no conflict in his "obligation" remarks and his trek to The Last Frontier.

"Nothing was happening," he said.

"I was ready to cancel the trip if we were doing something crucial."

Noye was back in Harrisburg in time to vote against the budget Aug. 4.

Observations and questions

1) Eshleman hangs Rep. Fred C. Noye on the legislator's own words, but they aren't just any words. Notice the forcefulness of the quotations Eshleman has selected. What are the key words punctuating Noye's speech in the first half of the story?

2) Compare Noye's tone to Eshleman's in the first half of the story. Then compare the tone of Noye's early comments to his remarks at the end of the story.

3) The kicker is more than just a statement of fact. It reads: "Noye was back in Harrisburg in time to vote against the budget Aug. 4." What are some of the messages in that short statement? Powerful writing puts the most important element at the end. Consider the difference in meaning if the sentence ended with the word "vote."

4) Surveys confirm the public's cynicism about politicians. What is the effect of this story? Should the press report inconsistencies in politicians' words and performance? What are the limits?

The LCB gives itself an A

DECEMBER 10, 1991

HARRISBURG—From the Let's-Pat-Ourselves-on-the-Back Department comes this: a report card on the state Liquor Control Board by, you guessed it, none other than the state Liquor Control Board.

How did the student fare? You won't be surprised.

"The results," says the report card's cover, "are impressive."

In what spokeswoman Donna Pinkham called a move to "clarify the misinformation that is out," the state-run liquor agency has drawn up a three-page brochure casting the LCB in rosy hues.

The Q-and-A format, which highlights everything from profit figures to the agency's concern for responsible drinking, comes just before the start of a year in which the LCB's very existence will be debated.

The LCB is among agencies whose purpose and performances will be reviewed next year as part of the state's sunset law. Those not meeting muster—and revived by a vote of the Legislature and signature of the governor—could be put out of business.

LCB-bashing is a popular sport in Harrisburg, particularly among suburban Philadelphia Republicans who view the agency as a dinosaur, unable to provide the right booze at the right price.

But the agency's defenders, who include Gov. Casey and the unions whose members work at the state's nearly 700 liquor stores, have opposed attempts to replace the LCB with a private system.

Pinkham said the report card, which went to 700 newspapers and radio and television stations, as well as legislators, was written, designed, and printed in-house at a cost of $123.

She said the timing of the report card had nothing to do with the LCB's future in the Legislature. Last year, the agency put out an annual report that recounted much of the same information.

The report card concept is new, however, although it meshes with many of the public relations
efforts the LCB has put into effect over the last four
years.

"Nothing in here that I can see is untrue or trying
to paint the picture a certain way," Pinkham said of
the report card. "It's all factual."

Observations and questions

1) Eshleman engages the reader quickly in the first two paragraphs. What are some of the techniques that he uses to get the reader into the story?

2) In the article "Flash! Sometimes, We Have to Write Long!" Richard Aregood says that a short sentence is not always the best way to send a message. Even in a short story, Eshleman uses some long sentences. Notice the lead. Although the sentence is long, it's not difficult to comprehend. What makes the sentence work for the reader?

3) This story works on two levels. It starts as an amusing look at bureaucratic self-promotion, then moves into an examination of why the agency issued a report card. What would be the effect of removing paragraphs five through eight? Short writing requires tough decisions on what to leave out. Could the story stand without that section?

4) The last word can leave a lasting impression with the reader. What is the effect of the kicker in this story?

Lottery has its own take on the story

DECEMBER 4, 1991

HARRISBURG—How do they love him? Let us count the days.

At least that's how a lot of Pennsylvania people paid respect Monday to Joseph Cicippio, who was released from captivity in Lebanon after 1,908 days—a number that showed up in news pictures taken of the signs outside the Norristown home of Cicippio's brother, Thomas.

Pennsylvania Lottery spokesman Mark Schreiber said yesterday that the number 1-9-0-8 was the most played number in Monday's Big Four drawing. It was bet 12,095 times.

"People will look for any kind of correlation," Schreiber said. He added that another frequently played number Monday was 1-9-4-1, which has been on many people's minds as Dec. 7, the 50th anniversary of Pearl Harbor, approaches.

Alas, hostage Cicippio's good fortune won no fortunes for lottery players, as the winning Big Four was 4-1-8-9.

Had 1-9-0-8 hit, Schreiber said, the total payout would have been more than $10.4 million.

"People wake up and look at their clocks, scores, accidents, plane numbers. People reach anywhere for their numbers," Schreiber said.

Even Norristown.

Observations on short newswriting

Somewhere between the old-fashioned, first-grade prose of "See Spot; see Spot run" and the meanderings of *Moby Dick*, the art of concise writing has foundered.

Newspapers know how to report concisely. Briefs of less than 500 words cover the obligatory bases: who, what, where, when, why, and how. In five paragraphs, we tell readers enough to get them through a conversation in the office coffee klatch.

We usually stumble when we write. It's as though we turn the key on a diesel engine, sluggish at first, taking hundreds of grinding words before the fuel warms enough to flow smoothly. By the time our stories are tooling along, we've far exceeded our limit for good writing under 500 words.

Writing short is easy; writing well within the confines of a 500-word limit is agonizingly difficult. The best short writing captures and explores a solitary idea, an isolated event. It resists the temptation to stray into interesting but essentially unrelated details and focuses precisely on that single moment. The best short writing looks through a microscope, not a kaleidoscope.

Much as a child's *Dick and Jane* once did, the best short writing relies on nouns and active verbs. The stronger the principal parts of speech, the stronger the writing. Simple and complex sentences twine together, crammed with pinpointed details that capture the senses. The best short writing is evocative. Its success grows from the simplicity of a solitary note, not from the cacophony of a jazz band.

This year's entries, found by the judges after hours of reading and worrying that there would be no entry that would meet the criteria, virtually jumped from its pages. Clear, concise, focused, detailed, evocative, it captured the essence of the best of short writing. We cheered when we shared it, for it sets the standard by which our newspapers' short writing must be measured.

Linda Grist Cunningham, Editor
Rockford (Ill.) *Register Star*

A conversation with Russell Eshleman Jr.

Tight, terse, and to the point

His byline is almost as long as some of his sentences. He is terse. He writes short. But good.
–James M. Naughton, Executive Editor
The Philadelphia Inquirer

KAREN BROWN: I noticed that you won a high school journalism award. Looks like you were interested in journalism early.

RUSSELL ESHLEMAN: Yes, even before high school. My junior high school had a little mimeographed newspaper, and I was the sports editor. I think what hooked me on journalism was seeing my name in print for the first time, probably about the eighth grade.

What did you do to continue your interest in newswriting?

Well, I took my first regular journalism class in 11th grade, and again, I just liked the idea of writing. I became the editor of the school newspaper in my senior year.

So when you started writing for the newspaper in junior high, you liked the byline. As you progressed, what did you like about writing?

I found I enjoy two things. First, I enjoy the actual writing, putting words together, the entertaining aspect of it. Number two, I like to tell people about things. You know, I'm not very good at keeping secrets, so if somebody tells me something, I guess one way to let that out is to write about it.

■ Russell Eshleman Jr., staff writer, *The Philadelphia Inquirer.*

■ **Born:** March 27, 1955, in Lancaster, Pa.

■ **Personal:** Married to Lisa Eshleman, a registered nurse; three children: Andrew, 11, Angela, 9, and Adam, 4.

■ **Education:** West Virginia University; graduated with degree in journalism and minors in political science and business.

■ **Newspaper Experience:** *The Gettysburg Times,* 1977; *Lancaster Sunday News* (part time), 1978; *Lancaster New Era,* 1979-84; *The Philadelphia Inquirer,* 1984-present.

In your early years as a student and a journalist, were there particular teachers who affected your writing?

Two of my high school teachers were very instrumental in terms of writing. They were the kind of teachers you wrote something for almost every day, and they were really tough. They wanted you to do the best job you could.

My journalism adviser, Dennis Schmid, was very excited about the idea of a journalism career, not only for me, but for other students. The other teacher was the stereotypical, quintessential schoolmarm, a woman by the name of Kathryn Buckwalter. She was about 5 feet tall and maybe 90 pounds, and she walked with a limp. She used to put the fear of God in everything we did.

How did she put the fear of God in you?

She demanded so much, and you had to come in and be able to recite. We had to diagram sentences and write regularly. She probably taught me more about grammar than anybody.

What about your editors? Did any of them have an impact on your writing or on your career?

One of the major influences on my career has been Pete Mekeel, who is now an editor at the *Lancaster New Era*. He was a terrific writer as a reporter. And as an editor, he is equally terrific, because he has something every writer needs: a vision of what a story is supposed to be about—the point of the story.

I know your interest in journalism led you to a degree at West Virginia University and to work at two small newspapers. How did you make the big step to *The Philadelphia Inquirer*?

I was the Family section editor at the *Lancaster New Era*. I had written a lot of fairly large feature stories that I thought were pretty good, and so I started sending them to the *Inquirer.* It seems I'd send them a packet of stuff once a month. Finally, maybe just to get rid of me, they said, "Well, come on down; we'll talk to you."

I had an initial interview, and I remember an editor at the *Inquirer* pointing to this filing cabinet that was about four drawers high, and saying the entire thing was filled with résumés and applications. Mine would be among those.

I went home thinking I'd probably never get there, but I kept sending them stuff. And for whatever reason, one time they called and said, "We'd like to talk to you again." So I went down and talked to them. The job that they had open at the time was in the Neighbors section. That would be local government reporting, which was fine with me.

I've heard several stories of award-winning journalists who got their jobs by bombarding editors with clips over a period of time. Is that really a route you would recommend?

I think it is. You know, a lot of people can write and a lot of people can report, but I think what you need to do is just keep after editors. If you want a job somewhere, you just have to keep harassing the editors to the point where they know you have perseverance.

How do you know when you're being obnoxious?

Well, it's a risk you've got to take. You do it in a nice way. There's a woman involved in hiring at the *Inquirer* named Arlene Morgan. I would call her once a month and say, "Anything new?" to keep my name in front of them.

One time, Arlene said to me that because of the sale of a major newspaper, they had gotten many letters and résumés from that city. They had gotten so many they could have chartered a plane for people to come in and interview. I said something like, "I'm with a small paper; how am I going to compete with these guys?" And she said, "Well, you know, we can't hire everybody from big papers." I think the *Inquirer* is always trying to hire a variety of people. They get lots of stars, but they also get people like me who come from smaller papers.

How did you move from the Neighbors section to covering the statehouse?

The Neighbors section was a nice transition for me, since I was coming from a small paper. I was very intimidated about coming to *The Philadelphia Inquirer*. I didn't really know how a big paper worked.

The frustrating part about working on the Neighbors section was that it didn't run in the main newspaper, so nobody saw your work but the people in the small towns you covered. A couple of things happened while I was working on that section. In about 1985, a series of tornadoes touched down in northwestern Pennsylvania. I was chosen to go out there with maybe eight or 10 other reporters, and I got my first page-one Sunday story covering that event.

Another big exposure for me was the baseball drug trials in 1985. A number of major league baseball players were caught up in this drug story; they were using cocaine. A U.S. attorney in Pittsburgh was prosecuting, and the newspaper sent me out to cover the trial.

I was writing stories, but at the same time, the *Inquirer*'s contracts with all the unions were expiring. I remember filing a story on a Friday night a little before midnight and then calling the copy desk, and they said, "Well, we have your story, but in five minutes we're not going to be reading it, because at midnight the strike starts." I thought, oh God, I'm finally getting into the paper, and now we're going on strike.

So did you get any benefit out of that big story?

Well, the benefit I got out of it was pre-strike exposure, and I was always a big baseball fan, so I got to see some people like Keith Hernandez.

Right after that, I was transferred to Delaware County as part of the suburban desk. I started covering county government and doing some features. I had an interest in coming to Harrisburg because I grew up in central Pennsylvania. For me, the best of both worlds would have been to work for the *Inquirer* and still live in my hometown, which is actually what I'm able to do now. And I also wanted to move to Harrisburg because, to me, the greatest beat in the world would be to cover state government.

About that time, Carol Morello, who is an ASNE Writing Award finalist this year in deadline writing, expressed a desire to leave the Harrisburg beat and go back to Philadelphia. The editors decided to let us trade places. Carol, of course, has gone on to do great things from abroad.

What are your hours as you cover the statehouse?

In this office, we generally start about 10:00 and go to 6:00, although we're at the mercy of the Legislature. The Legislature tends to start later and finish later.

How long are they in session?

They're in session most of the year. The only break they take is over the summer and around the holidays.

You talked about people who helped shape your writing early. What have been other influences on your writing?

Just reading a lot of people at the *Inquirer* has been helpful. We have a columnist named Steve Lopez, who is one of the best writers I've ever read. He is funny; he is witty; he is intelligent; he interprets things just as they should be interpreted. He writes a lot of Philadelphia government things. He sees things for what they are.

My boss, Doug Robinson, the state editor, has been very helpful. He's not the kind of editor who will dicker over a word. He lets me write any way I want as long as it makes sense. He's not one who wants to see every story in the paper read the same.

As a writer, what have you learned from those two?

Well, the overriding lesson from Doug Robinson is to keep things simple and make them understandable. And he has great news judgment in terms of what's a story and what's not a story. I just admire Lopez as a writer. I think he's very good.

Another writer I admire is John Irving. I've read everything he's written. He is one of the few people I've ever read who can move a reader to tears laughing. He gets all of the emotions flowing. Both Lopez and Irving write as though they're talking to you.

Your winning pieces capture that style of talking to the reader. Let's look at "Even for Trees, Age Could Have Its Privileges." Where did you get the idea for this story?

Well, one of my tasks in the Harrisburg bureau is to go through all the bills that are introduced. That means a few thousand bills per two-year legislative session. I look for anything that pertains to Philadelphia and the suburbs, or that has an interesting twist. The fact that a guy named Greenleaf was introducing something that had to do with trees just begged for mention somewhere.

I don't believe that government writing has to be dry and stodgy and lengthy all the time. I think you can do short stories and make your point and be just as effective and informative. A lot of times I'll write short, humorous stories that are actually about serious matters, and they can be effective.

For example, a few years ago, our Legislature approved a resolution allowing any Republican member to attend President Bush's inaugural, and the state would pick up the tab. This one legislator had this whole packet of receipts for meals and stuff, and I noticed that he had two dinners for one day. One receipt was clearly from a restaurant, and the other one, for $42, had just the name of a company.

I looked into it, and it turns out this place is a formal dress shop. The legislator had gone to Washington and forgot to take his formal shirt for his tux. So he bought one and billed the taxpayers.

I started writing the story very straight: "So-and-so billed taxpayers $42 for a formal shirt when he went to Washington last month." The editor, Doug Robinson, said to me, "Now wait a minute, you're making this out to be the crime of the century. There's something funny about this, that this guy went to Washington and billed the taxpayers for a formal shirt." He and Bob Zausner, my bureau chief, convinced me to write a story poking fun at this guy.

The story was effective. All these legislators know that every month I look through expenses, and I'm going to look for anything like that. By the way, this guy got teased to death by his colleagues, and he lost his next election. I don't think it was because of the story, but I think it was a contributing factor.

Tell me about the scope of your writing. You won the ASNE award for writing five short pieces, most of which are pretty funny.

Yeah. This is basically what I do on the side. My job is covering the Legislature, state agencies, the governor's office, and such. Right now, I'm up to my ears in how congressional districts are drawn.

What's the average length of the stories you write?

Probably 15 inches. Some stories are shorter. Some are longer, investigative pieces.

Do you have to shift gears when you're writing a short story, or is the process the same?

It's about the same process. Basically, I know as I'm walking back from the story what I'm going to write, and then it's a matter of sitting down and banging it out. And you do that for pretty much everything, whether it's a 25-inch piece or something short.

Your first story, "Even for Trees...," begins very generally: "Everybody complains about deadwood in state government, but a Montgomery County legislator wants to do something about it."

The reason that I start out very general like this without getting into specifics is because everybody can identify; everybody's complained about legislators and governors and presidents. So I'm saying, "Hey, I'm one of you. I'm complaining too. You want to read about another dumb thing in government, or a funny thing in government, here it is."

You also use several colorful phrases. In the second paragraph you wrote: "...that's enough to make a lumberjack wince..." And in the sixth paragraph: "At a time when lawmakers wish they could make money grow on trees since they're far from out of the woods yet on budgetary matters, Greenleaf's proposal might be just the sort of diversion that could make its way through the legislative thicket."
Is that kind of figurative language common in the writing that you do?

Well, not so much for serious news stories. I'll take some liberty with puns, and then my boss, Doug, will whack a couple out of it if he thinks I've put too many in.

A lot of writers and editors look at short writing as taking out everything except the very necessary. But in this example, you put in some things that aren't necessary, just to make the piece colorful. Would you talk a little bit about how to keep stories short but lively?

Well, a lot has to do with the subject. You have to choose the interesting element and expand on that whenever you can, whether it means using a pun or a name like Greenleaf.

Tell me how the pizza story, "Domino's Bites Back at Tax," came about.

It seems to me this was a natural little sidebar to a budget story.

So this story appeared along with a main story?

I guess this came a little bit later. This was a serious story about taxes. It was also one that was sort of humorous because we're talking about pizza as opposed to utility rates. You could take some liberties with it.

The tradition in newswriting has been to use the inverted pyramid. Increasingly, writers are realizing that it doesn't serve the reader well. In this story and in some of the others, you tend to use a diamond structure. That is, you start with something light, that's not essential, and the lead does not tell you what the piece is about. Then the story builds with increasing details to the middle. The bottom of the story narrows again with something that's light. It is an effective way to give information in a short, lively form.

Yeah. I could have written a story saying, "One hundred lobbyists came to the Capitol yesterday to denounce the imposition of a 6 percent sales tax on pizza," but that would have been a straight, stodgy way to do it, and nobody would want to read further than that.

You said government reporting doesn't have to be stodgy. But what if there isn't an element like pizza in the news? What if it's just utility tax receipts? How do you make it interesting?

You have to relate the news to the average citizen. The average citizen doesn't know what utility gross receipt taxes are. They do know that if they don't pay their tax bills, when they flick on their lights they won't go on, so you try to relate it to something they know.

You have two sources mentioned here, but you don't expend much space on their job titles. One element that bogs down writers is long titles. What's your technique for keeping the story moving around titles?

I differ with my bureau chief on this. He likes to use specific titles, and I don't think it's necessary, especially in this kind of story. For instance, Bob Deak might be a limited partner of the State College Pizza Hut. In this kind of story, that doesn't mean anything to anybody but him. This is a guy who runs a pizza place, and that's all you have to say. Why bog it down with a title?

In most of your stories, you have lively quotations, and often you use lively quotes as a "kicker," or ending. That's the case in your story titled "Lottery Has Its Own Take on the Story." You quote the lottery spokesman as saying, "People wake up and look at their clocks, scores, accidents, plane numbers. People reach anywhere for their numbers." How do you get such lively quotations?

I think it has a lot to do with whom you talk to. Sometimes the lively quote comes before you start the interview. You're just mentioning a topic, and a lot of times people come back with a lively quote.

How do you keep lively quotations from cluttering a story? Your stories seem to offer opportunities for many other details that could have been in the story. How do you decide which quotations and details to throw out?

In these kinds of stories, you just want to make

your point, get in and get out. You want to write a
6-inch story. If you used every quote you got, your
stories would go on forever. Plus, people tend to repeat themselves. So you use your quotes to bolster
the main points of your stories, and then cut it off.

How did this story come about?

Joseph Cicippio was from suburban Philadelphia,
from Norristown. Several papers had been running
pictures every time Cicippio's brother changed a
number on the sign indicating the number of days
Cicippio had been held captive. On the day he was
released, we ran a big picture. Actually I think Doug
Robinson caught the picture, and suggested I call the
lottery.

**The story titled "Legislator Buckles Down on
Jet Instead," about a legislator's trip to Alaska,
is one that could have been a longer, more serious story.**

Yeah, but remember the example I mentioned about
the guy with the formal shirt. This is another one of
those stories. When I found out that the legislator
went to Alaska, I thought, "I got him now." But
again, it's not the crime of the century. He's not going to go to jail for it, but it shows how hypocritical
politicians can be.

**I like the structure of this story. It has a suspend-
ed lead. About the fourth or fifth paragraph, the
reader finds out what the story is about.**

People know as they're reading this that this guy is
going to take a trip. It's obvious. You quote a politi-
cian as saying something, and readers know when
they see the story after the headline that this guy did
directly the opposite. So it wasn't like they were
surprised when they found out he went to Alaska.

**How long can you suspend information from the
reader? Here you delay for almost half the story.**

Yes, I'd say that's probably about it. I wouldn't want to go much further than that.

That's a nice lead, and a nice story. Do you have any kind of codes for the copy desk when you have a suspended lead like this, so that the headline doesn't subvert the story?

No; in fact, it's funny you mentioned that, because sometimes I'm concerned about a kicker or delayed fact. I don't want people on the copy desk to steal from it for the headline. They are pretty good at not doing that. Most of them have a sense of humor, and I think all of us who cover government and write the headlines and so forth look at government not with disdain, but with a question like, "What did government do this time?" or "What are they up to now?"

In a sense, that's responding to a certain mood in the country.

Oh yeah, I think this capitalizes on it. The Speaker of the Pennsylvania House and I have had differences over certain stories I've written and other people have written. He always accuses me of pandering to the public, but I keep saying to him, "I'm not pandering to the public; this is what upsets people about government."

Okay, let's go to the story "The LCB Gives Itself an A." In some ways, this story struck me as the one that could have been most easily written in a serious way, starting with, "The LCB spent $123 to send out mailings to 700 newspapers and radios to pump themselves." You create a metaphor for the reader through references to a report card, and you start with a very funny lead.

I think it's funny that, first of all, the state agency is giving itself a report card and spending taxpayer money to do it, even though it was only $123. But I think the strength of the story is that it puts the agency's act into context. It tells people that the reason this is going on is because at the end of this year, this agency is going to have to be reconstituted.

Well, you've found a way to speak to the reader, to share in their feelings toward government, and to help them see what government is doing.
Can you give some general guidelines about what makes good short writing?

I can't stress this enough. The key to good writing is to write with authority.

How do you define "writing with authority"?

I think it's knowing your subject and understanding the process. I've had the good fortune of being here in Harrisburg since 1986, so I've learned a lot in that time about how the place works. If you know your subject, and if you're confident you know the subject, you'll take risks with your writing. You won't be tentative. You have to understand the subject fully to be able to write with authority.

So the first rule is know the subject, understand the subject fully. The second thing you said is "take risks with your writing."

If you know your subject well, you can be confident of using words that you might not normally use. You can use words that might seem to accuse or defend because you are sure of the facts.

I want to separate short writing and bright writing. You mentioned the story about the legislator's formal shirt, but do you see short writing as an effective form for a variety of stories, including very serious ones?

Oh yes, I think so. A good example is a story I did last year. While going through records on payroll and expenses, I came upon the name of a new employee, Frank Oliver Jr. He had to be the kid of a legislator named Frank Oliver. I checked it out, and it turns out, yes, this is the guy's kid. There was no law forbidding the House from hiring a legislator's kid. I wrote basically a straight story saying, "The House has hired the son of a Philadelphia legislator." A state official confirmed on the record that this is the guy's son.

Then I quoted the Ethics Act, which says you can't use your position to enhance the finances of relatives. I asked the same official, was the dad involved in hiring the son? No, he did not hire him. Did the dad speak with the person who did hire his son? Yes, he did. I left it at that. My last line was, "Frank Oliver did not return a phone call for comment."

I basically left the impression with the reader that this guy may have violated the state Ethics Act, without actually having to say that. And that was a serious story that was about 6 inches long.

Many journalists have the belief that when you really get good, you get to write book-length pieces and win the big awards. Do you have any advice for convincing reporters that short writing can be good writing?

Every now and then, you think that you do this stuff but your colleagues don't take you seriously. But I don't consider these stories puff pieces because they do make a point about government. I think they tell the reader in a very easy fashion, "This is how government works."

Besides, if you have any talent as a writer, you have to be versatile. I can write a long story, I can write a short story, I can write a feature, I can write a hard news story. You have to be able to do that as a reporter. If you tend to write the same kind of story all the time, you're not really growing as a writer.

Marianne Costantinou

Finalist, Short Newswriting

A wise teacher inspired Marianne Costantinou to become a journalist when Costantinou was in the seventh grade at a New York City school. The teacher offered her the option of joining the newspaper staff or explaining a number of absences to her parents. She began getting paid for newspaper work while she was a freshman at Barnard College/Columbia University. The job was "hawking *The New York Times* on Manhattan street corners," she said. "The *Times* later let me come indoors" as a copyperson, news assistant, and free-lancer. In 1984, she went to *The Miami Herald,* and three years later to the *Philadelphia Daily News.* She's married and has a son.

Costantinou uses her position as a general assignment reporter to bring fresh touches to daily stories. Her editor says her strength is in taking risks in her writing. She writes short stories without losing the drama of events.

Racial slurs ended
her holiday picnic

JULY 6, 1991

It is a quiet street, Devereaux, a block where folks feel free to keep front doors unlocked, where the row houses are freshly painted and the sidewalks are swept daily.

It's the kind of block that makes parents feel good. Here, children are safe from many of the horrors of other city neighborhoods.

Or so Glenda Murphy thought.

Niggers!

The word landed on her patio Thursday afternoon like a bomb.

Niggers, go back where you came from!

The slurs came from three young men driving past her house off Torresdale Avenue in the Wissinoming section of the Northeast, she said last night.

As the only black family in the neighborhood, Murphy knew the white men were referring to her, her five children, and a dozen friends and relatives who had gathered for a Fourth of July cookout.

Within the hour, the epithets had turned uglier still. There was a confrontation across the street, in the playground, between her family and the men.

Other white residents gathered and joined in the shouting, she said. The police came, and the shouts turned to shoving and pushing and punching.

Nine people—five white and four black—were arrested in the melee, and a police officer was slightly injured, according to police.

For Murphy, 34, the incident was a bitter disillusionment. When she moved to the neighborhood two months ago from North Philadelphia, she thought she was sparing her children some of the city's ugliness.

"I moved to here because I came from a neighborhood with shooting, drugs," she said, crying. "I thought my children would have a better chance of life up here.

"I was proved wrong. Racism is worse than drugs."

Thursday was not the first time she or her children were called "nigger," she said. While most of her neighbors have been warm, some have made it clear that the family was unwelcome, she said.

"My children have been called 'nigger' since we moved here. 'Ni-guh, get the f___ away from here....' 'Ni-guh, go home.'"

Some of the residents can't understand the hostility. Ever since the Murphys moved into the $500-a-month, three-bedroom house, they've been friendly and quiet, said her next-door neighbor, Amentine Simpson, 60, who has lived on the block since 1957.

Glenda Murphy not only sweeps her own side of the sidewalk, but sweeps in front of the Simpson home as well, she said. And whenever they meet, they exchange pleasantries.

"All they were doing is having a barbeque for the Fourth of July, like everyone else," said Simpson, who witnessed the playground melee. "They did nothing wrong.

"It's a family. What difference does it make what color they are? It's a family."

"I'm not racially prejudiced, but they don't belong here," said a man whom neighbors identified as Freddie Neugebauer, 50, a resident of Van Dike Street for 18 years. "This is a lily-white neighborhood and they don't want outsiders in here....

"They have their neighborhoods. We have our neighborhoods. That's the way it's supposed to be.... They're in the wrong neighborhood. It's only gonna start trouble."

Tom Alex

Finalist, Short Newswriting

Tom Alex, a graduate of Northern Illinois University, chose a career not in writing, but as a climber with a tree service. He said a mishap in an oak tree in Iowa forced him to "fall back on a career in news reporting." He covered the police beat in Iowa for *The Ottumwa Courier*, the *Clinton Herald*, the *Cedar Rapids Gazette*, and the *Des Moines Tribune*. He joined *The Des Moines Register* in 1978.

Alex found a different career when he left tree climbing, but not necessarily a safer one. He fell while covering a story in 1982, and spent six months recovering. His writing competition entry included the story of a woman who fended off a burglar with a telephone receiver, and one on an 86-year-old woman who pulled her neighbor from a burning house. The story here tells of a family that finds a jewel in the rough.

An off-beet story with that certain special ring to it

JULY 30, 1991

As the dirt dropped away from a misshapen beet plucked from Richard Biddenstadt's garden, a bright metallic substance shone brightly underneath.

After some 50 years, a family mystery at a rural Keokuk residence finally was solved.

William Biddenstadt Sr. lost his wedding ring while gardening in the early 1940s, but he wasn't around last week to share in its discovery. He died in 1959 and his wife, Violet Inman Biddenstadt, died in 1973. Their wedding was March 20, 1919, so Biddenstadt wore the ring for 21 years or more before losing it.

Their son, Richard, now 62, lives next door to the old home place with his wife, Betty. The garden is located in front of the home place, which now is occupied by Richard Biddenstadt's sister, Frances Spiesz, 71.

Spiesz remembers looking for the ring some 50 years ago.

"It was 1940 or the early 1940s," she said. "I remember Dad talking about it. He was sorry he'd lost it and we went out there and looked for it. Finally we just gave up."

When Richard Biddenstadt pulled the "runt beet" from the ground last week, he couldn't help but notice its figure-eight shape. The reason was soon evident. The beet had a ring around its middle.

"The soil was completely dry and it just fell off. Otherwise I might have missed it," said Biddenstadt. "I planted the seeds with Dad's antique planter back in May. The ring must have been laying perfectly flat and that seed must have gone right in the middle of it."

He didn't remember that his father, a lifelong truck farmer, had lost the ring. When he talked to his older sister, she reminded him of that day years ago when the family searched the dirt for the wedding band.

Asked whether his father's initials were inside the band, Biddenstadt said, "I don't know. The ring is still around the beet and I'm keeping it in the refrigerator for now."

John Fensterwald
Editorial Writing

John Fensterwald won the Distinguished Writing Award after only one year of writing editorials. He's been a journalist for nearly 20 years, and was managing editor at the *Concord Monitor* prior to becoming editorial page editor.

His editorials explore national and international issues, including the Clarence Thomas hearings, changes in the Soviet Union, and presidential politics. He can hardly escape election coverage, for Concord is the capital of the state that hosts the first presidential primary. Yet, other topics draw much of his attention. His winning package focuses on the local community. "I look for a connection between people's lives and events in their community," Fensterwald said. He writes about the problems of residents, the things they think about, and the beauty of nature in Concord.

A teacher still

JANUARY 28, 1991

Five years later, Christa McAuliffe remains an inspiration.

It was five years ago today that the *Challenger* soared off into a cold morning sun and then plunged the nation into sorrow.

We knew then that memories of Christa McAuliffe would always fill a special, quiet corner of our minds. Now we know, from the poems and personal letters that still come occasionally to the newsroom from across the nation, that the same has been true for others.

Christa touched people in ways she could scarcely have imagined. From the day she was chosen to be the first teacher in space, people felt drawn to this open and warm woman from small-town New England. She had the gift of reaching out to fill an empty space in strangers' lives.

Too soon after came devastation and loss. The outpouring of emotion was surprising and deep; it continued long after her death. Then gradually the grief dissipated, and in its place grew a desire to preserve her memory with something lasting and meaningful.

Christa seemed bemused, if not embarrassed, by her celebrity and the adoration of people she hadn't met. But we know she would be proud of what others have done to further her life's work. There are schools and scholarships in her name, fellowships and sabbaticals for teachers in her honor. A magnificent planetarium in her hometown will inspire generations of New Hampshire children to explore life's infinite mysteries.

NASA's Teacher in Space program coincided with the growing awareness that education was in decline in America. An activist secretary of education and a report called "A Nation at Risk" jarred the nation and fueled a debate over what was to blame for lower test scores, a decline in basic skills, and a rise in the dropout rate.

Christa did not heal the divisions or change the direction of education; no one person could do that. She did, however, help to elevate the status of teachers. She was a firm advocate for their being paid well and respected for what they do. She embodied the qualities of excellence that others said were lacking in many of America's schools.

Her own strength was in the classroom—a global classroom, in the end—doing what she enjoyed most: reaching out to students, sharing the joy of learning with them, inspiring them, guiding them. By being herself she made people feel good about teachers, and she made teachers feel good about themselves.

Christa understood the nation's need to put her on a pedestal and turn a high school teacher into a heroine. In death, she has become a symbol and an ideal.

People in Concord, though, had a different relationship with her. They appreciated her simply for what she was—a true friend, a good neighbor, a caring teacher. She epitomized what was good about the community, and she made people proud to have known her.

Five years after her death, she is frozen in time like John Kennedy, the president she most admired, forever young, forever vibrant. We see her in our mind's eye as·if it were yesterday, thumbs up and smiling, leading a parade down Main Street toward a future that held such promise—and still does for those who follow her footsteps.

Observations and questions

1) Engaging writing emerges from the unexpected, the unpredictable. Fensterwald's lead would be appropriate and graceful if it said, "...the *Challenger* soared off into a cold morning sun and then plunged to earth." Instead he provides an unexpected ending. What are some of the effects of the lead's ending?

2) The paragraph beginning at the bottom of page 212 makes a transition from the discussion of Christa to the larger element of the state of American education. What is the key in this transition?

3) On page 213, the editorial reads: "By being herself she made people feel good about teachers, and she made teachers feel good about themselves." Unravel the complex of parallels here. Why does this sentence add punch to the editorial?

4) In using this picture, Fensterwald wrestled with the question of exploitation. He was able to stir special memories for the town with this moving image of her. Consider some of the memorable photos that linger in the public mind: the grimace of Lee Harvey Oswald, ministers pointing on a hotel balcony while the body of Martin Luther King lies at their feet, a clear blue sky with a V-shaped billow of smoke from a space shuttle. Sometimes the task of the writer is not to invoke new images, but to invoke memories or highlight those images that are already part of us.

Photo provided by the *Concord Monitor*

Velcome, Arnold

APRIL 26, 1991

It's time you put those big muscles to work for peace.

Arnold Schwarzenegger will be at the Beaver Meadow School Monday to pump up the president's campaign for physical fitness. Concord School Board members may want to keep their distance. Arnold will not be pleased to hear that they are considering dropping a half-credit from the PE requirement.

We had our misgivings when President Bush appointed Arnold chairman of his Council on Physical Fitness and Sports. True, he is a good Republican and, from what we can tell, a pleasant and intelligent man.

Yet his success in the weight room and on the screen have contributed to two of the forces undermining the well-being of our youth: narcissism and violence.

Arnold didn't get those 23-inch biceps and that 57-inch chest doing two dozen pushups and playing intramural soccer. He achieved it through an all-consuming, excessively vain, sometimes health-threatening regimen of body building. Although Arnold doesn't promote those practices now, his physique speaks for itself. He's a strange role model for a commission that advocates a balanced exercise program.

In most of his films, from *Conan* to *The Terminator*, Arnold has fed the stereotype in our culture that big muscles are to pummel and maim. As Hollywood's number one killer at the box office, he has elevated mindless violence to godlike heights. A kinder and gentler Arnold who can laugh at himself has emerged in his latest movies, like *Kindergarten Cop*, but even then, cute moments with kids are juxtaposed with disturbingly brutal scenes.

Yet it is for that reason we're pleased Concord's children will get to meet him in person. At least they'll see the human face behind the thug on film. Arnold can be charming off-screen; he has also been a conscientious advocate of fitness who has visited nearly every state for the president.

We hope someday he'll star as a nonviolent hero; maybe his trip to Beaver Meadow will inspire a new movie—*The Exterminator,* perhaps—about a strong man who rids an elementary school of malevolent microbes making teachers and students mysteriously ill.

[AUTHOR'S NOTE: Indoor pollution was the suspected cause of nausea and headaches at Beaver Meadow—a front-page news story at that time.]

Observations and questions

1) A standard form of editorial writing is to state the problem, explain the situation or offer opposing solutions, then state the preferred solution. Notice how this editorial includes the statement, explanation, and solution, but the elements are presented in creative ways. Where are the elements in this editorial?

2) The writer states two main concerns about Schwarzenegger: He promotes narcissism and violence. The editorial touches on broader concerns, however. What are some of the minor issues raised by the editorial?

3) This editorial is another example of how good writing is the peak of a mountain of research. What are some indications of the research supporting this piece?

4) After an editorial in which he calls the school board on the carpet and criticizes a hero of youth, Fensterwald ends with a new direction. What is gained by the reference to a school problem and by the light touch at the end?

Out of the loop

MAY 3, 1991

A lobby has outfoxed the governor on his "apple pie" issue.

Gov. Judd Gregg is no Carry Nation.

Wielding her hatchet with the relish of a fervid prohibitionist, Nation went around Kansas busting up bars in the 1890s. One of them was the Kansas Senate saloon.

Nation broke bottles; Gregg can't seem to get past the New Hampshire Senate's bottleneck.

On Tuesday, the Senate once again took the slippery way out when it put off an up-or-down vote on Gregg's proposal to lower the blood-alcohol level for legal intoxication from .10 to .08 percent. It also tabled action on another of the bills recommended by the Governor's Task Force To Prevent Impaired Driving—a ban on open containers of alcohol while in a motor vehicle. It is possible—but not likely—that the bills will resurface before the end of the session.

Having made a crusade against drunken driving his top legislative priority this year, Gregg has watched dourly from the sidelines as the restaurant lobby sweet-talked state senators under the table.

Asked the next day for his reaction, the governor was surprisingly restrained. "You have some interest groups which have communicated their concerns to the Senate. The Senate has apparently listened, and I think that's a very serious mistake."

The task force's bills, Gregg said, "are the motherhood and apple pie recommendations, and we should get on with it."

Good politicians, like good cooks, know that you get a half-baked pie unless you turn up the oven. Gregg's failure to put the heat on the Senate appears to have doomed the .08 legislation to oblivion for another year.

Some senators no doubt didn't like the idea of
.08 and were looking for a convenient way out.
Others, however, seemed earnestly confused by an
issue raised by the bar owners' lobby, the Hospitality Association. It said that lowering the breath-
alcohol level would create hardship for the already
financially hurting industry by making bars and
restaurants more vulnerable to suits by people
whom they didn't know were drunk. The lobby advocates a double standard—.08 for drinkers and
.12 as the threshold of protection for servers of
alcohol.

The liability issue was a smoke screen designed
to create doubt about .08, and it did. Current law already protects servers of alcohol from unwarranted
suits; the intoxicated person must be able to prove
that the server was reckless by intentionally serving
alcohol to someone he knew or should have known
would have been impaired.

Gregg and his aides should never have let the
Hospitality Association's assertions go unchal-
lenged. He should have sought clarification from
the attorney general's office on this point. And the
governor should have lobbied more vociferously
publicly and one-on-one with senators.

Gregg clearly doesn't enjoy the rough-and-tum-
ble of barroom or back room. That in itself does not
make him ineffective. But buttonhole politics and
the bully pulpit have their place, and this was it.

Observations and questions

1) A journalist writes for readers with various levels of knowledge and understanding. What type of responses might be evoked by the lead "Gov. Judd Gregg is no Carry Nation"? How can a writer be effective with readers whose knowledge varies?

2) Editorials not only challenge and inform readers, but also educate them. Notice that the snippet on Carry Nation tells a little history and sets the framework for comments on the governor.

3) Fensterwald undertakes one of the most difficult jobs for an editorial writer: explaining the legislative process. He outlines the legal battle and tells what the governor should have done. Where are the major sections of explanation? How does the writer clarify the situation?

4) The writer's point is given in the summary statement. Where does it appear in the body of the editorial? How does the kicker build on the summary statement?

A little night music

MAY 20, 1991

Nothing to do in Concord at night? Toads know better.

The sidewalks roll up at 9. Nothing for single people to do. Too quiet at night.

That common refrain to the *Monitor* questionnaire about Concord—certainly it was nothing new —came to mind while we took a late-night walk in White Park last week.

Actually, we could barely hear ourselves think, with the near-deafening chorus coming from the pond. And talk about nightlife: There was more slam-dancing and frenetic gyrations in that water than at the most uninhibited Village nightclub.

This is our favorite season at the park, when the lilacs are in bloom, the Little League is in full season, sunseekers return to the grass—and the American toads commence to mate.

The toads were what was making such a racket. There were dozens, if not hundreds, hidden among the cattails and swimming about. You could tell by the ripples on the surface and the reflections of their eyes.

The toads had come from all over the park and beyond to gather in water, as nature has decreed they must, for just a few days of raucous courtship. We don't know how, but their biological clocks keep synchronous time. All seem to know when to dig out of their dirt bunkers in neighboring yards to make the pilgrimage across Washington, Centre, and White streets. And at great peril: Even at night, when the sidewalks are supposed to be up, the traffic diminishes their number.

It's been said of the toads' smaller cousins, the tree frogs, better known as peepers: "A dozen make less than a human handful, but their voices can fill a whole evening." In the chorus of the pond, American toads are the baritones, less shrill and more melodious than peepers' annoying falsetto. To launch into a call to attract a mate, the male throws back his head, fills his enormous air sac, and lets loose.

On this particular night, the males appeared especially anxious to grab hold of anything toad (and, one day last week, onto the arm of a confused little boy who had thought *he* was trying to catch *them*). Gender and number were not an inhibitor. We saw three desperate males clenched to one poor female, who labored to shore to try to shake two of them off.

We never tire of watching this ritual. Nor, on this night, did a great blue heron, which arrived silently on a wingspan large enough to eclipse the young moon overhead. He waded slowly into the pond, then stood as still as a plastic flamingo, waiting to have his fill of toads and tadpoles.

There are few parks in the middle of a city of any size that can attract as shy a bird as the heron. And there are few cities where, a few blocks from downtown, the trills of toads can drown out almost all urban static.

The mating of toads does not substitute for the need for more entertainment and things to do after-hours in Concord, but it does provide a quiet diversion on nights when you're not quite ready to settle down to sleep.

Observations and questions

1) The first two sentences of the lead indicate that the editorial is a put-on, a lighthearted exaggeration. How does the writer build on this tone after the lead?

2) Fensterwald follows the lead with a transition that brings in local humankind: "This is our favorite season at the park, when the lilacs are in bloom, the Little League is in full season, sunseekers return to the grass—and the American toads commence to mate." What are the factors that bring rhythm to this list?

3) Much of the humor derives from the personification of toads. List some examples of this.

4) In addition to the humor, the editorial also tells quite a bit about nature. Consider the description of the heron on page 222. What lessons are taught about the heron and other animals in this piece?

Showing no mercy

OCTOBER 2, 1991

State was harsh, greedy in punishing disabled pot grower.

Greed has motivated many a big-time drug dealer. Greed may even have motivated Jim Jackson to grow a small crop of marijuana on his land in New Hampton.

But it was government greed that left him destitute and disoriented needlessly. And it was justice without compassion that broke his spirit.

Jackson is a 42-year-old unemployed man living on Social Security. He was growing three dozen pot plants on his property when the New Hampton police and the Belknap County Sheriff's Department busted him. They seized 10 pounds of dope— enough to charge him with manufacturing a controlled substance, a Class A felony. They claimed his crop had a street value of $40,000, though it was actually worth less than half that much.

Jackson pleaded guilty—the pot was right in his back yard, after all. His only defense was that he grew it to ease the pain from an artificial knee. You can believe whom you choose. That's not the point.

He was sentenced to a year in the county jail, although he could have gotten 20 in the state prison. The judge considered his plight and lack of criminal record (one DWI, nothing else). This month he got out to find that he no longer had his house and his land. He was nearly broke and he was homeless.

As its contribution to the war on drugs, the Legislature passed a law in the mid-1980s allowing the state to seize cash and sell property that a drug dealer might have benefited from or used to commit illegal dealings. A seizure is done in a separate proceeding, often before a different judge. It is a quick process. Sometimes, by the time criminal charges are dropped, a person's property has already been sold.

The intent is to deprive a drug dealer of his ill-gotten gains and the wherewithal to start over once he gets out of jail. But there's a big incentive for the police and the attorney general's office, which runs the program, to pursue it with zeal. The law enforcement agency that brought charges and the attorney general's office split 90 percent of the proceeds, with 10 percent going to programs for drug abuse and prevention. It is the only source of state money for drug enforcement and investigations.

Big-time cocaine dealers are usually smart enough to hide their cash, Porsches, and yachts in faraway places or secret bank accounts. Jackson, however, was no Pablo Escobar. He made for easy picking: You saw all he owned when you drove up the yard.

Jackson grew his pot in a garden plot, but the attorney general's office went after his whole property—5.5 acres and the little cottage he helped build. The state argued it was used in a drug manufacturing operation.

Jackson's lawyer pleaded hardship and asked the judge for only a partial forfeiture. He thought the judge would be sympathetic. But Judge William O'Neil ruled that under the law he had no discretion; it was either all or nothing (some lawyers disagree with his interpretation). So Jim Jackson's house and land were sold to a neighbor for about $50,000—more than twice as much as he could have made by selling every ounce of marijuana he grew and keeping none for himself.

The attorney general's drug division got its share of the take. The New Hampton police and the Belknap County sheriff's office did, too. And Jim Jackson is living out of a trailer at a friend's place, pondering a legal system that sent him to prison and then sentenced him to poverty.

Observations on editorial writing

If evaluating editorial writing were a science, we could simply tally up the scores: 7 points for clear language, 9 points for the logical progression of ideas, 3 points because the editorial is a half-inch shorter than 13 inches.

I wish this were a science. There'd be fewer opportunities for disagreement about the result, and editorial writers would have a measure of what they ought to be asking of the piece currently resisting them on the screen.

Somehow, we have never gotten around to declaring the criteria for the best editorial writing, but here is a sample of the questions one judge asks:

1) **Will a reader get the point?** Is the editorial built on simple, straightforward language that gets into the subject and back out with clarity? Does the editorial offer all the explanations and translations that are required?

2) **Will a reader *want* to get the point?** Is the reading itself an experience the reader might recommend to someone else? Will the reader feel satisfied when the editorial is over?

3) **Does the editorial take advantage of some of the tricks of the English language?** Will the piece change the reader's mind about the kind of words that are appropriate on the editorial page?

4) **Will a reader learn something about the debate?** Does the reader grasp that there are alternative arguments, and find the piece fair and unbiased?

5) **Will a reader feel respected?** Does the piece amount to a conversation between equals?

And so questions get answered, and great work gets anointed, and terrific work almost does. And the editorial writing judge goes back to wishing the evaluation could be done with a calculator.

Joann Byrd, Executive Editor
The Herald, Everett, Wash.

A conversation with John Fensterwald
A voice for the community

KAREN BROWN: You've been a reporter, managing editor, and editorial page editor. What are the major differences between newswriting and editorial writing?

JOHN FENSTERWALD: For me, editorial writing is an extension of the curiosity that I had when I first got into journalism: to look at subjects and answer basic questions that I had in mind. The biggest difference was getting used to writing every day. Editorial writing is never far from my mind. There's no vacation from it; I'm always looking for ideas. It's just become a part of me. And there's a discipline to it that's not my natural personality. I've enjoyed it in the long run.

How did you decide on your style and voice in the editorials?

I'd been reading editorial pages for many years, and I had several models of editorial writing that I wanted to avoid. I had read so many editorials that sounded as if your parents were lecturing to you. I felt all of us had had enough of that growing up. At the same time, I wanted to avoid the Andrew Dice Clay style of invective, which seems to be creeping into some editorials. That's simply name-calling and taking shotguns to politicians at every chance, picking your enemies and using insults and invective for the sake of making exciting copy. It's also just getting readers riled up based on the language, as opposed to the issue. Some editorial writers are being short and punchy and controversial as newspapers try to sell to their readers. I wanted to find my own voice, one that was also suit-

■ John Fensterwald, editorial page editor, *Concord Monitor.*

■ **Born:** December 12, 1951, in Baltimore, Md.

■ **Personal:** Married to Beth Fensterwald; one daughter, Molly.

■ **Education:** Tufts University, 1973.

■ **Newspaper Experience:** *Monadnock Ledger,* Peterborough, N.H., 1974-75, 1977-80; *The New Englander* (business monthly), Dublin, N.H., 1975-76; *Valley News,* Lebanon, N.H., 1981-85; *Concord Monitor,* 1985-present.

able for the community in which I was writing.

Let's talk a little more about the purposes of editorials. There seems to be a growing interest in commentaries that appear not just on editorial pages, but throughout the paper. Plenty of opinion is going in the newspaper. Why do newspapers need editorials?

The editorial is still the one place that serves as the conscience of the paper, a place where one can encourage the readers to take a look at certain issues both in and outside the community. The editorial page can encourage people to become part of the democratic process through participating in letters to the editor, sending their opinions to us, and also thinking about the subject that we're raising.

It's a vital part, and I think that the *Monitor*'s letters to the editor show that people have a tremendous interest in the editorial page. There are issues that we talk about and opinions that we express that people will not find anywhere else. We are the paper of record for our community, and we believe that people will always turn to the newspaper to see what the editors think about some of the key issues that they're facing.

Who reads your editorials?

I'm sure that those who are most active in affairs of the Legislature and the city government read the paper more frequently than others, but that's not to whom I'm writing, because that's when you become distanced from your readers. Then the editorial assumes a tone that's either lecturing or remote. I'm simply trying to write something in simple, clear terms that I think would be interesting to someone who may be familiar with the events in the community and the events in the world.

How do you get ideas for editorials?

A lot of my editorials start as questions; my curiosity drives me. I pursue leads and hope that I end up with a cogent opinion. I like the research part of this job. New Hampshire is a small state, so you can reach people you need for information without any trouble, from the governor on down. Except the governor doesn't like to talk to us.

How long do you spend writing your editorials?

Well, I am a procrastinator. In the back of my mind, I think that I do research as a way of putting off writing. The *Monitor* is an afternoon paper, so generally I spend several hours in the afternoon researching, and then I start writing late in the day or even at night at home.

Let me go on with the writing process. Do you tend to write in one quick draft, or do you first organize what you're going to write?

I tend to agonize. I take it home and mull it over. I know it's there in the back of my mind. Then I will sit down, usually around 10 o'clock, and start writing. I get to a certain point where I feel comfortable that I've earned a night's sleep, and then I will usually get up the next morning and finish it, which is sort of my second pass. Sometimes I think about it on the way to work, and I'll give it a third pass when I get there.

Let's look at your winning editorials, starting with "Showing No Mercy." Do you remember how you got the idea for this editorial?

That was the result of a front-page story that we had written about Jim Jackson. His story had angered me, so I wanted to find out more about the program and the reason the state seemed to be persecuting him.

Once you had the idea, what was your next step?

Well, in this case, I talked with the reporter about it at length, and then to find out a little more, I began making calls to learn the process by which the state confiscated Jim Jackson's property. I also talked with Jackson's lawyer.

Do you usually talk to the reporter and then do a little investigating on your own?

Yeah, I usually do. It's something I enjoy. And I find that it really helps me to clarify an issue and find a bit more depth. I really feel I have to master a subject.

You start with a slow, clear build: "Greed has motivated many a big-time drug dealer. Greed may even have motivated Jim Jackson to grow a small crop of marijuana on his land in New Hampton.

"But it was government greed that left him destitute and disoriented needlessly. And it was justice without compassion that broke his spirit."

This is a very interesting lead in that you introduce four ideas in four simple sentences, each a direct statement, each building the case you're going to make. And then in the third paragraph, you begin the explanation.

Would you talk a little bit about the lead and your thoughts in writing it?

I have a headline and I have a summary sentence or readout above the editorial. So I give the reader an understanding either of what the editorial is about or what the opinion is. That enables me to make a case in a slow, deliberate way and use language to build interest in the editorial before I get into specifics.

Do you write the head and the summary sentence?

Yes, usually.

Is the summary sentence above the editorial your design idea?

Yes. One of my jobs as managing editor was to lead the redesign for the paper, and I put a lot of thought into ways of making the paper accessible to readers.

This was one idea I brought to the editorial page when I took the job as the editorial page editor.

I'm interested in the tone used here. In the fourth paragraph, you say, "His only defense was that he grew it to ease the pain from an artificial knee. You can believe whom you choose. That's not the point." What's the tone you seek in your editorials?

Well, my editor, Mike Pride, has some good advice he gives our reporters, which is to write as if you're writing a letter to an intelligent friend. This was a point in the editorial that I felt I could almost talk to the reader one on one.

I know readers are going to say, "Well, sure, he's saying he has to smoke dope because he has a painful knee, but why isn't he working, what are his circumstances, why doesn't the guy have a job?" And because I know that readers are going to react that way, and I know that these questions are going through their minds, I want to direct them back to the point and say, "Don't let your mind wander— let's get back to the issue."

You're thinking ahead to your readers' responses. Overall, the editorial stands out for the simple language that you use, and the simple story.

Well, I like to relate government to people. Although he was in another town, Jackson was basically a neighbor. It would be one thing to do an editorial criticizing the program that the state has, but if you can relate it to a neighbor or a friend or someone readers might see on the street, it's much more effective.

The editorial titled "Out of the Loop" focuses on the governor and state politics. About midway through the piece, you quote the governor: "You have some interest groups which have communicated their concerns to the Senate. The Senate has apparently listened, and I think that's a very

serious mistake." Do you use quotations in editorials any differently than you did in newswriting?

Well, in either form there's got to be a reason for using a quote. In this one, the words that he used were telling. The issue is a hot issue, it's a controversial issue, and the words that he uses were bureaucratic and understated, saying things like "interest groups communicated their concerns."

I wanted to convey to the readers how, on this hot-button issue, a governor was using words that didn't convey any of that intensity.

The governor's later reference to motherhood and apple pie gives you some leeway to say, "Good politicians, like good cooks, know that you get a half-baked pie unless you turn up the oven." What's the point of playing with language like that?

I think it's fun. It's fun to write and, I hope, it's fun to read. You know, I had in the back of my mind the Harry Truman saying "If you can't stand the heat, get out of the kitchen," and I wanted to make the connection between apple pie and half-baked. So you lead the reader through language, making the connection from one idea to the next.

The last three paragraphs state your position on the issue. Do editorials need to take a position?

Well, that's interesting. I don't think that all editorials have to say "This is right or wrong" or "Yes" or "No." I think that editorials can encourage people to see the world differently, to step outside themselves, and to question certain assumptions, such as I did in the editorial on toads in White Park.

Sometimes the purpose of an editorial might be to articulate what many people may be feeling about a subject, such as Christa McAuliffe in that other editorial. So an editorial can serve many different functions in various forms. It could be narrative. It doesn't have to be very linear, saying, "This is my argument, this is why I believe in it, and this is what you should do to correct it."

Good point. Let's look at "A Little Night Music," the editorial on toads in the park. You start by making reference to a questionnaire. What was the questionnaire about?

Well, there was an organization that was going throughout the state developing a civic profile. They gathered a cross section of a couple of hundred people to talk about Concord and how they would like to see the city change. I thought, well, why don't we do our own questionnaire: What do you like about Concord? What do you dislike about Concord? One of the principal responses was that there is nothing to do. That was particularly mentioned by young people.

We'd already published the results of the questionnaire the week before, so this was picking up on that theme.

How would you describe Concord?

It's a very quiet city, and it's an hour from everywhere: from Boston, from the coast, from the mountains, from Dartmouth. You can get to most any place you want to go. As in much of New Hampshire, many of the people here are transplants.

It's a family town, very much oriented around schools. As the state capital, it's a politically active town. It has a population of about 35,000. It's a gem for a city its size, and it has a lot of parks and other places where you can take walks.

How did you get the idea for this editorial? Were you actually out walking at night and then thought about writing this?

At that point, my daughter was 2 months old, and my wife and I got to know every inch of that park at every hour of the day. We found that she responded to walks, that it would comfort her and put her to sleep, so we would take a lot of walks through White Park at night.

What did you want to do for the reader here?

Well, two things really. One was to explain to people that there's a lot of things going on right underneath their chins if they take a look at it, even in White Park, which is primarily used during the day to play soccer and take walks and have softball games. No one takes a walk after dark, but it's safe to do so. The other was just to have a little bit of fun.

You certainly had fun. You have a night of "raucous courtship," during which the toads are engaged in "slam-dancing and frenetic gyrations." In an effort to attract the female, "the male throws back his head, fills his enormous air sac, and lets loose" with a melodious, baritone call.
   You also have an erotic scene in which "three desperate males clenched to one poor female, who labored to shore to try to shake two of them off." I guess you have to know something about nature to appreciate all this.

My wife introduced me to a lot of aspects of nature, and I've learned to appreciate the environment more and more.
   You asked earlier what editorials should do. My feeling is that I've written about the ozone, I've written about diversity of species issues, and I've found it's one thing to write about issues in the abstract and another thing to write about nature in our readers' back yards. I hope that in focusing on the local environment, people might get interested and excited and therefore take an interest in larger issues such as global warming.

The editorial "Velcome, Arnold" attempts to balance some conflicting images of Arnold Schwarzenegger. Tell me a little bit about the background of this one.

Well, the whole issue of violence in our culture, in-cluding our movies, is one that concerns me. I felt that the world didn't need another preachy editorial. So I was going to have some fun doing this, and I started reading up about Arnold Schwarzenegger, and I watched *The Terminator*. I read a bunch of ar-ticles that said, "Gee, you know, Arnold is really a terrific guy," but I was trying to get people to go out-side of that connection with him as a Hollywood star and a good Republican, and look at the issue of violence and at what his movies say about society, and do it in a way that would be amusing, if I could.

And you chose to be somewhat ambiguous here.

The editorial had to be a little bit ambiguous about separating a person who is a nice person from the effect that person has on the culture as a whole.

Do you know how young people responded to this?

Mike told me the editorial was read by a class of sixth-graders, and they were furious. They said, "How could anyone criticize Arnold?"

The press can seem like a wet blanket. Yet it re-minds people of things they need to think about. Let's move on to the editorial on Christa Mc-Auliffe. My first questions is, how do you say something new in Concord about Christa?

With difficulty. Christa's death is very much a non-subject here; she is not talked about in Concord too much. It's something that people feel, but it's some-thing that is not openly discussed. Sort of like a death in the family.

And at the newspaper, we don't write something every time the anniversary of her death comes around, but the fifth anniversary of her death was different. A significant time had passed, and we were aware that the rest of the national media were going to be talking about it, so this was our opportu-nity to revisit that subject.

I wonder what some of your thoughts were in creating the mood here. You really did a beautiful job.

Thank you. Well, the purpose of this editorial was to crystallize a feeling that I know many people in this community shared, and put it in writing for them to read. That's an unusual purpose for an editorial because usually you don't try to fathom what people are thinking and then tailor the piece to the audience, but this was very special.

The piece begins: "It was five years ago today that the *Challenger* soared off into a cold morning sun and then plunged the nation into sorrow."
I want to talk about strong verbs in editorials. Here you picture the spacecraft as having soared and then plunged. In the lead, you're dealing with action. You've been a writer for years, and one of the first rules writers try to remember is to use strong verbs. Is that an appropriate guideline in editorial writing? Or does this particular piece represent one of the few chances you get to use strong verbs, because of the dramatic action?

I think good editorial writing is just an extension of good writing. As an editor, I learned the value of putting an emphasis on verbs instead of adjectives. And it's something that I personally have to work on, and it's usually something that I pick up on the second or final pass. The word choice isn't my preferred choice the first time I sit down and write the editorial.

But you're saying that in editorial writing, there is still the imperative and opportunity to use strong verbs.

Particularly so with opinions, yes.

Okay. Then we move on to the second paragraph: "We knew then that memories of Christa McAuliffe would always fill a special, quiet cor-

ner of our minds." I'm interested in your use of "we." In "Velcome, Arnold," you use the editorial "we," meaning "we the newspaper." In "A Little Night Music," the "we" seems more personal. But in "A Teacher Still," the "we" sounds more collective. It seems to translate to "we the people of this town." How did you interpret that "we"?

In this case, "we" referred to a relationship that I felt Concord as a city had with this person. It was one of the more personal editorials that the newspaper has carried.

Are you comfortable with the general editorial "we," or does it become cumbersome?

There's a tension that's created because I am writing for an institution, for the *Monitor* as a paper and as an editorial board, and I'm very comfortable in that role and in discussing opinions with both Tom Brown, the publisher, and Mike Pride, the editor.

I am also aware that there is a record of editorial stands, that my stand should be consistent with that of my predecessors. And I'm comfortable with that, but I also feel that editorials shouldn't come across as an institution. I try to reach readers as if I were talking to them.

And so it's hard sometimes to balance that sense of institution with that desire to be personal, and also to relate personal experiences. Obviously, the editorial board of the *Monitor* isn't out walking in White Park at two in the morning.

Besides the use of that pronoun, in what other ways did you try to build the Christa piece as a collective look at someone the community loved?

Later on in the piece, in the 10th paragraph, I talk a little bit about her relationship with Concord and try to summarize what she meant for the people who live here, for it was a different relationship from the Christa people saw on television or read about in magazines.

And in the third paragraph, we talked a little bit about how Christa had touched the lives of the people she had met here, and how she had a way of enriching all of our lives just by achieving the goal that she set out to accomplish and by bringing prominence and achievement to those around her, as neighbors and friends.

Let's go back to paragraph four. You talk about Christa and the effect she's had on the nation, and then you say, "Too soon after came devastation and loss." You never say the *Challenger* crashed, you never give the background, you never say she died. Were you tempted to include some elements traditionally presented in newspaper writing?

It really was unnecessary, and in fact would take away the personal approach that I was striving for.

You start the editorial by talking about a hometown hero, and then raise the issue to a higher level. You indicate there's something more involved here, not just Christa, but also an attitude toward education, and she had an effect on that, too.

Well, it would not have been necessary to write an editorial simply to say, "Christa died five years ago; gee, wasn't that tragic?" That's something that was a given, and everyone understood.

Christa saw her role as a teacher as having an effect on education, and this was an opportunity to look back at what has happened in education since her death, and to find out whether any of the ideals that she stood for have moved ahead.

At the end, the mood shifts again. You've taken the editorial to the broader national level, and now you bring it back home: "We see her in our mind's eye as if it were yesterday, thumbs up and smiling, leading a parade down Main Street toward a future that held such promise—and still does for those who follow her footsteps."

So, you end with hope instead of ending with the *Challenger* crash or the fact that it's been five years since the tragedy.

Yes. She had affected many people, particularly her students. One of the stories we have done is to talk with students who were in her classes. Several of them have been inspired by her to go into teaching, and that was part of what prompted my approach. I wanted to find out if perhaps her lasting value will be in some of the areas that she felt were important.

One little note, Karen, on this one. That picture I mention of Christa riding down Main Street ran at the top of the editorial. I try to use art and photos where appropriate with my editorials because I think they add another dimension. The art draws people to the editorial, and this was a picture that we had run. I was worried about the whole issue of exploitation of Christa. That is something that the media need to think about, and it gave me second thoughts before I ran that photo, but I decided that it was a tribute to her, and so it was appropriate.

It probably is the picture that people will remember her by: Christa and her children, Scott and Caroline, in a parade on Main Street. She's smiling and giving a "thumbs up" sign. It's a very moving picture, even to look at today.

Newsday

THE LONG ISLAND NEWSPAPER

Adrian Peracchio

Finalist, Editorial Writing

Adrian Peracchio is a member of the *Newsday* editorial board, specializing in foreign affairs. Before his current assignment, he was chief of the *Newsday* London bureau and headed a number of investigative project teams. He has been the recipient of several national journalism awards, including the 1984 Pulitzer Prize for general news reporting. He has worked at *Newsday* since 1978. Before that, he was a reporter for United Press International and the *Boston Herald*. Peracchio grew up in Italy and was educated in Europe and the United States. He is married and lives in Connecticut.

His work is an example of editorial pioneering at *Newsday*. The Sunday "cover" editorial moves away from traditional brevity. Once a week, the newspaper seeks to improve understanding of events with an in-depth editorial.

Tough enough to fight

MARCH 10, 1991

The Persian Gulf War has turned several military shibboleths on their heads. One of the most startling was the myth that women could serve in a war zone safe from the dangers of battle if they did not face direct combat. This war proved that on the modern battlefield women in non-combat roles are exposed to just as much danger as men in full combat.

At least five women were killed in the war zone. Mark their names. These soldiers may change forever the way we view women in war.

• Army Major Marie Rossi, 32, Oradell, N.J.: killed Feb. 24 when the Chinook supply helicopter she piloted crashed in Iraq.

• Army Private Adrienne L. Mitchell, 20, Moreno Valley, Calif.: killed when an Iraqi Scud missile crashed into a barracks near Dhahran, Saudi Arabia, Feb. 25.

• Army Specialist Beverly S. Clark, 23, Armagh, Pa.: killed in the same Scud attack.

• Army Specialist Christine Mayes, 23, Rochester Mills, Pa.: killed in the same Scud attack.

• Army Reserve Medical Technician Cindy Beaudoin, 19, Plainfield, Conn.: a college student, called up to serve on ambulances, died when she stepped on a mine.

Their deaths—and the capture and subsequent release last week of Major Rhonda Cornum of East Aurora, N.Y., and Private Melissa Rathburn-Nealy of Grand Rapids, Mich.—should become the spark for a push to redefine the role of American women in combat. And that should lead to equal opportunities for women to advance—and face danger; to win promotions—and get wounded; to attain glory —and yes, to die.

LET WOMEN VOLUNTEER FOR COMBAT?

As the dust of Desert Storm settles, U.S. armed forces must decide what to do about women who have made the military a career and wish to volunteer for combat. Ultimately, the military may be forced to conclude that if modern warfare exposes men and women to an equal danger of harm and capture, the women of a volunteer force must be allowed to be assigned to combat units if they wish—with the potential for promotions and professional advancement those assignments entail.

In other words: If capable women in the volunteer armed forces want to go into combat units, let them.

A recent TV interview with a young female Army captain made the issue clear. She had been first in her class at West Point, but she acknowledged that male officers who were inferior cadets stood a better chance than she at making general because they could volunteer for combat and she couldn't. Successful commands of combat units are to military officers what profitable sales campaigns are to company executives: Without them, they don't stand much of a chance to make it to the top.

Yet women in the American military forces have been exempted by law—some would say barred—from serving in combat units. The rationale was the legislative desire to expose women to a lesser level of risk. But, as the Persian Gulf War has shown, even women serving in combat-support roles are in harm's way.

It is a matter of simple equity, then, to make sure that if military women are exposed to equal danger, they must be given equal opportunities for career advancement. The argument is particularly cogent in this era of voluntary military service. Many women soldiers—particularly officers—intend to make a career out of the military. Should a draft be reinstituted, the issue would be different. Past drafts never applied to women, but if women were ever to be drafted, it's almost impossible to imagine Congress deciding that women who serve unwill-

ingly must fight. The women-in-combat issue must
be decided in the context of a volunteer military.

43-YEAR-OLD LAWS BAN
WOMEN WARRIORS

Legally, the armed services' treatment of women
warriors is hamstrung by combat-exclusion statutes dating back to 1948 that apply to the Navy,
Marine Corps, and Air Force. The Army has developed policies to exclude women from combat by
citing the implied congressional intent behind the
statutes governing the other services.

Women now make up nearly 11 percent of the
nation's 2.2 million uniformed personnel. The arguments against allowing women to serve in combat are anachronistic, but they surface every time
the issue makes it to the congressional floor, as it
last did in 1988. We don't think these arguments
should continue to frustrate military women's
wishes, and they ought to be re-examined:

• **Women can't handle war's physical demands.**
In the days of broadswords, that was quite true. But
modern combat is dependent not so much on brute
physical force as on the ability to handle sophisticated lethal equipment competently. Physical en-
durance and toughness are necessary, but so are
stamina and determination—both more dependent
on training, will, and desire than on sheer muscular
strength. Even carrying a wounded comrade can be
handled by a reasonably fit and capable woman.
No woman who can make it through basic military
training, let alone one of the military academies,
can qualify as a physical wimp.

Particularly when it comes to the Air Force and
the Navy, the physical requirements of combat differ not at all between the sexes. Flying an F-111
isn't a matter of muscles or hormones. Neither is
the piloting of a fighting ship, or the aiming of a
laser-guided missile.

• **Sex and sexual rivalries will spell trouble.**
Perhaps. Though if racial tensions are any indications, there will be a lot less of both in the front
lines than anyone imagines. The fact is that men

and women already live together in a war zone, with less privacy than in any coed dormitory. Somehow they manage it. The same arguments apply to privacy problems in general. Coed mountaineering teams and archaeological expeditions face the same difficulties and they cope. There will be some problems. Women in the gulf complained of the lack of female sanitary supplies. But that is just a matter of the armed forces adapting to changing needs.

• **Women shouldn't be forced into combat.** Congress will not agree to have men and women share risks with *absolute* equality in the military. That just isn't in the cards. In peacetime, men who volunteer for armed service have a choice of whether to serve in a combat arm or not—up to a point. Those who score below a certain level in basic intelligence and aptitude tests tend to be channeled into the infantry or a similar combat arm. In wartime, all bets are off. Men are sent where they are required. Should women be? Congress almost certainly won't let that happen.

But Congress may agree that women who *wish* to be assigned to combat units should be allowed to do so. This is particularly significant for officers. Non-coms can actually rise to the top of the enlisted ranks faster if they specialize in combat-support specialties, like radar guidance or nursing. Officers, instead, must serve in combat units if they aspire to the top of the heap.

• **Women in other armies don't have to fight.** Not so. Opponents of women in combat routinely cite the example of the Israeli army, whose policy is to exclude women from combat duty. But several NATO allied forces allow women to serve in combat roles: Belgium, Norway, and the Netherlands have opened all military specialties, including those involved directly in combat, to women. In fact, a Dutch woman was trained as a combat pilot in Texas in an Air Force program from which American women are excluded. Canada is experimenting with a program to allow women to serve in combat units.

THERE'S NO SAFETY ZONE

Modern warfare, characterized by great fluidity of battle zones and technological complexity, presents greater risks and opportunities for women. On a battlefield such as the Persian Gulf, it is nearly impossible to draw clear-cut lines of danger and safety, and therefore dictate which jobs military women can and cannot do.

The armed forces have already made great strides in ensuring equality of treatment for women. They must go the extra step, with Congress's help, and ensure that women are not stopped by an artificial barrier supported by archaic notions of chivalry ill-suited to a modern society, let alone an army.

Richmond Times-Dispatch

Thomas Harvey Holt

Finalist, Editorial Writing

Thomas Harvey Holt began journalistic writing at Northwestern University. He was majoring in industrial engineering and rhetorical theory at the time. He was sold on journalism by an internship at the National Journalism Center in Washington, D.C. It allowed him to work at the Washington bureau of *The Times* of London and *The Australian*. After graduating from Northwestern, he became a public relations writer at the Heritage Foundation, and later a consultant to Capital Research Center and other policy research groups. For two years, he was chief speech writer to the secretary of transportation in the Reagan and Bush administrations. He became assistant editorial page editor of the *Richmond Times-Dispatch* in 1989.

He said his writings emphasize economic liberty and the dangers of government power. This selection looks at the danger that legislators can pose to the economic health of taxpayers.

Greed in the night

JULY 19, 1991

After sundown Washington can be a decidedly dangerous place, especially for taxpayers. The world's most self-aggrandizing body waited until the later hours of Wednesday, by which time tourists and most members of the press had given up the Senate Gallery for Pennsylvania Avenue watering holes and scattered hostelries, to vote themselves a big, fat, $23,000 pay raise. This in exchange for agreeing not to shake down lobbyists for the same amount in "honorariums."

But that's not all. In the dead of night a sneaky and greedy Senate voted 53-45 (with Sens. John Warner and Charles Robb disgracing the frugal reputation of the Old Dominion by voting with the majority) for an amendment that also would make it illegal for future senators to be true citizen-legislators. Senators will be forbidden from making what the IRS calls "earned income" of more than 15 percent of Senate pay. By this formula, the gentlemen farmers who crafted the Constitution and constituted a substantial portion of Congress until recent times might hereafter be banished from public service. Although today's congressmen are full-time legislators, individuals who might be able to earn outside income ethically without neglecting their duties—farmers and authors, to cite two examples—should not be kept from joining the Senate. The ideal of a citizen legislature ought not be so cavalierly abandoned.

Count this anti-democratic device as one more incumbency-protection scam. From now on, barring a highly unlikely presidential veto, only professional pols need apply to the Senate.

The Beltway cognoscenti would say this is just as well: Today's Big Government ought not be entrusted to anyone but the sort of leeches who make politics, rather than productive endeavor, their primary careers. The inhabitants of today's Washington hold a dangerously high opinion of themselves. Dangerous to representative democracy, that is.

The Senate's gassy opinion of itself was eloquently encapsulated by Sen. Robert Byrd (D-W.Va.), who claimed that the Senate "is the most important board of directors of any business in the world." If it's a board of directors, as Sen. Charles Grassley (R-Iowa) pointed out, the Senate does an awful job and does not deserve a raise; it has failed even to pass a balanced budget. In any case, someone should remind Sen. Byrd that the Senate is not a productive business but "a necessary evil" tolerated by a people who believe in representative government.

But then the Senate demonstrated its great respect for representative government by holding its pay-raise vote in the dead of night, when the fewest of the represented might find out about it. We'd like to know who hollered into the Senate chamber, "The coast is clear!"

Henry Allen
Commentary

Friends describe Henry Allen as very intense. He describes himself as "fine-boned and kind of watchful-looking, a little ironic and oblique." He adds, "I really like to engage people."

He also likes journalism, a path he has followed for 26 years. His news stories and offbeat observations on life engage readers of *The Washington Post* and its news services. Allen's strong writing comes not only from his outlook and intense study of issues, but also from his ability to make the language picturesque. He sees journalism changing from a business of "craftsmen" who relish creative phrasing to a collection of "professionals concerned about their dignity and impact on public policy." "The idea of getting in there and noodling around with words for the sheer joy of it doesn't mean as much," Allen said. Maybe not for others, but for Henry Allen, there's still the noodling, and there's still the joy.

The gulf between media and military

FEBRUARY 21, 1991

The Persian Gulf press briefings are making reporters look like fools, nit-pickers, and egomaniacs; like dilettantes who have spent exactly none of
their lives on the end of a gun or even a shovel; dinner-party commandos, slouching inquisitors, collegiate spitball artists; people who have never been in
a fistfight much less combat; a whining, self-righteous, upper-middle-class mob jostling for whatever tiny flakes of fame may settle on their shoulders
like some sort of Pulitzer Prize dandruff.

They ask the same questions over and over. In
their frustration, they ask questions that no one
could answer; that anyone could answer; that no
one should answer if they could answer. They complain about getting no answers; they complain
about the answers they get. They are angry that the
military won't let them go anywhere, the way they
could in Vietnam. They talk about war as if it were
a matter of feelings to be hashed out with a psy-
chotherapist, or a matter of ethics to be discussed in
a philosophy seminar. A lot of them seem to care
more about Iraqi deaths than American deaths, and
after the big oil spill in the gulf, they seemed to care
more about animals than people—a greasy cor-
morant staggered around on CNN until it seemed
like a network logo, along the lines of the NBC
peacock.

They don't always seem to understand that the
war is real.

They don't seem to understand the military either. Meanwhile, the military seems to have their
number, perfectly. Media and military cultures are
clashing, the media are getting hurt, and it's all happening on television, live from Riyadh and the Pen-
tagon.

It is a silly spectacle.

It is so silly that 80 percent of Americans say

they approve of all the military restrictions on the reporting of the war, and 60 percent think there should be more. When a *Washington Post*–ABC News poll asked if we should bomb a Baghdad command and control center in a hotel where American reporters are staying, 62 percent said we should give a warning and then bomb even if the reporters are still there, and 5 percent said we should bomb with no warning.

Yesterday the *Los Angeles Times* quoted John Balzar, one of its correspondents in Saudi Arabia: "I was a sergeant in Vietnam and now I am a journalist here. In both wars, I feel like I'm in the wrong place at the wrong time, and I am going to go home and have people throw rocks at me."

It is so silly that *Saturday Night Live* recently went after the media with the same wise-guy irony it might have used on the military back in the '70s.

An actor playing a briefing officer says: "I am happy to take any questions you might have with the understanding that there are certain sensitive areas that I'm just not going to get into, particularly information that may be useful to the enemy."

A reporter asks: "I understand there are passwords our troops on the front lines use. Could you give us some examples of those?"

And so on, the point being that the reporters are either fools or traitors.

The point could just as well have been media self-righteousness, or their obsession with contradictions and ironies.

After a Marine reconnaissance team was trapped near Khafji, a reporter asked Gen. Pat Stevens IV: "You said recently our communications were 'superb,' but the Marine recon team was taken by surprise. How, then, can you call our communications 'superb'?"

In a briefing after U.S. planes bombed a building where civilians were hiding, one reporter adopted the Mike Wallace autograph-model tone of astonished innocence: "Are you saying, then, that you're not watching these buildings that you're going to target 24 hours a day?"

One reporter asked if we had put a limit on the number of Iraqi casualties we will inflict. Then there was the young woman with the National Public Radio accent, that elegant confection of crispness and offhandedness that you hear on *All Things Considered.* After the big oil spill, she wanted to know if Gen. Norman Schwarzkopf had been aware before the war began of the damage such a spill could do, and if so, had such a possibility entered his moral reasoning when he was deciding whether to start the war.

Why is this happening? Why do the reporters at the briefings seem to be on one side and the briefers on the other? And why do so many people cringe and hoot at the reporters, and admire the briefers?

Oil and water, dogs and cats, Hatfields and McCoys.

In *Battle Lines Report: Twentieth Century Fund Task Force on the Military and the Media,* Peter Braestrup, a former Marine and journalist, cites studies indicating that military values "are closer to those of Middle America than to those of the more permissive members of the media.... Not surprisingly, given the media's focus on conflict, deviance, and melodrama, most senior military men do not see the media as allies of civic peace and virtue.... There is no counterpart in journalism to 'duty, honor, country,' or to the military leader's ultimate responsibility for life and death and the nation's security."

The military demands team play. Journalists fight not only with the people they cover but with each other.

The military is hierarchical. Reporters have no rank. The military values loyalty and confidence in superiors. The press values objectivity and skepticism.

At a Senate hearing yesterday, former CBS anchor and war correspondent Walter Cronkite said the military "has the responsibility of giving all the information it possibly can to the press and the press has every right, to the point of insolence, to demand this."

Sen. John Heinz (R-Pa.) went to the point of insolence himself when he cited a long list of media
woe-sayings about the military before the war started, and a long list of successes since, concluding:
"Any advice for your colleagues?"

"No," Cronkite said.

The military is average guys who take pride in
their anonymity. The big-time press is high achiev-
ers struggling for the brief candle that passes for
stardom in the media. (When's the last time you
thought about Dorothy Kilgallen? Westbrook Peg-
ler? Chet Huntley?)

When the military makes a mistake in combat,
its own people die. When the press makes a mistake, it runs a correction.

For 20 years, they've been getting further apart,
each heading in its own direction, proud of becoming an island of virtue, unto itself.

But why do the reporters look so bad? What's
hard for viewers to understand is that they are
merely doing the poking, nagging, whining, demanding, posturing, and hustling that are the standard tricks of the reporting trade—people don't
have to tell them anything, after all, so they have to
worm it out of them. And there are many reporters
there who have never covered the military before.
It's an ugly business, and in the Persian Gulf they
do it on television, and they do it with the tone of
antagonism, paranoia, and moral superiority that
arose two decades ago in response to the lies and
failures of Vietnam and Watergate.

There is a lot of history here.

Back in the '70s, reporters were heroes of sorts
—one bumper sticker even said, "And Thank God
for *The Washington Post*."

Government officials and military officers were
the villains.

In the years since, the press has changed very little, and the military has changed a lot.

Besides polishing its public relations techniques
with courses at Fort Benjamin Harrison, the military seems to have studied the master, Ronald Reagan, and the way he buffaloed the press with his

nice-guy rope-a-doping—rope-a-dope, you recall, being how Muhammad Ali let George Foreman punch himself into exhaustion.

In the Persian Gulf briefings, the military briefers adopt the Reagan/Ali style, taking punch after punch, looking humble, cocking their heads, being polite, and playing the tar baby. They don't let the reporters get to them. They confess errors—deaths by friendly fire, bombs that missed. Like the Viet Cong, they only fight when they know they'll win. They come on like the silent majority in desert fatigues, while the reporters come on like Ivy League Puritans, pointing bony fingers and working themselves into rages.

Why, the reporters demand, can't they drive north and interview whatever troops they want? Why can't they talk to fighter pilots? Why are they restricted to pools? Why are so few journalists going to be allowed to cover the ground war?

This is not Vietnam, where combat was only a helicopter ride away—although it's interesting to note that one study says in Vietnam no more than about 40 reporters were ever out where the bullets were flying, except during the Tet Offensive of 1968 when the number might have gone to 70 or 80. Access to the siege of the Marines at Khe Sanh was limited to 10 or 12 reporters.

In Saudi Arabia, the military is keeping journalists on a short leash, but no shorter, probably, than it would keep them on in peacetime if they were doing stories at Fort Hood or Camp Pendleton. Corporations, professional football teams, police stations, and political conventions keep a close eye on journalists too. And no journalist would expect to get very far with businessmen and politicians by being as quarrelsome and ignorant as some of the journalists covering this war.

The parallel between other institutions and the military doesn't go very far, though. The military is a separate culture that is difficult to explain to anyone who hasn't been in it. As Bernard Trainor, a retired Marine lieutenant general, writes: "Whereas businessmen and politicians try to enlist journalists for their own purposes, the military man tries to avoid them, and when he cannot, he faces the prospect defensively with a mixture of fear, dread and contempt."

Trainor covered military affairs for *The New York Times* after he retired. He has seen the military-media war from both sides. Last December in *Parameters*, an Army War College magazine, he wrote: "Today's officer corps carries as part of its cultural baggage a loathing for the press…. Like racism, anti-Semitism, and all forms of bigotry, it is irrational but nonetheless real. The credo of the military seems to have become 'duty, honor, country, and hate the media.'"

With the end of the draft, Trainor says, the military "settled into the relative isolation of self-contained ghettos and lost touch with a changing America. It focused on warlike things and implicitly rejected the amorality of the outside world it was sworn to defend. In an age of selfishness, the professional soldier took pride in his image of his own selflessness. A sense of moral elitism emerged within the armed forces."

Hate! Scores to settle! As Secretary of Defense Dick Cheney recently told the U.S. Chamber of Commerce, "You might never know from all the stories we saw in recent years about $600 toilet seats that our defense industry was capable of producing effective systems and weapons to support our men and women in uniform." He went on about "doom and gloom reporting," and cited a 10-year-old story in *The Boston Globe* attacking the Tomahawk missile, even giving the exact date—Nov. 22, 1981.

The media have pulled away from mainstream America too.

Once, reporters were part of whatever team they covered, in a vague and unreliable way. They cut deals, they protected their favorites. But after Vietnam and Watergate, they declared a sort of ethical independence, and came to think of themselves as inhabiting a neutral territory of objectivity and value-free analysis. (It should be pointed out that objectivity is not an attitude that goes down well when there's an enemy shooting at American troops— hence the antagonism directed at Peter Arnett, the CNN reporter covering the war from Baghdad.)

Anyway, things changed in the '70s. Suddenly, the media had prestige. Instead of drawing their staffs from high school graduates, failed novelists, and the occasional aristocrat looking to get his hands smudged, big-time media were getting résumés from people who had grown up in the class segregation of upscale suburbs, day-school products who had never been in places where you don't let your mouth write checks that your butt can't cash, had never even been yelled at with the professional finesse of a drill sergeant, a construction boss, or a shop teacher. The most important experience in their life had been college. During the summers, they had internships, not jobs. A lot more of them were women. After the draft ended, virtually none of them even knew anyone who had been in the military, much less served themselves. They were part of what sociologists called the new class, the governing class, the professional class. They were a long way from most Americans.

The military came closer.

An Army infantry battalion commander in Saudi Arabia recently told his troops what kind of people they all are. "Like I told you before, this is not the Izod, Polo-shirt, Weejuns-loafers crowd. Not a whole lot of kids here whose dads are anesthesiologists or justices of the Supreme Court. We're the poor, white, middle class and the poor, black kids from the block and the Hispanics from the barrio. We're just as good as the...rest, because the honest thing is, that's who I want to go to war with, people like you."

Not people like the media.

But the military can't go to war without the media, either.

And oh, how the military wants to be honored, to have its deeds recorded for history. And how good journalists are at doing it, if their audiences and editors want to hear it. Both sides, in fact, like to sit around telling stories about their adventures, giving it all a mythological glow. Both feel they are underpaid and undervalued. Both feel they are sacrificing for a greater good. And in wars, journalists for once share a little of the risk with the people they are covering—in most peacetime stories, a story about an election or a stock speculator, say, this would be called a conflict of interest. Secretly, you suspect, the military admires the media's soldier-of-fortune independence, and the media admire the orderliness and blood-and-dirt courage of the military.

They're so close, you say. There's no reason they can't work together. And then you turn on the TV and watch the press briefings.

"General," a reporter drawls, "I wonder if you could dwell for a moment on the apparent contradiction between…"

Observations and questions

1) One way Allen builds unity in this piece is through the repetition of a word. Consider the word "silly" near the bottom of page 250. Notice how the word reappears. What are the effects on the reader?

2) Near the bottom of page 253, Allen writes: "...the military seems to have studied the master, Ronald Reagan, and the way he buffaloed the press with his nice-guy rope-a-doping—rope-a-dope, you recall, being how Muhammad Ali let George Foreman punch himself into exhaustion." How safe are writers in making assumptions about what readers know? Would they know what "rope-a-dope" is without an explanation? What lessons can be learned from the way Allen eases in an explanation of the term?

3) On page 256, the writer describes journalists who began entering the profession in the 1970s. He writes: "Instead of drawing their staffs from high school graduates, failed novelists, and the occasional aristocrat looking to get his hands smudged, big-time media were getting résumés from people who had grown up in the class segregation of upscale suburbs, day-school products who had never been in places where you don't let your mouth write checks that your butt can't cash, had never even been yelled at with the professional finesse of a drill sergeant, a construction boss, or a shop teacher. The most important experience in their life had been college." Go over the paragraph. What are the overt and subtle comments that Allen is making about the press?

4) Compare the reporters as described in Allen's commentary to the reporters in this book who covered the war. What are the differences?

Hail, and thunder, to the queen!

MAY 15, 1991

And then, after the talking-hat embarrassment with the lectern on the South Lawn of the White House, everything changed.

Queen Elizabeth II, this fusty cartoon, this up-holstered relic in white gloves, this corgi-bitten defender of an ill-kept faith, this walking logo for a country that looks like a theme park with riots, this highness, this majesty, drove across the Potomac River, got out of her limousine at the Tomb of the Unknowns, and Nature herself was enthralled.

Thunder rolled nicely through the playing of "God Save the Queen," cracked at just the right points in "The Star-Spangled Banner" (...*the rockets' red glare*...KA-BOOM), and then a rain that seemed as much ceremony as weather fell as she walked between the lush trees and the huge soldiers to the tomb. She carried her own umbrella, one of those touches that in a scene of English royalty seems miraculous, somehow. *Look! She breathes! She blinks! She carries her own umbrella!*

The Army had cranked up a "Full Honor Wreath Ceremony," known among the soldiers of Fort Myer as "a Mall job." There was a 21-gun salute thumping through the haze, there were single crashings of rifle butts and heels, there were commands coming across Arlington Cemetery with the airy precision of echoes, but the weather was the queen's, you couldn't help thinking.

This, of course, is what they pay her for—to be the big link at the top of the Great Chain of Being, not quite an angel, but somebody who can conjure up a thunderstorm when she needs one.

She wore a purple suit, with white piping, and a purple straw hat that shadowed her face, which looked powdered. She was the only one who looked utterly at ease, that offhanded calm of command, a look that makes you feel an urge to take

care of her at the same time you feel a little afraid
of her. Behind her, Prince Philip, Duke of Edin-
burgh, walked along in a white naval uniform and
did that British male thing of seeming to slightly
cantilever every body part in a different direction,
the effect being a hip-shot, lip-pursed, elbows-
flared, stiff-kneed acuteness—the sort of thing that
Joseph Verner Reed, chief of protocol at the State
Department, tries to get away with and often does,
at least until he's standing next to the Duke of Edin-
burgh.

A soldier, moving with the tense float of tomb
guards, brought a huge wreath. The queen touched
it. Together they set it before the tomb, where the
remains of unknown soldiers from four wars are at
rest.

Thunder!

Perfect!

Earlier, of course, on the South Lawn of the
White House, there had been spots of bother, spots
no bigger than all the prints and polka dots on all
the rayon dresses of all the women who seemed to
have agreed that this is what you wear, along with
endless straw hats, to watch the queen of England
arrive at the White House. Were they British or
were they only trying to look British? Then again,
aren't the British always trying to look British, isn't
that their real secret?

Anyway, the spots of bother.

The heat, for one thing, spotting all those dresses, and leaving one man on the South Lawn in a
faint. It was a great Washingtonian May heat, like
being trapped inside a fresh-baked pound cake, and
the Washingtonians at the ceremony took a certain
pride in it, knowing the British wouldn't quite understand it, in the way that the British took a certain
pride in the queen, at least to the extent that they
knew the Americans wouldn't quite understand
her.

Everyone waited in the heat, knowing the queen
had landed at Andrews Air Force Base minutes
ago, and was taking one of her rare helicopter rides
to downtown Washington. Chief of Staff John Su-

nunu wore one of the more preoccupied and impatient looks this city has seen since Lyndon Johnson stopped making appearances on the White House lawn. Marilyn Quayle, wife of the vice president, wore polka dots. The vice president wore a look of excitement, as if his parents had been promising him for months that he could come. The Kuwaiti ambassador looked grateful, which is his job. National security adviser Brent Scowcroft, as usual, stood out in the crowd for being so self-effacing.

Birds flew, smoke slipped out of the muzzles of cannons, and then the sound of the salute reached the lawn.

The queen! The president! Behind came Prince Philip and Barbara Bush, wearing a salmon suit and that sort of Will Rogers look she has—she is as American as the queen is British—as if she is about to put her hands in her pockets and rock back on her heels and say, "Well now." She said something to Prince Philip, who folded his hands behind his back and listened while cantilevering his head forward and sideways as if he were peering around a corner.

Anthems were played. Troops were reviewed.

The president spoke.

"A special relationship...standing fast with us for freedom...tested in the crucible...inseparable...the sands and seas of the Persian Gulf...naked aggression would not stand...there will always be a Britain."

(Why do we say this? Do we say there will always be a China? A Germany?)

The sound system fluttered for a while, and came back on.

"On behalf of an American people which reveres this mother country, I welcome you," he said, provoking a little grumbling from those who think of other countries as mother.

How tall he looked! Has he lost a little weight since his thyroid problem?

Or was it just how short the queen looked when she stepped behind the lectern—calamitously short, it turned out, for the photographers who pointed their telephoto lenses and saw what looked like a cluster of microphones wearing a purple hat. She is 5 foot 4, the president is 6 foot 3. Couldn't they have found a phone book for her to stand on?

She was witty: "It is 15 years since our last visit to Washington, when, with a gallant disregard for history, we shared wholeheartedly in the celebrations of the 200th anniversary of the founding of this great nation."

Laughter by the Americans, who like being made to feel naughty for rebelling.

But much muttering amid the British press. Was Bush supposed to have pressed some button or something to lower the lectern? Raise the podium? Boost the queen? Aren't Americans supposed to be good at gadgets like that? Protocol breach! Blunder! Immediately the *Times* of London man started cranking up the headline: "PRESIDENTIAL GAFFE TURNS QUEEN INTO TALKING HAT." The Reuters man would report a "giant talking mushroom." Later the White House press office would say that a step was available for the queen to step upon had she chosen to, and the palace briefing at the British Embassy referred all questions about it to the White House.

She was serene. She walked off to "Rule, Britannia," and gave that little tremble of a wave, that tiny conceptual karate chop that looks as though it might have been designed by royal doctors who feared that her constant waving might induce carpal tunnel syndrome.

Then lunch upstairs: minted purée of melon, red snapper with ginger and green peppercorn, green beans and diced tomatoes, and saffron rice timbale with the British ambassador, Antony Acland, and his wife, and Will Farish III and his wife—the Farishes board horses for the queen on their farm in Kentucky.

The president and the queen strolled out onto the Truman balcony. She carried her purse. Why?

The president spread his arms to a few media types wandering around below.

"Bless you, my children," he said. When one of

them tried to ask the queen how she liked the White House, the president said: "We're outta here."

Back to work.

Queen gave president Winston Churchill Award in Rose Garden. Then gave him four silver horseshoes over at the presidential horseshoe pit. Horseshoes marked E II R, for Elizabeth Regina the Second. Too nice to throw. President threw one of his own, missed by a foot. Prince Philip appeared fascinated by game of horseshoes.

Then the tree planting, of a little-leaf linden to replace one that had been planted in 1937 in honor of queen's father, George VI, but blew down last fall. Prince Philip appeared fascinated by leaf structure of little-leaf linden. Queen tossed three shovelfuls of dirt into pit with a Taper Forged Heat Tempered gold-colored True Temper No. 2 shovel with shaft made from original White House material removed in 1950, according to tiny plaque on shovel.

Then off to Arlington National Cemetery while the British press chaffed and gaffed away. Nothing to do after a bad lectern gaffe but throw a little thunder and rain at them. Let them know who's queen.

Observations and questions

1) Look at each word of the description of Queen Elizabeth II in the second paragraph. What do they mean? What does "fusty" mean, for example? Notice how the sound of the word carries about as much meaning as its definition. What is the image of the queen that Allen presents?

2) On page 260, Allen uses the term "spots of bother." What are the spots? Why use this phrase? Notice how the words add to the mood of the story.

3) The president is quoted in snatches on page 261. What is the reader supposed to get from this type of quoting?

4) Allen begins the story by referring to a "talking-hat embarrassment," but he doesn't explain the embarrassment until much later in the story. What holds the reader's interest to that point?

The Hill's ritual of passage

SEPTEMBER 11, 1991

For a moment there, before the hearing started, there was a sense of reality, or at least of surprise—you always feel a little surprised to see a famous face in the same room with you, even if it's the Senate Caucus Room, where the Senate Judiciary Committee gathered yesterday to enact the ritual of advice and consent in the case of Judge Clarence Thomas, nominee to the Supreme Court.

They strolled into the dead, perfect light of the television illumination—ambled in with that heavy, cushioned glide that senators tend to have, human Hovercrafts never touching the ground they walk on, but never able to escape it either.

There was Teddy, with his pained, pink face that seems to be getting smaller through the years while his head gets bigger, as if his face is about to implode into an infinitely small, dense, dimensionless point of pure Kennedyness kept warm by magnificent gray hair. There was Paul Simon with his bow tie, who looked like a precocious schoolboy on the verge of subsiding into the grumpiness of old age without ever having had a life in between. There was Howell Heflin, a small mountain of a man who has been coming to various small Muhammads for endless years, this being the task of the rulers of a democracy—his face is concave, bent in the middle so that his glasses seem to have slid down on his nose even when they haven't. And Orrin Hatch, with the wary aloofness of a man having his pants cuffed at a clothing store. And Strom Thurmond, with hair the color of the paneling you cover your basement walls with, and features vanishing into the racelessness of old age, a face that is shrewd and calm.

For a moment, they seemed real, or pleasantly startling, tiny under the lights and the huge coffered ceiling of the Caucus Room, but deeply recognizable, as if you were seeing them on postage stamps dropped on a sidewalk.

Congress is back. The hearing season has started, and a promising season it is—grandees and scoundrels will be filing into hearing rooms to talk about the CIA, the BCCI banking scandal (Clark Clifford this morning, the *éminence grise* himself, the gray cardinal of the Democratic Party, intoning responses through that little church of fingers he tends to erect in front of his face), and, as it happens, about 4,000 other things in the coming year, generating more than 400,000 pages of transcripts from the Government Printing Office, most of which will remain unread forever, part of a quasi-religious entity known as "the record."

"A hearing is a very simple morality play, a ritual, like a Noh play," says a lawyer who was involved with the confirmation hearings of Supreme Court Justices Anthony Kennedy and Antonin Scalia.

"Putting on a hearing is like putting on a Broadway play, except nobody comes to the practices," says Peter Stockton, a research analyst with the House Energy and Commerce oversight and investigation subcommittee.

Of course, with a Supreme Court nomination, the ritual has become so complex and demanding that it can provoke the spending of millions of dollars and thousands of person-hours of investigation, the writing and rewriting of questions and answers, mock hearings, press leaks, op-ed articles, press conferences, and fund drives, even when the nomination is considered to be nearly a sure thing, as it was yesterday with Clarence Thomas. Every conceivable reality has been foreseen, tamed, packaged (Ken Duberstein is the outside consultant called in by the White House to handle Thomas's side)—hence the unreal feeling in the hearing room as soon as Thomas entered to a sparkle of photographers' flashes that grew so numerous they became a sort of sheen in the air.

Thomas, a wide, intense, affable man, seemed not to lead his entourage in but be led by it, this being the proper humble stance of either a democratic aspirant or the central figure of a ritual, Thomas being both.

He was accompanied by his wife, his son, his mother and a sister, Sen. John Danforth of Missouri, Duberstein, and Fred McClure, the White House's head of congressional affairs.

Photographers assembled in a semicircle, leaning forward with crisp cheer, a little reminiscent of the odd posture of the Whiffenpoofs at Yale, as if one of them was about to sound a tone on a pitch pipe and they'd all start singing "I Talk to the Trees."

There was much self-effacement of the sort that demonstrates precisely how much power is being thrown around.

"You'll hear from 20 senators before you get to speak," Sen. Joseph Biden, committee chairman, told Thomas. "It may be the most painful part of the process."

When Biden commented on Thomas's youth—he's 43—Thomas replied, "I've aged in the last 10 weeks."

Within half an hour, reporters were walking around and reading newspapers. It was hard to see why the press was there at all. They could scarcely see the senators over one another's heads, and they couldn't see Thomas at all—he sat with his back to them, facing the senators. Photographers watched, but not from the floor in front of the witness, as they often do. In *The Tempting of America,* Judge Robert Bork's account of his failure to win approval by the committee, he claims that photographers were banned from shooting up from the floor at witnesses after Lt. Col. Oliver North made fools out of the Iran-contra committee by turning himself into a hero, partly in pictures shot from below, giving him the noble, foreshortened aspect of a recruiting poster.

Soon senators were chatting with each other and gliding discreetly in and out of the room. The hearing had acquired the offhanded gravity of true ritual, rather than the frantic superficiality that tends to accompany the gathering of facts. If facts were the point of hearings, there would be no need for hearings, as a committee headed by Sen. Warren Magnuson figured out in 1976, when it entered 4,500 pages of testimony, questions, and answers into the record without a hearing ever happening at all, except for documents being submitted.

In 1981, anthropologist J. McIver Weatherford wrote in a book called *Tribes on the Hill:* "The last great spectacle of the era, the Watergate hearings, showed the system for what it was—an orchestrated performance. The degree to which the hearings were planned in advance was apparent to everyone who could read in the morning newspaper what 'dramatic revelations' would be forthcoming in that afternoon's hearings."

There have been great hearings in the Caucus Room—the Titanic, Teapot Dome—but the golden age may have come after the Legislative Reorganization Act of 1946 opened all hearings to the public, and the new medium of television turned them into a national spectacle, an endlessly startling reality.

Back in the 1950s, you had the feeling not so much that you were learning something from the sight of McCarthy going after commies, Kefauver and McLellan going after mobsters and juvenile delinquents, but that you were peering through an electronic keyhole, squinting through tiny electric snowstorms (remember when "snow" was a big problem on your TV?) at final and secret fact.

It had been decades since anybody thought that anything real happened on the floor of the House or the Senate, but people knew stuff happened in the committees, in the hearings. Real gangsters! Real pinkos! Gritty Armageddon rendered in the black-and-white that always made things seem realer than our own lives!

Plus, those were the days when we got excited just to be watching television. We'd watch a test pattern if there was nothing else on. Real television!

The select committee investigating the Iran-contra scandal in 1987 failed to understand the reality of television until it was too late. To a lot of them, Ollie North was a screwball criminal, but on television he was a folk hero. Television made another folk hero out of an obscure senator named Sam Ervin during Watergate. It made a presidential contender, or so we thought, out of another one named Howard Baker. It persuaded a lot of viewers that Robert Bork was a cold-hearted smarty-pants. His goatee didn't help.

"People came to us and said he should shave it off," says Tom Korologos, who handled the Bork nomination for the White House. "We said, 'What, he's had it all these years and now he shaves it off?'"

It was not a question of principle, it was a question of image. Korologos recalls getting a tablecloth to hide the fact that one of his witnesses had a tendency to jig his leg while answering questions. Anyone testifying at any of the many hearings run by Rep. John Dingell is cautioned not to drink coffee or anything else—Dingell has been known to go all day without a bathroom break. The ritual is too powerful to be interrupted.

In his book about the Watergate hearings, John Dean tells of having a secret set of signals to prompt a break, but being told in a whisper, "Dammit, just keep going." It was Dean who brought along one of the greatest of the category known as "the obligatory wife," the cool and impeccable Maureen. Another was Betsy North, at the Iran-contra hearings. When Alexander Haig was nominated as secretary of state, he brought along a relative in a clerical collar.

Image is everything. Neither side wants any new information to be revealed. When Alexander Butterfield told the Watergate committee about the taping of presidential conversations, it seemed to be a moment of spontaneous drama, but it was nothing new to the investigators. As lawyers say, never ask a question to which you don't know the answer.

Korologos says: "One of the first things you ask anyone going in front of a committee is, 'What have you done that you're not too proud of?' When Gerald Ford nominated Nelson Rockefeller as vice president, we asked him if there was anything he was worried about people finding out. He said there was. He said, 'My biggest concern is that people will see I'm not as rich as they think I am.'"

Anthropologist Weatherford argues that reality tends to become ritual in politics. Floor debate in the House and Senate became so ritualized after the brawls and nation-changing oratory of the 19th century that the real business of politics moved more and more into caucus and committee. One arena of political reality became the hearing. But now the hearing too is more and more a ritual.

After the morning's speechifying yesterday, Heflin was confronted outside the hearing room by Joseph Rauh, the old pillar of liberal activism in Washington, and an opponent of Thomas.

"But Joe," Heflin said, "you're sentencing him before the trial!"

Then he smiled a smile that suggested he knew that Rauh knew that he knew that Rauh knew they were talking about something else entirely, the sort of indescribable something else that makes it necessary to enact the hearing ritual, over and over.

Down the hallways of the Russell Senate Office Building, television technicians stared at monitors, watching senators and abortion rights advocates giving press conferences, checking tape of the hearing. There was Thomas, invisible all morning to spectators in the hearing room! There was the whole scene, democracy itself, the people's tribunes speaking out! Facts! Quotes! Suddenly, for the first time in hours, it seemed so real.

Observations on commentary

When I look at a personal opinion piece, I look for a point of view. I look for the writer who examines a set of circumstances and finds things I've never thought of before, or examines them in a way that is different from what I have seen before. Mike Royko, for instance, is good at taking something that is common and making it universal.

I also look to see if there is an opinion there. You can't write a successful neutral column. A commentary has to be more than a truncated feature story. It should comment on something.

Next, I look for basic good writing. Is the piece clear? Does it express a thought vividly? Does the writer use figures of speech and other colorful language? Most people who write well are people who have been writers for a while. They have often worked at several positions in the newsroom. People who write clearly are also people who think clearly. They can sort through issues and express themselves lucidly.

Finally, I ask whether the writer can produce compelling commentaries consistently. The columnist has to fill a certain amount of space time after time. Can the writer successfully sustain the interest of an audience?

Judges desperately look for something different as they review commentaries. They look for something that breaks out of a mold. They look for comments that are sharp, pointed, or maybe comic. Too many columns and Op-Ed pieces are too much alike. They are dull. We look for something that is not generic, something that tells of the colorful events in this world.

Don Marsh, Editor
The Charleston Gazette

A conversation with Henry Allen
The ideas beat

KAREN BROWN: With your interest in writing fiction and becoming a novelist, did you major in English at college?

HENRY ALLEN: Yes. But I'll tell you, I was an awful student. The only thing I could do well was take aptitude tests, and that I was really good at. And so I got into college on the strength of that, and I majored in English because I spoke the language and I wrote with some fluency.

So you decided to take your act out of college and into the military?

I quit college with a year to go in one of those things that young men do, and joined the Marine Corps in 1963. I spent a little over three years in the Marine Corps, ending up in Vietnam, where I decided that if I wanted to be a writer, I'd better get writing. I'd always tried to engineer things in the Marines so that I could end up in the neighborhood of a typewriter, and then I would write and write and write, mostly fiction. But none of it went anywhere. My dream was to be a novelist, living the life of adventure, wandering from café to café, being glamorously bleak and existential.

In Chu Lai, I said to myself, "Either you've got to get serious about this writing business, or you'd better get into aluminum siding sales." So I thought, "Well, what's going to make you write? Go someplace where you've got to write," and newspapers seemed like the place. I wrote to a bunch of newspapers in Connecticut, where my parents were living at the time, and I came up with a résumé that made it sound as if I had some ex-

■ Henry Allen, editor, Style section of *The Washington Post.*

■ **Born:** May 23, 1941, in Summit, N.J.

■ **Personal:** Married to Deborah Allen; three children: Hannah, Peter, and Nicholas.

■ **Education:** Graduated from Hamilton College, Clinton, N.Y., in 1967 with degree in English.

■ **Newspaper Experience:** *New Haven Register,* 1966; *New York Daily News,* 1967-69; AP-Dow Jones,1969-70; *The Washington Post,* 1970-present.

■ **Awards:** National Endowment for the Humanities Fellowship, Univ. of Michigan, 1975-76.

Finalist, ASNE Distinguished Writing Awards competition, 1988,1989.

perience. I got real lucky with the *New Haven Register.*

An editor there could see that I really had no experience, but he gave me a one-week tryout on the copy desk. I had three days before my tryout started, and a friend used a cocktail napkin in a bar to show me how to write headlines.

For three days, I bought two copies of the *New Haven Register,* cut all the headlines out of one copy, read the stories, wrote headlines for them, and then compared them to the headlines in the *Register.*

At the end of three days, I had the rudiments down, so when I showed up they were astonished at the speed with which I learned how to write headlines. I stayed there from May 1966 until September, when I went back to college to finish my last year.

Was there something that appealed to you about headline writing?

Yeah. I thought headline writing was great. I liked the regular form of it. I liked the challenge of it. I liked learning the jargon. You know, "Eastern Star Sets Fete."

At the same time, I was going home at night and writing endlessly, getting about four hours of sleep.

What were you writing?

I started these notebooks where I was just teaching myself how to write. I'd pick out things to describe, from a pencil to a man's shoe, to the way a streetlight looks reflected in a puddle of water. I'd put down wisecracks and quips, the dialogue that I'd overheard, the way things sound, trying to reproduce reality in words. I'd be doing that all day, and writing on slips of paper that I'd stick in my shirt pocket.

Then I'd go home at night, take out the slips of paper, type them out, and amplify them and edit them and so on, because I wanted to learn how to write. I also read to see how others wrote.

You've mentioned three qualities that I've heard a lot in this year's Distinguished Writers interviews. They're nothing new about writing, but they stand out. One quality is that good writers write a lot. They keep writing. The second is good writers read a lot. Who were some of the people you were reading at this time?

Early in my life, I was interested in F. Scott Fitzgerald, Ernest Hemingway, William Faulkner, that romance period of American writing. Later, I read Allen Ginsberg and Jack Kerouac. Kerouac was very interested in writing about America as it is, the way people are, and the actual gritty truth of things. So that was a slightly different romance from the Hemingway-Fitzgerald romance.

By the time I wrote for newspapers, Tom Wolfe and the New Journalism had come along. I first read Tom Wolfe while I was still in the Marine Corps, and his writing was just astonishing, just the pure pleasure of it, the acuteness of his vision, and the humor of it. Then there were Gay Talese and Jimmy Breslin. Breslin was the only journalist I read in Vietnam who understood a thing about what was going on there. He came over and just wrote about what he saw. So few journalists did that then, and so few do it now.

The third point that keeps coming up as a quality of a good writer is enthusiasm. How important is that to a writer, and why?

It's everything. We're not in this for the money, baby. It's like being a musician. You just got to like sitting at a piano and hitting the keys. Or being a painter. You just got to like mucking around with paint. You got to enjoy it.

A poet named Stephen Spender said there are two kinds of people who want to be great poets. The first kind just wants to screw around with words, and the second kind has a great message to bring to the world. But it's really only the first kind who ever ends up becoming a great poet.

To be a writer, you've got to like the material that you're working with, which is the English language.

You eventually left the *New Haven Register*, finished your college degree, and started as a trainee at the *New York Daily News*. What did you learn as a trainee?

It was a wonderful experience, and I got some good coaching, too. They taught me little tricks, like whenever you can work food into copy, it's good. In other words, instead of saying, "The man's hat was dark brown," say, "It was chocolate brown." It increases the impact.

Anyway, I ended up on the financial page, and they would let me write these little tiny items. And in each one, I would always try to work in a particularly effective verb. I'd try to make it a bit more vivid, give a little more punch in these shorts.

Your winning pieces are long, but let's talk a little about short writing, because you've done a lot of it. What makes good short writing? You said strong verbs, for one.

I used to check my copy to try to get my verb percentage real high. And I tried to keep my adverb percentage real low. People tell you that it's adjectives that make copy dead. It isn't. It's adverbs.

Anything else on short writing?

Yeah. You can always make it shorter. Also, you've got to tell the reader right off that he or she is in safe hands. You say, "Reader, I know what I'm talking about. Trust me," and bang, off you go. You've got to do that with a good lead.

What happened when your training period at the *Daily News* ended?

Well, in the years that followed, I went to Europe and spent a couple of months in a hotel in Crete trying to write a novel. I bummed around India, then returned to the *New York Daily News* as a city reporter. I was mainly interested in the counterculture. I bummed around in the United States and ended up living in a friend's loft in Washington, D.C. I applied to *The Washington Post* for a copyeditor's job. It was easier to get a job as a copyeditor than as a reporter.

They gave me a job in the Style section, which was a new adventure in feature journalism. I realized this was something special; it was what I wanted to do. I cleaned up my act so I could do better work, and six months later, they made me a reporter.

When did you get into writing commentary?

Well, I never did get into commentary. That's the mystery, you know. I used to write stuff for Outlook, the Sunday opinion section, and I would write the occasional piece for the Op-Ed page. But the strange thing is that the pieces that I write, such as those in the winning package, are intended merely as descriptions of situations.

Along the way, I had acquired a kind of cultural perspective, starting in 1975 when I had a National Endowment for the Humanities fellowship at the University of Michigan, then with a lot of reading, and then with the two years that I spent as editor of Outlook. By "cultural," I don't mean opera or Picasso. I mean culture in the anthropological sense, the way any given bunch of people sees the world, the way they define reality.

And that was the viewpoint that I tried to bring to stories, because what people think about something is just as important as what it really is. And so I would analyze and describe and write features about things from this perspective.

How frequently do you write?

Well, I probably end up writing, on average, about one story a week, maybe a little more.

Are most of your stories similar to those in the

winning package?

I used to do more profiles, then I got interested in the ideas beat, and the *Post* wanted me to keep doing that. But I'm also a great believer in writing what we call "day hits." I'll be working on a long piece and an editor will run over and say, "Hey, we heard that this is going on down on the corner of 16th and K," and I'll take a notepad and run out and do it, and then come back and write the story on deadline. You've got to mix up the long and daily pieces.

What's the ideas beat? Is that a formal title?

No, that's just a name I use for the stories that I do, the stories that look at the cultural perspective.

I want to look at your stories, beginning with "The Gulf Between Media and Military." How did the idea come about?

The idea came from the editor.

What was the next step?

The next step was that I started doing research, including watching the briefings on C-Span, reading other newspapers, and reading all the polls. I went up to the Hill and covered the Senate hearings, where Walter Cronkite testified about media coverage of the war. I was calling experts on the media, including Peter Braestrup at the Library of Congress who wrote that great two-volume book on the coverage of Tet.

As you were doing the research, did you have a sense of what the piece would look like, what the point would be?

No. I never do. See, I jump into a huge pile of research. For every quote you see in here, I'll bet there were 10 that I didn't use. For every book or article you see cited, there are five more that I don't mention. I do a huge amount of research.

How much time does all that take?

On this one? I would guess I spent maybe five days.
But when I say days, I'm talking 7:30 in the morning till midnight, just going all the time.

When the research stops, what happens next?

I go get another cup of coffee, take a lot of deep
breaths, and start looking for a lead in that pile. You
know, it's like the huge pile of manure. You know
there's got to be a pony in there somewhere.

   You start fooling around with a sentence, and that
sentence kind of grows and it makes another sentence come out of it, and eventually you say, "Oh, I
see where I'm going." My feeling is that the English
language is a computer unto itself, and it will start
telling you how to write the story.

**Your piece begins: "The Persian Gulf press brief-
ings are making reporters look like fools, nit-
pickers, and egomaniacs; like dilettantes who
have spent exactly none of their lives on the end
of a gun or even a shovel; dinner-party commandos, slouching inquisitors, collegiate spitball
artists; people who have never been in a fistfight
much less combat; a whining, self-righteous, upper-middle-class mob jostling for whatever tiny
flakes of fame may settle on their shoulders like
some sort of Pulitzer Prize dandruff."**

Poetry. Sheer poetry.

[Laughter] Such modesty. Why is the lead so long?

Why is it so long? It's not long. It's exactly the right
length. There is no long or short when something
works. And that lead really works. I like to think
that I was speaking for a large segment of the American population when I wrote it.

   I'm poking the readers by using language that

they're not used to. I'm trying to wake people up. I suppose I'm just trying to wake up my own profession, too. And I'm trying to write lively, engaging, entertaining copy.

Good point. Would you say a little bit about the complexity of the structure there?

Okay. Let's talk nitty-gritty craft here, huh?

All those phrases and clauses go against the general teaching on lead writing. Why did you choose to use them?

I like lists, for one thing. It's actually a very simple structure. Basically, I say, "The following things belong to this list," and I just list them. So it's really a very easy lead to read.

You build rhythm in several ways in your piece. For instance, in the second paragraph there's repetition: "They complain about getting no answers; they complain about the answers they get. They are angry that the military won't let them go anywhere, the way they could in Vietnam. They talk about war as if it were a matter of feelings..."

The key in writing that was the word "answers." I thought about questions so simple that anyone could answer them, and questions that no one could answer. And the rhythm built from spinning that word around. It's like improvising on a refrain in music.

You also pace the piece with long and short paragraphs. The very long second paragraph is followed by a short third one. It reads, "They don't always seem to understand that the war is real."

That pace gradually emerges as I edit, because I know the timing devices that I want. You set up a rhythm, then you break it. The break emphasizes the existence of the rhythm. And when you get a rhythm going, then the reader knows that you're in control, that you know what you're doing.

One technique that also helps the reader as you build is the use of what my teacher of rhetoric would call proofs. You start with some statistics that show that the public is not happy with the press. You have a quotation saying that the public is not happy with the press. Then you use *Saturday Night Live* to make the same point. The latter is an unexpected source for a proof in a serious article for *The Washington Post.*

Well, but it does demonstrate that people who are attempting to reach millions of people, who have years of practice at it and know what they're doing, have a sense of their readers.

You said you have at least five times as much research material as you use. How do you select what to include in the article? How do you decide which proofs to use?

You look for the ones that best illustrate the situation. You look for sources that are well researched, verifiable, and true in some way; for material that resonates in the mind of the reader; for proofs that make sense.

The next section of proofs is quoting three reporters. You let the sources hang themselves there by quoting them exactly.

If a truth is self-evident, you don't need to do anything else to it.

The section of proofs is convincing. In the middle of the article, you have a transition: "Why is this happening? Why do the reporters at the briefings seem to be on one side and the briefers on the other? And why do so many people cringe and hoot at the reporters, and admire the briefers?" Do you remember your thinking as

you reached this point in the writing?

What I have to do here is explain cultural perspective. I'm saying that we have two sides here. We have one side that thinks one way; we have one side that thinks the other way. These are two cultures.

In that paragraph, you're slowing the pace and telling the reader, "We're taking a turn here." As I look at this piece, I think I see four elements of good commentary writing. I'm going to list them, and you let me know whether you agree. The first is that the commentary has a sense of righteous indignation.

Yeah. Boy, I hate that word "righteous," but I cannot deny that there's a tone of indignation.

Let me approach it another way. Is it important to you to feel passionately about the subject?

Oh, yes. I feel passionately about everything I write about. When I stop feeling passionate about stories, I'm going to go sell cars.

The second element is a store of knowledge on the topic.

I want to have the subject thoroughly covered, because that gives me the confidence to make stronger statements.

The third element is a contemporary feel or an adaptation to current culture, followed by clarity of purpose in writing.

You're saying the reader knows what the point is?

Yes. And the final element is the willingness to turn a phrase, or to write in an interesting manner.

Oh, yes. You go along in the story and you kind of feel a dead spot. You have to try shorter sentences or longer sentences, cut something, or move a section; you have to figure out ways to enliven the writing.

Would you tell me a little bit about the background of the piece "The Hill's Ritual of Passage"?

I was just going to do a piece on the culture of congressional hearings. So that's why I started doing the research. And I always look for anthropologists and cultural historians to help me. So I'd done all this research. I go up there and I'm standing in the back of the Senate Caucus Room, figuring I've got to cover it live to see what's going on.

I'm a little deaf. When you stand in the back of the room, you can't hear what anybody's saying, so I'm watching their faces. I'm realizing how familiar these faces are in the minds of Americans. Even if they can't quite put the name with the face of Joe Biden, they know it's the face of somebody important. That face has a little niche in their minds. So I thought, what's interesting about those faces? If I write about them in a certain way, that face pops into a reader's mind. Make it happen. Let them actually re-create the face in their minds.

Do they see the face, or do they see the character, or both?

Well, you hope a little bit of both, I guess, because with somebody as old as Strom Thurmond, there's character in that face.

It's no accident that you wrote about the "racelessness of old age" in his face.

I was fooling around a little there. In a way, I'm doing with words what caricaturists and cartoonists do with drawings.

What about the theme of this piece? In the lead, you say, "For a moment there, before the hearing started, there was a sense of reality…" And then

in paragraph four, it says, "For a moment, they seemed real…" The references to reality appear in the eighth paragraph, and the last statement in the piece reads, "Suddenly, for the first time in hours, it seemed so real." You said earlier that your ideas beat looks at what is real.

Yeah. That's what the piece is about. What I want to point out to the reader is that what seems to be a fact-finding session is actually a ritual. And that one reality doesn't necessarily fit with the other reality. There's a point at which the hearing becomes pure theater, an acting out of roles, of pretense.

In "Hail, and Thunder, to the Queen!" the first paragraph is extremely vague. It begins: "And then, after the talking-hat embarrassment with the lectern on the South Lawn of the White House, everything changed."

That's a classic tease lead. I figured the phrase "talking-hat embarrassment" was enough to prick up people's ears. They'll want to know what that is. I've got talking-hat embarrassment. I've got White House. And then, boom, I go to Queen Elizabeth.

This piece includes unique descriptions, things that we see but never stop to think about. How do you happen to notice those things?

The words that the queen said were not that important. I was supposed to do the scene, to observe and write the things I saw.

There are a lot of little tricks to writing descriptions. And you can learn them by reading. George Orwell once pointed out that description is essentially a technology that has been perfected over time. In 18th-century novels, for instance, you'll see very little landscape description. But by the time you get to the 20th century, Hemingway can go on for pages about what the mountains looked like.

Faulkner uses a trick of description when he puts together two words, two objects, or two concepts that ordinarily do not belong together. For instance, he describes pigeons flying around a courthouse steeple as looking like paint smears. And in the effort that your mind makes to get from one to the other, the illusion is created of something very vivid and alive in your mind.

I'm convinced that there is an electrical or chemical reaction in the mind that you can create with words. I mention all this to say that when you learn techniques for describing things, then you really see the thing, you are able to observe better.

Earlier in this conversation, you talked about the language telling you what to write. You said that as you explore your research and dabble with interesting words and phrases, the language tells you the story. Consider an analogy: When I get dressed most mornings, I open the closet and wait for an outfit to call me.

Exactly.

But there's a problem when nothing calls me.

Oh, yes. God, it's the worst, right?

What do you do when nothing calls your name, when the language doesn't speak to you?

What do I do then? I'll walk around the newsroom, and I'll see my friends, and they ask that same question that journalists always ask each other when they don't have anything else to talk about, and that is, "What are you working on?" And I'll tell them. Then I see another friend. He asks me the same question. And I tell him, and I listen to what I say, and usually what I say is the lead. But I'm just saying it in conversation. It's a way of forcing yourself just to come up with the lead.

As you're talking to people, you're getting coaching from others, in a sense. But there can be a problem. As a reporter, I learned one time that a

very good story I was working on came out awfully flat because I had talked it out. How do you avoid that?

Oh, that's a terrible danger. You've just got to watch it. If you tell people the whole story, and you keep doing it, then you don't want to write it anymore, because you've already told it.

So you have an instinct about when you've talked enough about it?

Yeah. Also, I don't know what the story is until I've written it. There is some discovery in the writing.

Are there any other methods that you use to overcome writer's block?

I keep going through my notes, and I look for words that look like they're fun to play with, some good sentences. I start expanding them, and that will sometimes turn into a lead.

Then there's the method when I come home and I sit at the dining room table with my head in my hands, telling my wife that my career is finished, my talent is gone, that I never should have done this to start with, because the story is hopeless and impossible. She'll say, "Why?" And I'll say, "Well, it's hopeless, because of X, Y, Z." And all of a sudden, I'll figure the reason for the block.

You come at it from a different angle, and talk it out.

I come from a different angle, and it very often comes out of feeling just utterly hopeless and confused.

Well, how can you keep functioning year after year if you still have these negative voices tearing at you?

It really starts to grind you down after a while, and that's why I like to mix up the length of the stories.

The long ones tend to be harder and more complicated. The short ones have a deadline, and so you
don't have any choice. You've got to write the
thing, and you get it out of the way.

The mixing helps, but if you're going to play pro
football, you're going to get some bruises. And if
you're going to play pro writing, you're going to
have some moments of doubt and anxiety.

**You've been an editor, and you've been in the
business for a while. How does the journalism
profession keep people for a lifetime career?**

You know, that word "career" troubles me a lot. I
think about corporate executives having careers, surgeons having careers, but to me, journalism is an adventure, and as long as it's an adventure, and you're
having fun at it and learning things, then it's good.
But as a career, like being a civil servant or a cop or
anything else, I think that makes bad journalism.

**What do you do when you're not writing? What
do you do for fun?**

Oh, I windsurf. I play squash. My wife, Deborah, is
arguably the greatest cook in America, and we like
to have people sitting around our dining room table
horsing around and doing a lot of laughing and a lot
of arguing.

So you're able to get away from your writing.

When I'm working on a piece, I can't. I'm thinking
about it all the time. I remember driving home from
the marina pulling a sailboat on a trailer. All of a
sudden, I had to pull the car over from the middle of
the road to the curb. I was blocking traffic, but I had
suddenly realized what I had to say in a piece that I
was working on, and I didn't care. Let the people
honk their horns. I pulled out a little pocket notebook, and I think I filled something like 20 or 30
pages with stuff. It just came to me right then.

And so I keep a notebook by the side of my bed,

and when I'm really working on a piece, I'll wake up in the middle of the night and write down ideas, images, and transitions. I've gotten pretty good at writing things down in the dark.

How have editors affected your writing?

Ah, man. You cannot do it without good editors. A good editor is heaven and a bad editor is hell. I've had some really good ones. I had a guy named Curt Suplee. He would understand what I was trying to get at, and he would show me how I could do it better. He would help me explain the story to myself.

And then Mary Hadar, my editor right now, has helped. One time I was writing a piece, and I knew the point of the piece, and so I quoted five different people making the point. I just found proper sources to say what I wanted to say. She came walking out of her office waving the copy at me, and she said, "There are all these quotes up there at the top."

And I said, "Yeah, that's the way you're supposed to do it, right? That's the way we're all taught you're supposed to do it." She said, "Well, why don't you just say it?" That was a great epiphany in my career.

One other editor was Joel Garreau, who is now a reporter at the *Post*. He would look at a piece, and he'd look up and say, "Why am I reading this?" And I wish that every editor in America, every time he or she sat down to edit a story, would ask that question.

We journalists have been taking care of ourselves for a long time, worrying about our dignity and our stature in the community, and our responsibility and our ethics, and all of that's important. But hey, the most important person, the single most important person, is the reader.

The Sacramento Bee

Peter Dexter

Finalist, Commentary

Pete Dexter joined *The Sacramento Bee* in 1986 after 12 years at the *Philadelphia Daily News*. He worked for newspapers in Florida before going to Philadelphia. Dexter is author of four novels: *Brotherly Love, God's Pocket, Deadwood,* and *Paris Trout*, which won the 1988 National Book Award. The book was also made into an award-winning cable television movie. Dexter wrote the screenplay for the movie *Rush,* and has written for *Esquire, Inside Sports, Playboy,* and *Sports Illustrated.*

His column is syndicated by Universal Press. It's been said that the three subjects he talks about seriously are his wife, his daughter, and his writing. Dexter said you can also add his dog, cat, boxing, and maybe the family parrot. His collection of writing includes some of the above, but also takes a sober tone. Here he ponders the values in an impending conflict.

Kuwait not worth 5,000 U.S. lives

JANUARY 13, 1991

And so, having perhaps decided that Saddam Hussein is not so much another Hitler as Rosemary's second baby, the president of the United States has announced that the time has come to go in there and get the little fellow out before he develops horns and is that much harder to remove.

Yes, five months after the cravings for raw liver began, Mr. Bush and his yes-man chorus of advisers have decided they can't wait nine months, which, as it happens, was the amount of time that even the optimists said it would take for economic sanctions to coax Saddam out.

Meaning if Iraq isn't exiting Kuwait in two days, very soon 20-year-old kids are going to start dying in the desert.

Another way to put that, of course, is that Saddam Hussein's ass is about to get kicked. At least that is the way the president put it a few weeks ago.

And as filling as those words are to a patriot's chest, it may be worth noting now, before fighting commences, that they are not quite accurate. As is often the case with President Bush.

It is not the president who is going to kick Mr. Hussein in the behind. The president is going to stay in Washington, or, if it lasts long enough, I suppose there will be vacations to Maine.

And it is not actually Saddam himself whose behind is going to be kicked. If anything has come into focus in five months of watching the man on CNN, it is that he takes excellent care of his own behind. He is not a kamikaze; he is not waiting for the next life to be rewarded.

The holy war—the mother of all wars—that Saddam is preparing his people to fight may in fact last as long as there is a 12-year-old kid somewhere in Iraq who can still hold a rifle, but will end before anything happens to one of Saddam's good suits.

At any rate, President Bush isn't going this alone, as he is wont to point out. Specifically, the United Nations has overwhelmingly committed itself to the principle of Americans dying in the desert to punish an aggressor nation. It has also indicated that it's all right for America to pay for it.

And with that mandate—not to mention yesterday's vote in both houses of Congress that authorizes him to declare war—the president has everything he needs to legally start the killing. My own guess is that, not wanting another unpopular war, he will not initiate hostilities until a couple of hours after the Super Bowl.

Giving us two weeks to reconsider.

And there are some things that need reconsidering. With all due respect for the remarkable intellects that were on display during the recent "debate" in Congress, it is certainly fair to say that most members of Congress couldn't have found Kuwait on a map at this time last year.

It is also fair to say that most members of Congress do not have independent understanding of our military capability or Iraq's, or of the long-term effects of economic sanctions, or of the nature of the conflict between Iraq and Kuwait that preceded Saddam's invasion.

Except for age and citizenship, there are no qualifications I know of for going to Congress, and more and more, as television replaces newspapers, it shows.

Who are these people—the Saudis and Kuwaitis—we are suddenly calling our friends? What ties do we have that obligate us to step in with anything beyond economic sanctions?

The only ties we have to the whole Middle East —save Israel—are economic.

All right, and Danny Thomas.

Are 5,000 kids going to die to preserve governments that condone the torture of prisoners—some of them Americans, incidentally—and amputation? That don't recognize women as citizens?

The number 5,000, by the way, came from one of the members of Congress I listened to last week during the "debates" on war with Iraq.

This particular member of Congress—and I can't remember who it was—argued that Iraq could be brought to its knees with the probable loss of only 5,000 American lives.

Five thousand lives, of course, is an acceptable figure only as long as it remains a figure. When one of those 5,000 is someone you love, the number is not acceptable at all.

And before 5,000 faceless families are asked to bear the sorrow and hopelessness that goes with losing someone they love so George Bush can say he kicked Saddam's ass, all of us ought to be asking some questions that do not have answers like "for freedom" or "to deter aggression" or "to protect our national interests."

Our primary national interest is to protect the ones we love.

If I may borrow from the presidential vocabulary, Kuwait, my ass.

Robert Jones

Finalist, Commentary

Robert Jones wrote for the *San Francisco Bay Guardian* and *Newsweek* before coming to the *Los Angeles Times* in 1972. He started with the *Times* as a staff writer in the Metro section, then began covering the environment and special projects. He's been a columnist since 1989, writing "On California" for three years, then "Coast Letters" starting in 1991.

Jones studied at Cornell University, and has a bachelor's degree in English and history from San Francisco State University. He's a native of Memphis, Tenn. Jones has won awards for a series of articles on rain forests and an article on earthquakes.

He also won the Nixon Newspapers Inc. National Journalism Writing Award from Ball State University for a two-part *Los Angeles Times Magazine* article, "The White Salamander Murders," and he's won a city press club award for personal column/commentary.

The column included in this collection looks at the fictional past and troubling presence of the Los Angeles Police Department.

Jack Webb doesn't live here anymore

MARCH 20, 1991

I remember the show ran on Monday nights and I remember my father loved it. He was the family's biggest fan of *Dragnet*. My mother refused to watch, probably on religious grounds, but the rest of us did, every week. *Dragnet* was part of our routine.

That took place in Memphis, Tenn., 1953 or '54. We had one of the first TV sets on the block and *Dragnet* was our introduction to California. We saw palm trees growing out of the sidewalks and crooks wearing Hawaiian shirts.

But the important part was something else. Something we didn't recognize at the time. We were watching the invention of the LAPD.

* * *

The uniformed officers on *Dragnet* were unlike anything I had ever seen in Memphis. These cops were tall, had flat stomachs, and showed respect at the crime scene. They seemed professional. They addressed detectives with a "Sir" and displayed no cynicism. They visited victims in the hospital.

The LAPD was being created for the first time. I am not referring here to the Los Angeles Police Department. That's a real police force with real people. The Los Angeles Police Department had existed for 100 years by the time *Dragnet* first appeared.

The LAPD is different. It was invented by television and to this day is still being invented by television. After *Dragnet* there was *Adam 12* and then *S.W.A.T.* and *T.J. Hooker* and *Police Woman* and a dozen others. There has never been a television season without an LAPD cop show on the air.

This invented world was a place of simple moralities, simple virtues, and clean living. Every uniformed cop had a blond girlfriend and worried at night about the people he was hired to serve and protect.

And all this raises a question: After 30 years of having a mythical LAPD piped into our homes and our brains, did we come to believe the myth? Did we buy the notion that our clean, California cops behaved like *Adam 12?* And that only places like Philadelphia or Chicago had the other kind of cops, the kind who would accept a $10 bill to forget a speeding ticket?

I think we did believe in that invented LAPD, as did the rest of the world. And the shattering of that belief explains, in part, the sense of betrayal in Los Angeles over the past two weeks. Those officers swinging their clubs cannot be reconciled with the television version.

The next time you watch the videotape—which could be in five or 10 minutes if you have the television on—ask yourself just why the horror bites so sharply. After all, you have seen violence worse than the beating being administered to Rodney G. King. Unless you have been living on the moon, your television has shown you people—real people—being gunned down on the streets or burned to death.

Monks have immolated themselves in Asia, blacks have set one another afire in South Africa, soccer fans have been crushed to death in front of our eyes.

There's usually a reaction of some sort, but nothing like this. So what explains the Rodney G. King affair?

I think it's this: The King beating destroyed not only the way we thought of the LAPD but the way we thought of ourselves here in California. And we sense, with some anger, that there will be no going back. The California that was a separate world from the East, that had clean government and clean cops, has slipped away.

Not entirely, perhaps. I am not arguing that L.A. has turned into Philadelphia. But the sense of remove about California has been eroded in a serious way. We have watched our cops using their batons like rubber hoses just as, a year ago, we watched our Sacramento legislators taking their bribes in fat envelopes.

So it's become much harder to believe that California is exempt from the petty corruptions and viciousness of the old world back East. The distinctions between their world and ours have blurred.

* * *

And maybe that's not all bad, if we finally see the lies behind the television version of ourselves.

I remember one episode of *Dragnet* in which Sgt. Friday was forced to visit the East Coast during an investigation. He had a terrible time. It snowed, the crooks turned out to have connections in the Police Department, and Joe caught a cold.

He was so happy to get home. Life was simply better here, he said. In L.A. you knew who the good guys were and who the crooks were.

No more, Joe. But thanks for the memories.

Editing the meaning of news

BY KAREN F. BROWN

At first we ignored it, the feeling that something is wrong with the news we're presenting. We ignored the sense that we're missing the real stories, the creeping frustration with traditional categories of news, and we ignored the fact that readers and viewers are turning away.

Then economic reality overcame inertia. An industry recognized the need for change, but as we approach a new century, wise men and women of the press have trouble pinpointing what news should be. We produce studies, workshops, and special reports, often grasping at any experiment, inspecting to see if there's a model for us all.

The best models might not be found in seminars or survey results. The best models might be emerging all around us in stories that grip readers and bring understanding. In many ways, these stories follow old forms of good journalism. In some ways, they plug the holes in traditional coverage.

During a recent conference on "Redefining the News," New York University professor Mitchell Stephens and Poynter Institute associate Don Fry explored the way we think of news. Stephens said traditional definitions include stories that have impact, emotional appeal, conflict, timeliness, proximity, prominence, and deal with the unusual. Fry said holes in coverage include stories that tell what actually happened, explain the process, explore religion on a personal level, report on education beyond the school board, show the effect of history, and tell about people in social classes other than our own.

Here are examples of stories that are filling the holes.

What actually happened. Journalists laugh when you say one thing missed in news coverage is what actually happened. What, then, is all that stuff filling so much news space and time? they ask. It's what immediately happened, what seems to have happened, what sources say is happening. It's the best report that we can give at that time.

We can do better. We can look back and give a reasonable report on what shaped events, a report on the fuller picture formed by discrete acts.

For instance, we knew the nation's spirits were sagging. Monthly figures proved unemployment was up. Daily reports regularly listed job closings and bankruptcies, even of long-standing firms. Take-outs and special reports alluded to the problems of the middle class. But the in-depth investigative series "America: What Went Wrong?" by Donald L. Barlett and James B. Steele of *The Philadelphia Inquirer* explained what actually happened. They explained that tax payments aren't just going up; the proportion of taxes on certain family incomes increased from 17.8 percent to 24.3 percent between 1970 and 1989. Laws have encouraged business practices that weaken the U.S. economy. The reporters' findings were controversial, but they were an example of making sense of the world, instead of giving daily pieces of news. Their findings also proved that people will attend to news that explains what actually happened.

Process. A few years ago, television programmers scored big points by creating a Saturday-morning interlude of jingles and cartoon characters to explain how a bill becomes a law. Journalists need to remember the child in all of us. We can dispense with the cartoons, but we have a continuing curiosity about how things work, about what happens on the *inside*. One newspaper revealed a process by using a stand-alone graphic to explain the route of a check from the time it's written until it returns cancelled.

Another type of process story is G. Wayne Miller's story "Working Wonders" in the *Providence Journal-Bulletin.* In his explanation of how the deformed insides of a little girl are made normal, he wrote:

"Using a combination of cutting cautery, scissors, and blade, he proceeds through skin, fat, a layer of tissue called the rectus sheath, finally piercing the peritoneum, a thin but tough membrane that lines the abdominal cavity. There is no hesitation in his work, no false starts, not a single wasted motion. Hendren is as unflappable at his table as he was in a plane.

He places a metal ring around the wound and attaches several retractors to pry it wide open. He has to be able to get two hands and a multitude of instruments down in there."

Religion. We approach the subject of religion like faithful church-attenders who've never felt spiritually moved. Usually, religion sections offer only bulletin boards of church events. Anything beyond announcements or articles on denominational activities seems too weird for a daily newspaper. Yet millions of people wrestle with spiritual questions every day.

Newsweek took the plunge on the issue the week after Christmas 1991. A cover story titled "Talking to God: An Intimate Look at the Way We Pray" included this:

"Talking to God: in America, as the prophet Amos put it, those conversations flow like a mighty river. This week, if you believe at all in opinion surveys, more of us will pray than will go to work, or exercise, or have sexual relations."

Education. Writers cover education, as they do religion, from a safe distance. Most stories are from meetings or administrative offices, while most of the action of schools is in classrooms.

"South of Heaven: A Year in the Life of a High School" was the *St. Petersburg Times*'s attempt to tell readers what goes on in schools today. Writer Thomas French focused his story on five high school students, including an honor student and a dropout-to-be. Of the latter two, French wrote:

"They both walk the same long halls, weaving through the same crush of teen-age bodies. They sit in classrooms only a hundred yards from each other, trapped behind weathered desks scrawled with the same declarations of love and lust. They rail against the same mind-numbing rules, make cracks about the same principal, sneak off the same campus at lunchtime, just to escape whatever's being dished out in the cafeteria.

"The truth is, though, the two of them don't go to the same school at all. Even if they brushed shoulders in front of their lockers, they probably wouldn't notice each other. They are invisible to each other."

The seven-part series told about student and teacher motivations, race relations, social class distinctions, school budgets and curriculum, parental frustration, and success in spite of obstacles.

History. News is what's new, many journalists believe. But sometimes news is the history of an event. One newspaper faced tough criticism for the paper's honest reporting of problems at an African-American university. The complaint was less about the current problems than about the newspaper's failure to tell the history of the institution, and the failure to relate problems to past neglect of the institution.

Henry Allen's writing in *The Washington Post* presents a model for including history in coverage. In "The Hill's Ritual of Passage," he wrote:

"There have been great hearings in the Caucus Room—the Titanic, Teapot Dome—but the golden age may have come after the Legislative Reorganization Act of 1946 opened all hearings to the public, and the new medium of television turned them into a national spectacle, an endlessly startling reality."

He continued by tracing other hearings up to the Clarence Thomas confirmation. Sometimes the needed history is a complete story; sometimes it's a section giving context to a story.

Other people. We still have problems seeing people who are not like us. The issue applies to social classes, but also to race, ethnic groups, gender, etc. Some of us are getting better, but as a group, the American press still acts as though large segments of the population are invisible. The proof is in the absence of daily life stories on people who are poor or non-white. When they appear in the news, it's usually in stories of misfortune or crime.

The Chattanooga Times used a different approach in a story about a local community. Writer Carolyn Mitchell's story appeared under the headline "Family spirit: Shepherd is known for caring." She wrote: "Freeways are tombstones for thousands of communities crushed by the relentless unfurling of the superslab.

"But when Highway 153 rolled through the middle of Shepherd, the small, mostly black community refused to wither in fragmented clusters of houses.

"Many people displaced by the road construction found new homes in the century-old neighborhood that residents claim has the feel of a family."

She explained that Shepherd residents recognize local achievement and have organized a recreation program that state officials cited as Tennessee's best.

There is little mystery why the stories mentioned here succeeded. Writers and editors decided to edit the *meaning* of news to try different approaches. They went beyond the usual boundaries, and in the process brought compelling stories to readers.

Annual bibliography

BY LUZ NELIDA MIRANDA

This selected bibliography of recent books and periodical articles focuses on the art and craft of writing for newspapers. Also included are items on reporting, composition, coaching, editing, and the teaching of writing.

CLASSICS

Blundell, William E. *The Art and Craft of Feature Writing: Based on The Wall Street Journal*. New York: New American Library, 1988.

Elbow, Peter. *Writing With Power: Techniques for Mastering the Writing Process*. New York: Oxford University Press, 1981.

Franklin, Jon. *Writing for Story: Craft Secrets of Dramatic Nonfiction*. New York: Atheneum, 1986.

Murray, Donald. *Writing for Your Readers: Notes on the Writer's Craft from The Boston Globe*. Chester, CT: Globe Pequot, 1983.

Zinsser, William. *Writing to Learn*. New York: Harper and Row, 1988.

BOOKS

Adler, Elizabeth. *Print That Works: The First Step-by-Step Guide That Integrates Writing, Design, and Marketing*. Menlo Park, CA: Bull Publishing, 1991.

Burgett, Gordon. *The Travel Writer's Guide: How to Earn at Least Twice What You Spend on Trav-

el by Writing Newspaper and Magazine Articles. Rocklin, CA: Prima Publishing, 1991.

Campbell, Don. *Inside the Beltway: A Guide to Washington Reporting.* Ames, IA: Iowa State University Press, 1991.

Cappon, Rene J. *Associated Press Guide to News Writing.* Englewood Cliffs, NJ: Prentice-Hall, 1991.

Cates, Jo A. *Journalism: A Guide to the Reference Literature.* Englewood, CO: Libraries Unlimited, 1990.

Clark, Roy P., and Don Fry. *Coaching Writers: The Essential Guide for Editors and Reporters.* New York: St. Martin's Press, 1991.

Edelstein, Scott. *Writer's Book of Checklists.* Cincinnati, OH: Writer's Digest, 1991.

Fensch, Thomas, ed. *Nonfiction for the 1990s.* Hillsdale, NJ: Lawrence Erlbaum Associates, 1991.

Griffin, Robert J., and Dayle H. Molen, with others. *Interpreting Public Issues.* Ames, IA: Iowa State University Press, 1991.

Halberstam, David, ed., and Glenn Stout. *The Best American Sports Writing 1991.* Boston: Houghton Mifflin, 1991.

Hay, Vicky. *The Essential Feature: Writing for Magazines and Newspapers.* New York: Columbia University Press, 1990.

Izard, Ralph S., and Marilyn S. Greenwald. *Public Affairs Reporting: The Citizens' News.* Dubque, IA: William C. Brown, 1991.

Jacobi, Peter. *The Magazine Article: How to Think*

It, Plan It, Write It. Cincinnati, OH: Writer's Digest, 1991.

Jones, Bill, ed., and Bill Martin. *A Spectrum Reader: Five Years of Iconoclastic Reporting, Criticism, and Essays.* Little Rock, AR: August House, 1991.

Keir, Gerry, and Maxwell McCombs. *Advanced Reporting: Beyond News Events.* Prospect Heights, IL: Waveland Press, 1991.

Killenberg, George M. *Public Affairs Reporting: Covering the News in the Information Age.* New York: St. Martin's Press, 1991.

Klaidman, Stephen. *Health in the Headlines: The Stories Behind the Stories.* New York: Oxford University Press, 1991.

Kluge, P. H., ed. *The Columbia Knight-Bagehot Guide to Business and Economics Journalism.* New York: Columbia University Press, 1991.

McIntrye, Bruce T. *Advanced Newsgathering.* New York: Praeger, 1991.

Mencher, Melvin. *News Reporting and Writing.* Dubuque, IA: William C. Brown, 1991.

Potter, Clarkson N. *Writing for Publication.* New York: NAL-Dutton, 1991.

Protess, David L., and Fay L. Cook. *The Journalism of Outrage.* New York: Guilford, 1991.

Ricchiardi, Sherry, and Virginia Young. *Women on Deadline: A Collection of America's Best.* Ames, IA: Iowa State University Press, 1991.

Rothmyer, Karen. *Winning Pulitzers: The Stories Behind Some of the Best News Coverage of Our Time.* New York: Columbia University Press, 1991.

Rushin, Pat. *Puzzling Through the News.* Baltimore, MD: Galileo, 1991.

Sims, Norman, ed. *Literary Journalism in the Twentieth Century.* New York: Oxford University Press, 1990.

Sternburg, Janet. *Writer on Her Work.* New York: Norton, 1991.

Willis, Jim. *The Shadow World: Life Between the News Media and Reality.* Westport, CT: Greenwood, 1991.

Witt, Leonard. *Complete Book of Feature Writing.* Cincinnati, OH: Writer's Digest, 1991.

Zinsser, William, ed. *They Went: The Art and Craft of Travel Writing.* Boston: Houghton Mifflin, 1991.

MAGAZINE AND PERIODICAL ARTICLES

Abrahamson, David. "Teaching Journalism as Literature and Possibilities of Artistic Growth." *Journalism Educator* 46.2 (Summer 1991): 54-60.

Aregood, Richard. "Flash! Sometimes, We Have to Write Long!" *ASNE Bulletin* 734 (September 1991): 11.

Blonston, Gary. "We Mustn't Let Words Fail Us." *ASNE Bulletin* 731 (April 1991): 4-6.

Bowman, Sally-Jo. "Moving Readers With Ease." *Writer's Digest* 71.12 (December 1991): 38-40.

Brown, Karen F., and Roy Peter Clark. "Tips for Increasing Minority Coverage." *The Quill* 79.6 (July/August 1991): 25.

Christian, Darrell. "Our Best Sports Writing Stretches Beyond the Basics." *APME News* 188 (February 15, 1991): 15-16.

Clark, Roy Peter. "O Brave Newsroom, That Has Such People In't!" *ASNE Bulletin* 735 (October 1991): 4-5.

"The Coach as an Editor: Part 1. An Interview With Marilyn Moyer, Writing Coach and Projects Editor at the Arkansas Gazette." *The Coaches' Corner* 6.3 (September 1991): 3.

Dreier, Peter, and Alec Dubro. "Housing: The Invisible Crisis." *Washington Journalism Review* 13.4 (May 1991): 21- 24.

Harkrider, Jack. "Learning to Edit." *C:JET* 25.2 (Winter 1991): 19-22.

Harrigan, Jane. "Five Frames to Support Your Articles." *Writer's Digest* 71.7 (July 1991): 24-25.

Hart, Jack. "Finishing the Story With a Happy Ending." *The Coaches' Corner* 6.1 (March 1991): 1+.

Hedley, David. "Mapping: A New Way to Consider Readability." *The Coaches' Corner* 6.4 (December 1991): 1+.

Jaspin, Elliot G. "Just Do It!" *ASNE Bulletin* 737 (December 1991): 4-8.

Kress, Nancy. "Using the Flashback." *Writer's Digest* 71.4 (April 1991): 8-10.

Larsen, Elizabeth. "Watching Between the Lines." *Utne Reader* 46 (May/June 1991): 26-28.

Meyer, Philip. "Stop Pulling Punches With Polls." *Columbia Journalism Review* 30.4 (November/ December 1991): 64-67.

Peck, Louis. "Anger in the Newsroom." *Washington Journalism Review* 13.10 (December 1991): 23-27.

Ruffini, Gene. "Reporting a New Kind of War." *Washington Journalism Review* 13.2 (March 1991): 20-23.

Ryan, Leland. "Goodbye, Copy Desk. Hello, Display Desk." *ASNE Bulletin* 731 (April 1991): 7-12.

Seals, Louise. "Rx for AP." *APME News* 191 (August 1, 1991): 3-7.

Seattle Times Staff. "A Vital Connection." *The Quill* 79.6 (July/August 1991): 24-25.

Smith, Steve. "When to Use Racial, Ethnic IDs." *The Coaches' Corner* 6.4 (December 1991): 1+.

Steele, Bob. "Ethics Clinic: A 10-Step Approach to Good Decision-Making." *The Quill* 79.2 (March 1991): 36.

Stephens, Mitchell. "Deconstruction and the Get-Real Press." *Columbia Journalism Review* 30.3 (September/October 1991): 38- 42.

Stepp, Carl Sessions. "When Readers Design the News." *Washington Journalism Review* 13.3 (April 1991): 20-24.

Streckfus, Richard. "Good Writing Can Be Taught with Critiques and Rewrites." *Journalism Educator* 46.3 (Autumn 1991): 64-68.

Weinberg, Steve. "The Kitty Kelley Syndrome: Why You Can't Always Trust What You Read In Books." *Columbia Journalism Review* 30.2 (July/August 1991): 36-40.